Arrival Survival Canada

A Handbook for New Immigrants

Arrival Survival Canada

A Handbook for New Immigrants

Naeem "Nick" Noorani   **Sabrina Noorani**

OXFORD
UNIVERSITY PRESS

OXFORD
UNIVERSITY PRESS

70 Wynford Drive, Don Mills, Ontario M3C 1J9
www.oup.com/ca

Oxford University Press is a department of the University of Oxford. It furthers the University's
objective of excellence in research, scholarship, and education by publishing worldwide in

Oxford   New York
Auckland   Cape Town   Dar es Salaam   Hong Kong   Karachi
Kuala Lumpur   Madrid   Melbourne   Mexico City   Nairobi
New Delhi   Shanghai   Taipei   Toronto

With offices in
Argentina   Austria   Brazil   Chile   Czech Republic   France   Greece
Guatemala   Hungary   Italy   Japan   Poland   Portugal   Singapore
South Korea   Switzerland   Thailand   Turkey   Ukraine   Vietnam

Oxford is a trade mark of Oxford University Press in the UK and in certain other countries

Published in Canada
by Oxford University Press

Copyright © Oxford University Press Canada 2008

The moral rights of the author have been asserted

Database right Oxford University Press (maker)

First published 2008

Library and Archives Canada Cataloguing in Publication

Noorani, Naeem, 1957-
Arrival survival Canada / Naeem Noorani and Sabrina Noorani.

(Canadian newcomer series)
Includes bibliographical references and index.
ISBN 978-0-19-542891-9

1. Immigrants—Services for—Canada. 2. Immigrants—Cultural
assimilation—Canada. I. Noorani, Sabrina, 1955– II. Title. III. Series.
HV4013.C2N66 2008   362.84'00971   C2007-906128-1

1 2 3 4 – 11 10 09 08

Cover design: Sherill Chapman
Cover image: iStockphoto
This book is printed on permanent (acid-free) paper ∞.

Printed and bound in Canada

Dedication

This book is dedicated to the Native Canadians who have been hosts to immigrants through the years, to the millions of immigrants who have come to this wonderful country, and to the many immigrants we met along our way, some of whom are featured in this book and in the *Canadian Immigrant* magazine. Thank you for being our motivation.

A special thanks goes out to Adrienne Clarkson, our former Governor General, for her foreword. She epitomizes the heights an immigrant can aspire to. Thank you for motivating a generation of immigrants!

Last, but not least, this book is dedicated to our parents, siblings, and children, and to our families and friends back in India.

Acknowledgements

This journey began many years ago and so the list of people involved is long. Impossible as it may be, we are going to try to include as many as we possibly can.

Cindy Angelini, David Bai, Debbie Catherwood, Frank & Sandra Cumming, Lynda Cumming, Dr. Godwin Eni, Nancy Forrest, Alla Gordeeva, Susan Gordon, John Halani, Dave Hayer, Kelly & Maggie Ip, Margaret Jetelina, Massood Joomratty, Stephanie Kewin, Kexin Lu, Steve & Jane Mayall, Lynn Moran, Suneel and Jaya Mehra, John Nuraney, Carol O'Dell, Bethany Or, Bunty & Kavita Pundit, Late Dave Quackenbusch, Deirdre Rowland, Manoj & Bhavana Sabharwal, Balwant Sanghera, Jason Tomassini, Praveen Varshney, Julie Wade, Josephine Wong, Tim Welsh, Sandra Wilking, Morena Zanotto, and our friends at channel m and Radio Canada International (RCI).

Thank you all from the deepest corners of our hearts!

Table of Contents

Look for these features throughout the book. They give interesting and fun facts about Canada.

Look for these features throughout the book. They will answer some of the most commonly asked questions about Canada.

A note on the language: As English is the second language of many newcomers to Canada this book was written in straightforward language. In addition, at the end of each chapter readers will find a **Key Words** section that defines some of the important words and terms for that topic. For clear definitions at the appropriate language level the *Oxford ESL Dictionary* was used.

Foreword

Everyone who comes to Canada will benefit from this book. All the practical information that newcomers to Canada need is presented in a simple, helpful way. Everything from searching for a job to shopping for groceries to buying and selling a house are dealt with here. This book is not just information, it is a friend, a guide, and a support. Use it and you'll find that you'll know more, and be able to do things with confidence. Good luck!

The Right Honourable Adrienne Clarkson, P.C. C.C. C.M.M. C.O.M. C.D.
Twenty-Sixth Governor-General of Canada

The Rt. Hon. Adrienne Clarkson, PC, CC, CMM, CD, 26th Governor-General of Canada, came to Canada as a refugee from Hong Kong during the Second World War. After a long and distinguished journalism career and many contributions to Canadian life and culture, she was appointed Governer General in 1999 by Prime Minister Jean Chrétien.

Introduction

Only an immigrant to Canada would be astonished that it takes nearly a week to drive across this vast country, and only an immigrant would be surprised to discover that most of the 33 million residents of Canada live within a few hundred kilometres of the American border. Canadians take such facts for granted.

Also, only immigrants would be surprised at how easy it is to leave Canada and cross that boundary to the United States, which is often called the longest undefended border in the world. Of course, border security has increased since September 11, 2001 and identification, such as a Permanent Resident Card or passport, is required. But it's still fairly easy—border crossings in many countries aren't quite so straightforward.

Immigrants might be shocked at the variety of government services available in Canada. There are many government departments, and the services they offer often differ from province to province.

The aim of this book is to simplify the newcomer's first year in Canada. It answers many questions and addresses some of the dilemmas that may confront newcomers to this incredible country. This book is more than just the result of research, however; it is based on my wife Sabrina's and my own experiences as immigrants, as well as many stories that we have been privileged to hear. This book was originally written a year after we migrated. What you now have in your hands is the product of many years of experience.

I moved here in November of 1998, three months after Sabrina and our two kids came to pave the way. The problems Sabrina had to face were very different from mine; I simply followed along. However, I have used our collective experience, and the experiences of many other immigrants, in the writing of this book.

We were raised in Bombay, which is now called Mumbai, on the west coast of India. Although we loved it and still have many relatives and friends there, we wanted to explore the world. In 1992, we moved to the Middle East, where we lived until we moved to Canada in 1998.

I have worked in advertising and marketing for 22 years. This field, in which my wife and I believe I excel, is really nothing more than finding an ideal match between a product and a consumer.

In much the same way, this book is also a match between a product and the consumer. The product is the information we have gathered on how to settle in Canada. The consumer is you, the new immigrant or the potential immigrant.

There are many, many surprises you will face once you land in Canada. Take the health care system, for example. We had heard that Canada was very generous with its health care services. This is appealing when you're approaching middle age, as I am, and it played a role in our decision to choose Canada as the country in which we wanted to live.

To my surprise, I learned that in Canada, like everywhere else, you only get what you pay for. Just one month after we arrived, my rambunctious 14-year-old son, Dan, took a tumble while rollerblading and ended up with a sprained wrist. We hustled him off to the hospital, expecting the country's health care system to cover the expenses. Judging from the reception we received, it seemed that the hospital staff thought we had just arrived from the planet Mars. As it turned out, we weren't covered by the Medical Services Plan of BC.

The Medical Services Plan is the all-encompassing health care plan that British Columbia's residents support with monthly payments. Since the plan doesn't actually activate until three months after the applicant applies, we had to cover all the medical expenses for Dan's wrist. Our bill for that small accident was $500; this was much less than it would have been in many other countries, but was still substantial.

My first word of advice for immigrants is to contact your provincial health care supplier immediately upon your arrival in Canada—the first day, if possible. And obtain private medical insurance for the period before your provincial health plan kicks in. Medical services in Canada, which vary from province to province, will be covered at length in Chapter 6—Medical Coverage.

My lawyer in Dubai helped my family get to the shores of this country. But when I arrived, I still didn't know how to rent an apartment, get a job, buy a car, get a credit card, obtain car insurance, or open a bank account.

While the answers to those questions are free for the asking in Canada, you have to know whom to ask. There were several books on the subject written by provincial governments, but none written by an immigrant—someone who has experienced the challenges of walking the same road. This book compiles answers in an easy-to-read, practical format.

Arrival Survival Canada will cover survival basics for new immigrants: how to select a place to live, find work, and get health care coverage. It will also explain a little bit of the history of Canada and some of the strange customs Canadians have. Take, for instance, the Polar Bear Swim: people in many Canadian cities celebrate the first day of the New Year with a loud and lively party on the shore of a very cold body of water into which hundreds of rum-soaked citizens plunge themselves.

The book will also cover some basics of Canadian law—your rights, your responsibilities, and the best course to follow in the event of, say, a minor traffic accident or a break-in at your house.

It will include information on settling in this country, on the various tax structures, on registering your child for school, on taking night school courses, on obtaining financial assistance from the government, on Canada pension plans, and much more.

It is based on my own challenging and sometimes frustrating experiences as a newcomer. If it helps you to eliminate the stress from your experiences, then I'll be happy.

As well, the book shares the personal stories of many other immigrants in Canada, from Senator Mobina Jaffer, to Olympic wrestler Daniel Igali, to immigrants from all walks of life.

After writing this book, I wanted to continue to help immigrants in their first several years of life in Canada by providing lots of information, resources, and profiles of successful immigrants in Canada to serve as inspiration. In April 2004 Sabrina and I started a monthly magazine called *Canadian Immigrant* (www.CanadianImmigrant.ca). The magazine has grown from 7,000 copies to 80,000 copies per issue and continues to help numerous immigrants succeed.

In November 2006, I was invited by RCI (Radio Canada International—one of the Canadian Broadcasting Corporation's radio stations) to participate in a new show for immigrants called *The Link*. The show allowed me to answer questions from potential Canadian immigrants from all over the world. I have included some of these throughout each chapter.

I am constantly asked one question: "What makes immigrants succeed?" In my opinion, there are five major conditions for success:

Learn the language. Let's face it, if you don't learn English all your skills will be hidden away like a gem in a cave. If you moved to Germany or Japan, you would make a conscious decision to learn your new country's language. Why then do some immigrants settle for less than the best that Canada has to offer by refusing to learn English? I encourage immigrants to make a real effort to learn English and to speak it at least three to four hours a day.

Stay positive. I have seen the same situation so often that it has become predictable: a new immigrant meets with resistance and barriers in job-finding and then sits with friends from the same ethnic community who moan about life in Canada. Before you know it, the negativity seeps into the newcomer's being. If this starts happening to you, think about why you were excited about moving to Canada, and focus on all the great things you want to accomplish here.

Embrace Canada. Remember your dreams about coming to Canada? Well, they have come true. Now go out and enjoy all that is Canadian. The very act of going out and discovering the sights of the city you have adopted will make you value and enjoy the beauty of Canada and its people.

Have a Plan B. Some people think that in order for immigrants to succeed, they need to start at the bottom. I do not agree with this, but believe you should have a Plan B for your life in Canada. Plan B means having flexibility in what you intend to do in Canada. That very flexibility changed me from an advertising professional to a publisher! I should add, however, that in order to have a Plan B, you must have a Plan A!

Stay clear of ethnic silos. I do understand that moving to a new country can be very scary. A lot of immigrants tend to move into an ethnic community that matches their own background. While this may be comfortable, I personally believe your true growth in a new country will come from moving out of your comfort zone. When you have friends of all nationalities, you will learn a lot more. Usually, when your friends are from your own country, many of your discussions centre on the past and life "back home." You need to look at the future and at Canada, your new home!

This book will not attempt to cover every angle of every possible question a newcomer might have—what book could? I hope it will go a long way toward helping newcomers deal with some of those early problems.

And when you have survived your first few weeks in Canada and have figured out the basics, you'll realize there is still much to learn.

In closing, I will say those three words you will hear very often:

Welcome to Canada!

Naeem "Nick" Noorani

Chapter 1

Welcome to Canada

In This Chapter

- What do you mean by "multicultural"?
- Canada is how big?
- It gets how cold?
- What is a Governor General?

Canadians are proud that their country embraces many cultures. It is, in fact, one of the most ethnically and racially diverse countries in the world. You and your unique background will add to the **mosaic** that makes this land of about 33 million people truly **multicultural**.

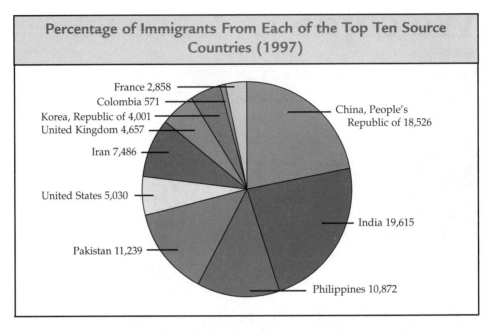

Percentage of Immigrants From Each of the Top Ten Source Countries (1997)

France 2,858
Colombia 571
Korea, Republic of 4,001
United Kingdom 4,657
Iran 7,486
United States 5,030
Pakistan 11,239
China, People's Republic of 18,526
India 19,615
Philippines 10,872

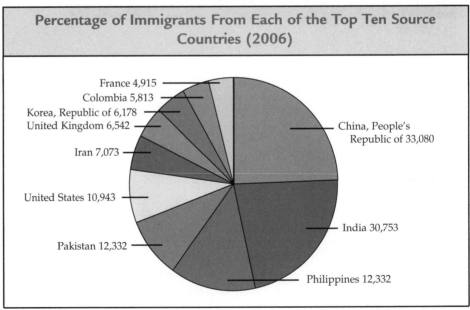

Percentage of Immigrants From Each of the Top Ten Source Countries (2006)

France 4,915
Colombia 5,813
Korea, Republic of 6,178
United Kingdom 6,542
Iran 7,073
United States 10,943
Pakistan 12,332
China, People's Republic of 33,080
India 30,753
Philippines 12,332

Source: Citizenship and Immigration Canada

Canada, often called a "nation of immigrants," has always been a land of ethnic diversity, from as early as the 1880s when Chinese men came to work on the transnational railway connecting Canada's east and west. Some people say that Canada is a unique country that was created not through war and bloodshed, but through the creation of the railway. While it would be inaccurate and simplistic to suggest that its people have lived side by side in perfect harmony through the years, they have lived in relative peace. Also, most have prospered: Canada ranks near the top of the United Nations' list of the best countries in which to live, and it ranks high in the world in terms of **Gross Domestic Product** per capita.

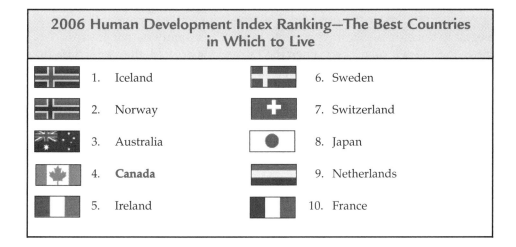

2006 Human Development Index Ranking—The Best Countries in Which to Live			
1.	Iceland	6.	Sweden
2.	Norway	7.	Switzerland
3.	Australia	8.	Japan
4.	**Canada**	9.	Netherlands
5.	Ireland	10.	France

Source: United Nations Development Programme

As the country grows through immigration, Canadians of every ethnicity and background are finding places for themselves and learning to enjoy and celebrate their diversity. Under the Canadian Multiculturalism Act, all are encouraged to practise their traditions, customs, and religious beliefs as long as they respect Canadian law.

Canada is sometimes referred to as the *Great White North*, a phrase that was popularized in a movie about two not-so-clever brothers with an obsession for beer, called *Strange Brew*. Canadians use this term affectionately when talking about their country.

In the Beginning

Native Canadians are descendants of Canada's original immigrants who probably came here from Siberia during the last ice age, and have lived here for thousands of years. These individuals are a diverse group, with many tribes who have their own languages and cultures derived from their unique histories and regional differences. It is believed that the name "Canada" is derived from the word "Kanata," which in the Huron-Iroquois language means "village" or "settlement."

Traditionally, these people relied on hunting and gathering in order to survive, although by the time the first European settlers arrived, they had begun to develop agriculture as well. In addition, many native groups traded with each other, and when the Europeans arrived, they joined in. In exchange for fish and tools, the Native Canadians gave these newcomers animal furs, which were highly valued in Europe.

The majority of Europeans who came to what is now Canada were from Britain and France. These British and French settlers needed the Native Canadians to help them with exploration, trade, and their initial survival, but also often warred with them, creating difficult relationships among the groups. Competition among the Europeans also led the Native Canadians, at various times, to join either the British or the French in their fighting with one another.

Canada's Aboriginal people are known by many names, and this can be confusing. The term "First Nations" encompasses many Aboriginal people, but does not include the Inuit (those living in Canada's northern regions) or the Metis (those of mixed Aboriginal and European descent).

Europeans began to move into North America in the 15th and 16th centuries, although there were no permanent British or French settlements in Canada until the 17th century. The French set up villages in Newfoundland, Nova Scotia, and Quebec, and the British established colonies all along the Atlantic coast.

When these settlers first arrived, Canada was considered an unimportant rural region, with its only value coming from the rich furs of its many beavers, foxes, wolves, and other small mammals. Fur trading posts, most of which were developed by the Hudson's Bay Company (still a popular department store across Canada today), were created across the country, beginning in the east and eventually spreading across the north and into what is now British Columbia.

Relations between the English and the French had been difficult in Europe, and this did not change when the groups settled in North America. They often fought over land, the fur trade with First Nations people, and religious differences.

In 1756, the Seven Years' War broke out between the English and the French around the world. This set the British and French in Canada fighting against each other. The British side won, and the French no longer had any significant power in Canada. In spite of this, a strong French influence is felt throughout Canada, although there is still tension between many Canadians of English and French descent.

The Dominion of Canada was formed in 1867 when Ontario, Quebec, Nova Scotia, and New Brunswick joined together under a new Canadian constitution, then called the British North America Act. The anniversary of the country's creation is celebrated each year on July 1, a national holiday known as Canada Day. It is generally marked by fireworks and other celebrations in communities across the country. Although Canada has been self-governing within the British Empire since 1867, it wasn't granted full independence until 1931 by the Statute of Westminster.

Size and Population

Canada is a massive country. It takes the average driver more than seven days to drive across it on transcontinental Highway 1 or 101, all the way from Vancouver to Halifax; it takes about seven hours to fly across it. The country encompasses nearly 10 million square kilometres of land and there is a distance of more than 7,000 kilometres between its westernmost provincial capital and its easternmost capital. Only the Russian Federation spans more territory than Canada.

Canada is divided into ten provinces and three **territories**. But it also has five unofficial but distinct regions: the West Coast of British Columbia; the Prairies, made up of Alberta, Saskatchewan, and Manitoba; Central Canada, which is Ontario and Quebec; Atlantic Canada, which is composed of New Brunswick, Nova Scotia, Prince Edward Island, and Newfoundland and

Distances Between Canada's Capital Cities (in kilometres)

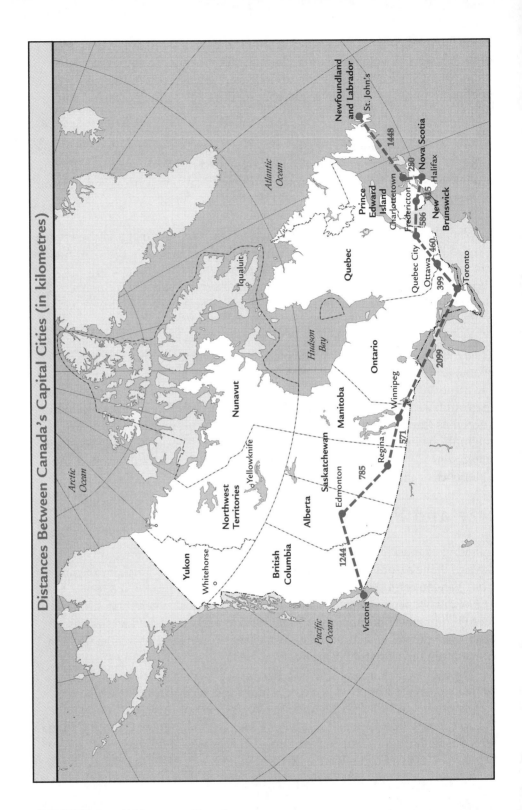

Q: Why do so many Canadians live near the US border?

A: There are two main reasons why the Canadian population lives close to the border. The first is the fact that the US is Canada's number one trade partner and Canadians living close to the border are able to conduct business or cross over and shop in the US fairly easily. The other reason is that the weather does tend to be a bit harsher in more northern areas. Cities like Vancouver are known for their mild winters compared to places like Edmonton.

Labrador; and the North, which consists of the Yukon, the Northwest Territories, and Nunavut.

About 33 million people live in this country, with about 80 percent living within 250 kilometres of the American border, including all the inhabitants of Canada's three largest cities and their suburbs: Toronto (with about 5.1 million), Montreal (with about 3.6 million) and Vancouver (with about 2 million). Ottawa, located in Ontario near the Quebec border, is the nation's capital.

Canada's population is heavily concentrated in Ontario and Quebec, as is much of its industry. These two provinces produce more than three-quarters of all the manufactured goods made in the country.

Canada has two official languages, English and French. An official policy of **bilingualism** guarantees everyone the right to communicate in either of those two languages when dealing with the **federal government**. This explains why all federal signs and documents are printed in both languages. At last count, 59 percent of all Canadians listed English as their first language; 23 percent listed French; and 18 percent listed another language.

Long regarded as a land of natural resources, Canada has developed a much more diverse economy over the past few decades. Now, in addition to such traditional industries as forestry, mining, energy, agriculture, and fishing, Canada is well known for its high technology industries such as communications, and its growing tourism industry.

Currency

The dollar is the basic unit of currency in Canada. The most common paper bills are the 5-dollar, 10-dollar, and 20-dollar, but 50-dollar and 100-dollar bills are also used. Canadian coins include the penny (1 cent), nickel (5 cents), dime (10 cents), quarter (25 cents), loonie (1-dollar coin), and the toonie (2-dollar coin).

Climate

Temperatures are measured using the Celsius (or Centigrade) thermometer.

With such a large area of land, which is bordered by three oceans and the Great Lakes, Canada's climate varies dramatically across the country. But all regions enjoy (or endure) four distinct seasons: spring, summer, autumn, and winter. The coldest regions of the country are in the north and central regions; January and February in those areas can produce subfreezing temperatures and blinding blizzards. Summer in most parts of Canada can get very warm and can also bring lots of mosquitoes, so depending on where you are in the country, you might want to carry sunscreen as well as insect repellent.

Summer days in Canada can be very hot, and are often quite uncomfortable when the air is humid rather than dry. In 1965, Canadian meteorologists created a new measurement, called the humidex, which reflects how the combination of high temperatures and humidity feels to the average person. The highest humidex reading in Canada was recorded in a town near Winnipeg, Manitoba, on July 25, 2007, when the humidex reached 53 degrees Celsius. Fortunately, readings this high are quite rare!

While the climate across the country varies, the following description of the four seasons in Canada might help you prepare for some of the seasonal differences.

Spring (officially lasting from March 21 to June 21) is frequently rainy with daytime temperatures getting warm, while nights remain cool. In central and southern Canada, the first flowers usually bloom in March, with leaves

forming on the trees in February or March on the West Coast and about two months later in the rest of Canada.

Summer (June 21 to September 21) is the hot season. In southern Canada, daytime temperatures normally stay above 20 degrees Celsius, and can sometimes rise above 30 degrees. Toronto and Montreal can get extremely hot and humid in the summer.

Autumn (September 21 to December 21) in Canada is also called fall and can be beautiful and balmy. As the temperature drops, leaves on the trees begin to turn colour from green to gold, red, and yellow. Central and Eastern Canada, which boast thousands of kilometres of maple tree forests, offer a brilliant show of fall colours, attracting tourists from around the world. However, in the later weeks of autumn, rain and sleet can become common. In many parts of the country, snow begins to fall and accumulate in November and December.

Winter (December 21 to March 21) can be a challenge. During the winter months of December, January, February, and March, the temperature usually stays below freezing (zero degrees Celsius) day and night, except on the West Coast, where freezing temperatures are rare. Temperatures in some parts of the country drop under 25 degrees below freezing. In Vancouver and Victoria, snow will sometimes accumulate, while in many other parts of Canada snow generally stays on the ground from late December to the middle of March. In the winter, the wind chill factor can make the cold temperatures feel considerably colder. Caution is advised when venturing outdoors—but more about that later.

How We Are Governed

Canada has three levels of government: the federal government, ten **provincial** and three **territorial governments**, and hundreds of **municipal governments**. As a citizen, you will be allowed, and encouraged, to vote during elections for all these levels of government.

The Federal Government

The federal government is responsible for such national matters as foreign policy, national defence, trade and commerce, criminal justice, social benefits, the banking and monetary system, fisheries, postal services, aeronautics, shipping, railways, telecommunications, and atomic energy.

The federal government shares responsibility with the provinces on such matters as immigration, agriculture, and health. The federal government consists of three branches: executive, legislative, and **judiciary**.

The executive branch consists of the **Governor General** (the official representative of the British monarchy), the **Prime Minister** (the leader of the political party that elects the most Members of Parliament during a federal election), and the **Cabinet** (members of the governing party, appointed to the position of ministers within various federal departments by the Prime Minister). Government departments are also part of the executive body.

The legislative branch is the Parliament, which consists of two chambers: the House of Commons and the Senate.

The House of Commons (or the Lower House) is composed of 308 Members of Parliament (MPs), who are elected during federal elections to represent each federal riding in Canada. Elections can be called by the ruling party at any time, but no party can remain in power for longer than five years between elections. MPs have the primary responsibility for proposing, debating, and voting on the laws that govern the country.

The Senate (or the Upper House) is made up of 105 Senators appointed by the Governor General, on the advice of the Prime Minister. Senators review and suggest changes to any proposed **legislation**, giving such proposals "a sober second thought" before they become law.

The judiciary body includes the Supreme Court of Canada, Canada's highest court, made up of appointed senior judges.

Provincial and Territorial Governments

The provincial governments are responsible for education, property and civil rights, the administration of justice, the hospital system, **natural resources** within their province's borders, social security, health, and municipal institutions. The provinces also share many powers and responsibilities with the federal government.

The structure of the provincial governments is similar to that of the federal government, except that the provinces do not have a senate.

Mobina Jaffer: From Refugee to Senator

Senator Mobina Jaffer's origins are in Uganda and India. She came to Canada from England, where she first fled as a refugee from Uganda in 1972.

It was in Canada that she fulfilled her longtime dreams of getting into politics.

"I love politics," she says. "My father was a member of parliament in Uganda, and I just loved the work."

She began volunteering with the National Women's Liberal Commission and then ran as a candidate in two federal elections. She lost both times, but her work with the Liberal Party of Canada caught then–Prime Minister Jean Chrétien's attention, and she was appointed as a senator in 2001. She was the first Indian, first Muslim woman, and first African to be appointed to the Senate of Canada.

"I feel very blessed that Canada has given me this opportunity," Jaffer says.

—Margaret Jetelina

The provincial executive body includes the Lieutenant-Governor, a representative for the Queen. The leader of the party with the most members elected during a provincial election assumes the role of **Premier**.

In each province, the elected members sit in a legislature located in the province's capital city to debate laws and issues. The elected officials are called Members of the Legislature (MLAs) or Members of Provincial Parliament (MPPs), except in Quebec, where they sit in the National Assembly. The ruling party must call an election within five years of the previous election.

The governments of the Yukon, the Northwest Territories, and Nunavut also have elected legislative assemblies, but have fewer powers and responsibilities than the provinces.

Municipal Governments

Municipal governments are directed by elected mayors, councillors, and parks board commissioners who usually hold weekly public meetings to debate and form policy on such matters as building bylaws, police, the

Q: What is the difference between a province and a territory?

A: Although the territories cover 40 percent of Canada's landmass, only 3 percent of the population lives in this area. This has led to some distinct differences between provinces and territories. The provinces own provincial land, while the federal government owns territorial land. In territories, the federal government may get involved in matters such as education which are traditionally a provincial responsibility. The way territories are run is changing rapidly and Nunavut is an example of how the territories are slowly being permitted to make decisions in self-governance.

distribution of water, sewage, garbage collection, transit, fire services, and parks.

In most districts, the operation of schools is guided by elected school trustees who set policy in their school districts and decide how to spend their budgets.

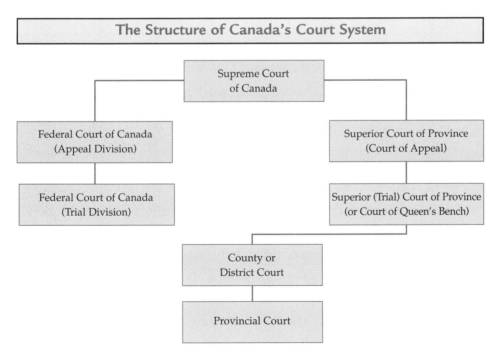

The Structure of Canada's Court System

- Supreme Court of Canada
- Federal Court of Canada (Appeal Division)
- Superior Court of Province (Court of Appeal)
- Federal Court of Canada (Trial Division)
- Superior (Trial) Court of Province (or Court of Queen's Bench)
- County or District Court
- Provincial Court

Source: Canada, Department of Justice, *Canada's System of Justice* (Ottawa: Supply and Services, 1988), 20.

Learning More About Canada

It is often said that the best way to learn about your new country is to get involved in it. Read Canadian newspapers, watch the television news, and participate in—or at least attend—community functions and meetings. These could be church gatherings, farmers' markets, gardening classes, athletic events, charity bazaars, or anything else that catches your fancy. You can also get involved in local politics and volunteering. Who knows— maybe you could end up on **Parliament Hill** in Ottawa too.

Key Words

bilingual: having or using two languages (n. bilingualism)

Cabinet (usually "the Cabinet"): the most important leaders of departments or senior ministers in the government, who have regular meetings with the President/Prime Minister

federal government: the governing body connected with the national government rather than the local government of an individual state or province

Governor General: the representative of the Crown in Canada and other Commonwealth countries which regard the Queen as the head of state

Gross Domestic Product: (abbr. GDP) the total value of all the goods and services produced by a country in one year

judiciary: the group of judges in a country or province

legislation: a law or a group of laws

mosaic: something made up of many diverse parts

multicultural: for or including people from several different races, religions, languages, or traditions

municipal government: the governing body of a town or city

natural resource: something from nature that has value to a country, such as minerals or oil

Parliament Hill: the hill in Ottawa on which the Parliament Buildings stand; the federal government of Canada

premier: the first minister of a province or territory

Prime Minister: the leader of the government in countries that have a parliament, e.g. Canada

provincial government: the governing body of a province

territorial government: the governing body of a territory

territory: an area of land

Note: Entries taken or adapted from the Oxford ESL Dictionary

Creating Your Canadian Experience

At the end of every chapter you will find a section called Creating Your Canadian Experience. This section asks questions to help you make the information in the book specific to you. Some of them require Internet research and others might ask you to go out into your community to find answers. Answering these questions will help you to create your Canadian experience.

1. Use a mapping website, such as www.mapquest.ca or maps.google.ca to find out the distance from your new home to the following cities:

    a. Ottawa, ON: _____

    b. Victoria, BC: _____

    c. St. John's, NF: _____

    d. The city you moved from: _____

2. Research on the Internet to find out what the top three industries are in your province.
    Tip: type the name of your province and "Top Industry" into a search engine.

    _____

    _____

    _____

3. Research the weather in your new Canadian city and compare it to the city you moved from. Websites such as www.theweathernetwork.com can be helpful for finding this information.

Canadian City	Jan	Feb	Mar	Apr	May	June	July	Aug	Sept	Oct	Nov	Dec
Average Temperature												
Average Precipitation												

City You Moved From	Jan	Feb	Mar	Apr	May	June	July	Aug	Sept	Oct	Nov	Dec
Average Temperature												
Average Precipitation												

4. Who is the current Prime Minister and what party is he or she from?

_____

5. Find out the name of your local Member of Parliament and the party he or she represents.

_____

6. Go to the website www.cic.gc.ca and find the name of the current federal Minister of Citizenship and Immigration.

_____

7. Who is the Premier of your province and what party is he or she from?

_____

8. Find the name of the current provincial minister who handles immigration issues.
   Tip: type the name of your province and "immigration minister" into a search engine.

   _____

9. What is the name of your city's mayor?

   _____

Chapter 2

Canada's Major Cities

In This Chapter

- What are Canada's major cities?
- What are the major industries in each city?
- How does the climate vary across the country?
- What kinds of cultural events and entertainment does each city have to offer?

Canada is a huge country. From the time you decide which city to settle in, you will want to know about the city you have chosen, its **population**, industries, transportation, climate, places of interest, cultural events and festivals, as well as some of the popular local sports. This chapter is meant to give you a general idea of your new home, as well as the other major cities of Canada. I would strongly suggest you familiarize yourself with Canada's provinces and major cities, as this will help you know your new country better.

British Columbia

BC is one of Canada's most popular provinces for travellers, as it has a great tradition of multiculturalism, a warm climate, and incredible natural beauty. BC's many **amenities** and its reputation as an exciting tourist spot earned it the honour of hosting the 2010 Winter Olympics.

Vancouver

Vancouver is BC's biggest city and Canada's third-largest city. It is well-known for its spectacular beauty, outdoor activities, and excellent living conditions. The city is definitely attractive to newcomers; more than one-third of Vancouver's population is made up of immigrants.

At a Glance

Population	Average Annual Growth	Population Density	Unemployment Rate	Average Home Price	Average Rent (2 bedroom)
2,116,581	1.3%	735.6/sq.km	3.8% (Dec. 2005)	$587,483	$1,045/month

Note: The information for the At a Glance boxes is from Statistics Canada.

Industry

The film industry is very important to Vancouver's economy, and the city has become the third-largest film production centre in North America, after Los Angeles and New York. Tourism is equally important to the city, as people are attracted to its skiing, scuba diving, and wide variety of performing arts productions.

Recently, there has been a boom in the **high-tech** industries, with some major software companies, such as Microsoft and EA Sports, establishing offices in Vancouver.

Transportation

Vancouver has an extensive **public transportation** system, so getting around the city without a car is fairly easy. The SkyTrain is an automated **light rapid transit train** that runs from the city's waterfront to Surrey, BC. A network of buses also operates in the city, with many of the lines running until the early hours of the morning.

Water travel is often necessary to get around Vancouver and its surrounding areas. The city has SeaBuses which operate between the downtown core and North Vancouver, as well as frequent ferry service to Victoria, the provincial **capital**.

Climate

Sheltered by the mountains of Vancouver Island, Vancouver has a moderate oceanic climate. It experiences a lot of rain, yet despite the high rainfall it is one of the warmest cities in Canada.

Temperature (°C)

	J	F	M	A	M	J	J	A	S	O	N	D
Maximum	6	8	10	13	16	19	22	22	18	14	9	6
Minimum	0	1	3	5	8	11	13	13	10	6	3	1
Average	3	5	6	9	12	15	17	17	14	10	6	4

Precipitation

	J	F	M	A	M	J	J	A	S	O	N	D
Rain (mm)	132	116	105	75	62	46	36	38	64	115	167	161
Snow (cm)	21	9	4	1	0	0	0	0	0	0	3	19

Note: The information for the Temperature (°C) boxes and the Precipitation boxes is from Environment Canada.

Places of Interest

Grouse Mountain (situated in North Vancouver) and Cypress Mountain (in West Vancouver) are great for skiing. Popular locations for water sports include English Bay, Spanish Banks, Jericho Beach, Kitsilano, Ambleside, White Cliff Beach, Wreck Beach, and Stanley Park. Each has a unique appeal; for example, White Cliff is overlooked by huge white cliffs which are commonly used for cliff diving.

Other popular attractions for children and adults include the Vancouver Aquarium, the Vancouver Art Gallery, and the Greater Vancouver Zoo. All of these are open year-round.

Cultural Events and Festivals

Every year, at least three countries take part in a fireworks display called the Celebration of Light. This competition gives each country an opportunity, over the course of nearly two weeks, to showcase its creativity. The free event draws spectators to Vancouver's beaches and parks to watch the fireworks displays. Over one million people take part in the Celebration of Light each year.

Due to its diversity, Vancouver hosts several annual cultural festivals. Some of them are the Chinese New Year celebrations, the Punjabi New Year, the Vancouver Asian Film Festival, and the Caribbean Days Festival. This last festival is one of the city's largest cultural celebrations, attracting tens of thousands of people with its food, music, and multicultural street parade.

Sports

Some popular sports among both locals and tourists are skiing, snowboarding, rock climbing, mountain biking, rafting, and hiking. Vancouver's beautiful waters and mountains provide scenic settings for these activities.

Vancouver's Sports Teams:
• Vancouver Canucks (hockey)
• Vancouver Whitecaps FC (soccer)
• BC Lions (football)
• Vancouver Canadians (baseball)

Victoria

Victoria is the capital of British Columbia, and is located on the south side of Vancouver Island. Although it has a much smaller population than Vancouver, the city is popular with tourists, hosting more than 3.5 million visitors each year.

Known as The Garden City, Victoria offers a serene setting in which to enjoy its many cafes and restaurants, or activities such as golfing, cycling, and bird watching. You will also find examples of Aboriginal art throughout the city.

At a Glance

Population	Average Annual Growth	Population Density	Unemployment Rate	Average Home Price	Average Rent (2 bedroom)
330,088	1.16%	695.35/sq.km	3.7% (Dec. 2005)	$565,685	$874/month

Industry
Tourism is the biggest industry in Victoria, as the large number of yearly visitors suggests, although there are also many jobs with the provincial and federal governments and the education system. The University of Victoria, or UVic, is a highly respected post-secondary institute and is also the source of many jobs in the city.

Transportation
Victoria was named in honour of Queen Victoria and the city has a certain British feel to it, as its transportation demonstrates: double-decker buses are commonly used for everyday service within the city.

To get to Victoria from the mainland, you can travel by water or air. Ferry service from Vancouver is convenient and reliable, with boats departing several times daily. Planes and helicopters between the two cities operate more frequently than ferries, but trips can be quite expensive, often costing more than ten times as much as a boat trip.

Climate
Victoria usually has moderate temperatures all year round. These moderate temperatures mean that the city has an eight month frost-free season. There is also very little rain in Victoria; the average monthly rainfall is five centimetres in winter, and two and a half centimetres in summer.

Temperature (°C)

	J	F	M	A	M	J	J	A	S	O	N	D
Maximum	7	8	10	12	14	16	18	19	17	13	9	7
Minimum	2	2	3	4	7	9	10	10	9	6	4	2
Average	4	5	7	8	11	13	14	14	13	10	7	5

Precipitation

	J	F	M	A	M	J	J	A	S	O	N	D
Rain (mm)	182	138	107	75	45	29	21	27	55	121	209	189
Snow (cm)	12	4	2	0	0	0	0	0	0	0	3	8

Places of Interest
Victoria and the surrounding area is home to many unique tourist attractions. At Mineral World, you can pan for gold or collect shells and gemstones; Victoria Bug Zoo and Pacific Undersea Gardens provide you

with the opportunity to safely observe, and sometimes interact with, a variety of interesting creatures without leaving downtown Victoria. For those interested in history and government, the city is home to BC's Parliament buildings and Government House, the Lieutenant-Governor's official residence, both of which are available for tours. Victoria also has many art galleries, museums, and an IMAX theatre.

Cultural Events and Festivals

In keeping with the British feel of the city, Victoria hosts the Tartan Parade, the Victoria Highland Games, and a Celtic music celebration called Ceilidh in the Park. Victoria also adds some Caribbean flavour with its annual SKA Fest.

Sports

Because Victoria is located on an island, water sports are very popular here, and you will often see people sailing or kayaking. Cycling and cricket are also common pastimes in the city.

Victoria's Sports Teams:
• Victoria Lions (football)
• Victoria Salmon Kings (hockey)
• Bays United FC (soccer)

Alberta

The province of Alberta is named after Princess Louise Caroline Alberta, the fourth daughter of Queen Victoria. Lake Louise, the Village of Caroline, and Mount Alberta were all named in honour of the princess.

Calgary

Calgary is the largest city in the province of Alberta and is located in the south, approximately 80 kilometres east of the front ranges of the Rocky Mountains. The city is known for its winter sports and year-round eco-tourism.

An economic boom has attracted thousands of people to the city in recent years; Calgary has more than one million residents, and is continuing to grow.

At a Glance

Population	Average Annual Growth	Population Density	Unemployment Rate	Average Home Price	Average Rent (2 bedroom)
1,079,310	2.68%	5,107.43/ sq.km	4.4% (Dec. 2005)	$423,801	$960/month

Industry

Calgary started to profit from the oil industry in 1947 when huge reserves of oil were discovered. Petroleum is still the main source of industrial activity in the city, and the reason for Calgary's continuing economic growth. Other important sectors for the city are manufacturing, information and communication technology, and tourism.

Transportation

Both buses and light rail transit are available in the city. You can travel on the light rail within Calgary's downtown for free, although you will need to pay for trips that go outside of the downtown area. The city is also very bike-friendly; there is a large interconnected network of paved multi-use paths spanning over 635 kilometres, as well as another 260 kilometres of on-street bike lanes.

Climate

The climate in Calgary is generally cold. Winters are long and dry, while summers are short and moderately warm. However, chinook winds routinely blow in from the Pacific Ocean. This can be a huge relief to Calgary's residents in the winter, as the warm winds can dramatically raise the air temperature within a very short period of time.

Temperature (°C)

	J	F	M	A	M	J	J	A	S	O	N	D
Maximum	-3	0	3	11	16	21	23	23	17	13	3	-1
Minimum	-15	-11	-7	-1	3	7	10	9	4	0	-8	-13
Average	-9	-5	-2	4	10	14	16	16	11	6	-2	-7

Precipitation

	J	F	M	A	M	J	J	A	S	O	N	D
Rain (mm)	0	0	2	9	44	77	70	49	43	6	1	0
Snow (cm)	18	15	19	20	10	0	0	0	6	12	16	19

Places of Interest

Calgary has a unique atmosphere when compared to the rest of Canada: hotel saloons and western bars are popular, and the city harbours great musical talent; it is sometimes referred to as the Nashville of the North. The Southern Alberta Jubilee Auditorium is a 2,500-seat performing arts facility. The auditorium was opened in 1957 and has been host to numerous Broadway musicals and annual Remembrance Day celebrations.

Cultural Events and Festivals

The world-renowned Calgary Stampede and Exhibition is an annual fair and rodeo which takes place every July and is one of the largest festivals in Canada. The event began in 1912, and currently attracts more than one million spectators each year. Other festivals include the Calgary Greek Festival; GlobalFest, which celebrates cultural diversity in Calgary; Expo Latino; and Pride Calgary, which includes a street gala and a gay pride parade.

Sports

Calgary hosted the Winter Olympics in 1988 and continues to make use of facilities that were built for the games. At the Canada Olympic Park, you can ski, snowboard, or mountain bike, as well as take introductory lessons in the more unusual sports of bobsleigh, skeleton, and luge. The Olympic Oval was built for speed skating competitions, but also contains track and field facilities.

Calgary's Sports Teams:
• Calgary Flames (hockey)
• Calgary Stampeders (football)
• Calgary Roughnecks (lacrosse)
• Calgary Vipers (baseball)

Edmonton

Edmonton is the capital of the province of Alberta and is located on the North Saskatchewan River in the central region of the province. It is known as the City of Champions because of the impressive number of successful sports teams that have originated here.

At a Glance

Population	Average Annual Growth	Population Density	Unemployment Rate	Average Home Price	Average Rent (2 bedroom)
1,034,945	2.08%	109.9/sq.km	4.4% (Dec. 2005)	$345,809	$808/month

Industry

Like Calgary, Edmonton went through a large oil boom in 1947, earning it the nickname of Oil Capital of Canada. The city is a major supply and service point for Alberta's natural resources, including its oil sands. Much like Calgary, Edmonton's population is rising steadily and there is growth in nearly all industries.

Transportation

Edmonton is a large city, so walking isn't always a convenient way to get around. Fortunately, the city has a transportation system consisting of buses and light rail transit. There are also hundreds of kilometres of bike paths and trails for the city's cyclists.

Climate

Summers in Edmonton are mild, while winters are cold. The city is fairly dry all year, never receiving much rain or snow.

Temperature (°C)

	J	F	M	A	M	J	J	A	S	O	N	D
Maximum	-8	-4	0	10	17	21	12	22	17	11	0	-6
Minimum	-19	-16	-10	-2	3	7	9	8	3	-1	-10	-17
Average	-13	-10	-4	4	10	14	16	15	10	5	-5	-11

Precipitation

	J	F	M	A	M	J	J	A	S	O	N	D
Rain (mm)	2	1	1	10	39	76	101	70	45	10	2	1
Snow (cm)	26	19	18	12	4	0	0	0	3	8	17	22

Places of Interest

The city is famous for its West Edmonton Mall. The mall is not only a shopping centre; the enormous facility contains an amusement park, ice skating rink, and water park.

Art lovers will enjoy the Peter Robertson Gallery, which primarily features Canadian artists. Whyte Avenue is a great source of entertainment, both day and night. It has lots of great shops and cafes, as well as an interesting mix of bars, art house theatres, and music venues.

Cultural Events and Festivals

The Festival City, as Edmonton is known, hosts numerous events each year. These diverse events range from the Edmonton International Fringe Theatre Festival to the Canadian Finals Rodeo. Edmonton is also home to Vinok Worldance and the Volya Ukrainian Dance Ensemble, two dance companies that showcase international music and dancing.

Sports

During the brief warmer months, golf is a favourite sport in Edmonton. Throughout the winter, curling becomes a popular pastime for the city's residents, both to play and watch.

Edmonton's Sports Teams:
• Edmonton Oilers (hockey)
• Edmonton Eskimos (football)
• Edmonton Rush (lacrosse)

Saskatchewan

The name Saskatchewan comes from the Plains Indians' word for the river that runs swiftly, "kisiskatchewan." This refers to the province's most important rivers, the North and South Saskatchewan rivers.

Regina

Regina is the provincial capital of Saskatchewan and the major commercial centre of the province. The city was named after Queen Victoria (or Victoria Regina), by her daughter, Princess Louise, in 1882.

At a Glance

Population	Average Annual Growth	Population Density	Unemployment Rate	Average Home Price	Average Rent (2 bedroom)
194,971	0.22%	57.2/sq.km	4.9% (Dec. 2005)	$174,719	$619/month

Industry

Agriculture plays a major part in the city's economy; Viterra, the country's largest agricultural company, has its headquarters here. The mining industry is another major source of jobs in Regina and throughout the province, with Saskatchewan producing a large portion of the world's potash and uranium.

Transportation
Although Regina is a fairly small city, it has an extensive system of bus routes. This method of transportation will be especially appealing to seniors, who are eligible for yearly bus passes at a dramatically reduced rate.

Climate
Regina has a continental climate; its summers are warm and its winters are cold and dry. With an average of 2,365 hours of sunshine each year, it is considered Canada's sunniest capital city.

Temperature (°C)

	J	F	M	A	M	J	J	A	S	O	N	D
Maximum	-10	-7	0	10	19	24	26	25	18	12	0	-8
Minimum	-22	-19	-11	-2	4	9	11	10	4	-2	-10	-19
Average	-16	-13	-6	4	11	16	19	18	11	4	-5	-13

Precipitation

	J	F	M	A	M	J	J	A	S	O	N	D
Rain (mm)	1	0	3	14	48	61	59	39	33	16	2	1
Snow (cm)	19	14	14	7	2	0	0	0	2	5	12	19

Places of Interest
Popular attractions in Regina include the Royal Saskatchewan Museum, the Saskatchewan Science Centre, and the Norman Mackenzie Art Gallery. IPSCO Place is home to the Buffalo Days Exhibition, an annual summertime festival and parade.

Cultural Events and Festivals
The highlight of Regina's festivals is Kona-Fest, a winter celebration of music, arts, sports, and culture. Among other things, it includes snowboarding competitions, ice sculpture displays, and concerts.

Sports
As in many cities across the country, soccer is popular in Regina, and the city has several leagues. In the winter, you'll find the locals engaged in sports such as ice skating and curling.

Regina's Sports Teams:
• Saskatchewan Roughriders (football)
• Regina Pats (hockey)

Manitoba

Manitoba's name probably comes from the Cree word "maniotwapow," meaning the strait of the spirit, and refers to the sound of Lake Manitoba's waves crashing on the shore. The noise was supposed to sound like the voice or drumbeat of the Great Spirit, or Manitou.

Winnipeg

Winnipeg is the capital of Manitoba, and is located at the eastern edge of the great plains of western Canada and the geographic centre of North America. The city lies in close proximity to hundreds of lakes, including Lake Winnipeg, Lake Manitoba, and Lake of the Woods. More than half of Manitoba's residents live in Winnipeg.

At a Glance

Population	Average Annual Growth	Population Density	Unemployment Rate	Average Home Price	Average Rent (2 bedroom)
694,668	0.54%	131.0/sq.km	3.6% (Dec. 2005)	$167,774	$709/month

Industry

The city is a regional centre for commerce, industry, culture, finance, and government. The primary employers in Winnipeg are the government and government-funded institutions.

Transportation

The city of Winnipeg has a network of buses operating downtown, with limited service to the city's suburbs.

Climate

Winters here are long, cold, and windy, so the city is sometimes referred to as "Winterpeg." Summer temperatures can get very warm, but the season is short.

Temperature (°C)

	J	F	M	A	M	J	J	A	S	O	N	D
Maximum	-12	-9	-1	10	19	23	26	25	19	11	0	-9
Minimum	-23	-20	-11	-1	5	10	13	12	6	0	-8	-18
Average	-17	-14	-6	4	12	17	20	18	12	6	-4	-14

Precipitation

	J	F	M	A	M	J	J	A	S	O	N	D
Rain (mm)	0	0	6	26	58	84	72	75	51	25	5	2
Snow (cm)	23	17	19	9	2	0	0	0	0	5	19	20

Places of Interest

Winnipeg has a vibrant arts culture, and is home to the Royal Winnipeg Ballet, the Winnipeg Art Gallery, the Manitoba Opera, and the Manitoba Museum.

Cultural Events and Festivals

Some popular events in the city are an annual Icelandic festival, called Islendingadagurinn, and the Winnipeg Music Festival.

Sports

Winnipeg locals enjoy similar sports to those in other Canadian cities. Soccer, hockey, and many water sports are popular.

Winnipeg's Sports Teams:
- Winnipeg Blue Bombers (football)
- Manitoba Moose (hockey)

Ontario

Ontario's name comes from a native word, possibly "onitariio" or "kanadario," which loosely translate to beautiful or sparkling water or lake.

Ontario is the most heavily populated province in all of Canada, and is the second-largest in total area. Much like BC, Ontario has a large immigrant population made up of people from a wide variety of ethnic backgrounds.

Toronto

Toronto is the capital of Ontario and Canada's largest city, and its diverse ethnic makeup makes it attractive to many newcomers; about half of its residents are foreign-born.

At a Glance

Population	Average Annual Growth	Population Density	Unemployment Rate	Average Home Price	Average Rent (2 bedroom)
5,113,149	1.84%	866.1/sq.km	5.6% (Dec. 2005)	$361,898	$1,067/month

Industry
Commerce is a major contributor to Toronto's economy, and many major banks have their headquarters here. Tourism is also extremely important to the city, with millions of visitors visiting Toronto each year.

Transportation
Many people who live in Toronto do not own cars; they instead rely on the city's public transit system. This includes several subway lines, as well as many streetcars and buses. The transit system is generally fast and reliable, but it is expensive when compared to that of other Canadian cities.

Climate
Toronto has a fairly mild climate. Summers are warm, and average temperatures throughout the winter usually remain just below freezing.

Temperature (°C)

	J	F	M	A	M	J	J	A	S	O	N	D
Maximum	0	0	4	10	16	22	25	24	20	13	7	1
Minimum	-7	-6	-2	3	8	13	16	16	13	7	2	-4
Average	-4	-3	1	6	12	17	21	20	16	10	5	-1

Precipitation

	J	F	M	A	M	J	J	A	S	O	N	D
Rain (mm)	23	26	40	57	67	68	69	80	76	60	67	45
Snow (cm)	29	25	19	6	0	0	0	0	0	0	5	27

Places of Interest
Numerous dance companies, opera companies, and symphony orchestras contribute to the city's arts scene. As well, Toronto has many museums and art galleries, the most popular being the Royal Ontario Museum and the Art Gallery of Ontario. The city is also known for its landmark downtown mall, the Toronto Eaton Centre.

Cultural Events and Festivals
The Toronto Caribbean Carnival Festival, or Caribana, takes place from July to August. This event attracts hundreds of thousands of tourists, and brings millions of dollars into the city. Toronto's Chinese Lantern Festival takes place on the waterfront at Ontario Place from September to October, and is the largest of its kind outside of Asia.

Each year, the Toronto International Film Festival shows hundreds of movies throughout the city's downtown and attracts celebrities from around the world.

Sports
Toronto's residents play a variety of indoor and outdoor sports; some of the most popular are golf, hockey, and soccer.

Toronto's Sports Teams:
• Toronto Maple Leafs (hockey)
• Toronto Blue Jays (baseball)
• Toronto Raptors (basketball)
• Toronto Argonauts (football)
• Toronto FC (soccer)
• Toronto Rock (lacrosse)

Ottawa
Ottawa is the capital of Canada; government buildings, historic sites, and national museums can be found everywhere. This ethnically diverse city is located close to Ontario's border with Quebec. A short drive over the Prince of Wales bridge will take you to Gatineau, Quebec.

At a Glance

Population	Average Annual Growth	Population Density	Unemployment Rate	Average Home Price	Average Rent (2 bedroom)
1,130,761	1.18%	197.8/sq.km	4.6% (Dec. 2005)	$267,765	$941/month

Industry
The national parliament buildings are here, and the Prime Minister resides in Ottawa, so the Federal Government is a major source of employment. Tourism is also very important to the city's economy.

Transportation

Transportation services in Ottawa include the Transitway, which is a network of high-frequency bus rapid transit lanes with full stations, and a light rail system called the O-Train. There are also connections to buses that serve the surrounding rural areas.

Climate

Ottawa is situated on the south bank of the Ottawa River; the Rideau River and Rideau Canal also run through the city, so it can get very windy at times. The nation's capital does get a lot of snow in the winter, and despite the summer season being short, it is very warm and humid.

Temperature (°C)

	J	F	M	A	M	J	J	A	S	O	N	D
Maximum	-5	-4	2	11	19	24	26	25	20	13	5	-3
Minimum	-14	-13	-6	1	7	13	15	14	10	4	-1	-10
Average	-10	-8	-2	6	13	18	21	19	15	8	2	-6

Precipitation

	J	F	M	A	M	J	J	A	S	O	N	D
Rain (mm)	14	15	30	58	76	84	87	88	84	72	64	30
Snow (cm)	46	41	27	7	1	0	0	0	0	3	19	54

Places of Interest

As well as the government buildings, which include the Parliament of Canada, Confederation Building, and Rideau Hall, Ottawa is also home to a large number of embassies.

Cultural Events and Festivals

The Tulip Festival takes place throughout the city each spring. It was originally inspired by a gift of tulips that Holland's Princess Juliana gave to the city in 1945.

The Carnival of Cultures consists of cultural performances featuring music, song, and dance from around the world. Many countries participate in this annual event.

Sports

Winter sports are very popular in the city. Many people play hockey or skate on the Rideau Canal, which is known as the world's largest skating rink.

Ottawa's Sports Teams:
- Ottawa Senators (hockey)
- Ottawa 67's (hockey)

Quebec

Quebec is the only province in Canada where the primary language spoken is French. Quebec's residents often call it "La belle province," or "the beautiful province," demonstrating the pride they have in their home.

Montreal

The city has one of the world's largest French-speaking populations. Many residents, however, are bilingual, so English speakers will not have trouble communicating in Montreal.

At a Glance

Population	Average Annual Growth	Population Density	Unemployment Rate	Average Home Price	Average Rent (2 bedroom)
3,635,571	1.06%	853.6/sq.km	9.6% (Dec. 2005)	$228,006	$636/month

Industry

Although tourism is crucial to the city, Montreal excels in many different industries. Aerospace, telecommunications, electronic goods, software engineering, textiles, and tobacco all play a significant part, and the film industry and video game industry are gaining importance.

Transportation

The city's bus and subway systems are among the best in Canada, extending across several municipalities.

Climate

High humidity is very common during summer, and it's not unusual to experience heat-waves late in the season; these are called "Indian summers." Some snow falls during spring and autumn, with temperatures dropping drastically in January.

Temperature (°C)

	J	F	M	A	M	J	J	A	S	O	N	D
Maximum	-5	-3	2	11	19	23	26	25	20	13	5	-2
Minimum	-14	-13	-6	1	7	13	15	14	9	4	-1	-10
Average	-9	-8	-1	6	13	18	21	19	15	8	2	-6

Precipitation

	J	F	M	A	M	J	J	A	S	O	N	D
Rain (mm)	21	19	34	63	67	83	86	100	87	73	70	35
Snow (cm)	48	41	31	11	2	0	0	0	0	3	24	55

Places of Interest

Montreal provides plenty of art and culture with its many theatres and museums. Some highlights are the Montreal Museum of Fine Arts, which is one of Canada's oldest museums, and the Place des Arts, a major venue for music, theatre, dance, and comedy.

The Biosphere, in Parc Jean Drapeau, is the city's most unusual attraction. It was the US contribution to the 1967 World's Fair and was later donated to the city of Montreal. It has since become a popular tourist attraction.

Cultural Events and Festivals

Montreal hosts various festivals throughout the year. Fete Des Neiges de Montreal is a celebration of winter and involves lots of outdoor activities, including building snow sculptures. Festivalissimo is a Latin and Portuguese showcase of film, visual art, literature, and music. In the summer, Montreal's Italian Week celebrates Italy through comedy, music, fashion, and art.

Sports

Hockey is very important to Montreal's residents, and many enjoy playing or watching the sport during the city's long winters. Montreal is also home to several motor racing events, the Canadian Grand Prix and the Champ Car series.

Montreal's Sports Teams:
• Montreal Canadiens (hockey)
• Montreal Alouettes (football)
• Montreal Impact (soccer)

Quebec City

Quebec City is one of the oldest cities in Canada, founded in 1608. It is the capital of Quebec and the second-largest city in the province.

At a Glance

Population	Average Annual Growth	Population Density	Unemployment Rate	Average Home Price	Average Rent (2 bedroom)
715,515	0.84%	218.4/sq.km	4.3% (Dec. 2005)	$165,088	$637/month

Industry

As the provincial capital, a large number of the city's jobs are in public administration. Transport and the service industry are other major employers.

Transportation

Quebec City's transit system consists of a fleet of buses. Many of the routes run late on weekends to ensure that travellers get home safely.

Climate

Quebec City has a humid climate, with lots of precipitation. Summers are warm and sunny, but winters are very cold. The city often gets snow until May.

Temperature (°C)

	J	F	M	A	M	J	J	A	S	O	N	D
Maximum	-7	-5	0	8	17	22	25	23	18	11	3	-4
Minimum	-16	-15	-8	-1	5	10	13	12	7	2	-3	-12
Average	-11	-10	-4	3	11	16	19	18	13	7	0	-8

Precipitation

	J	F	M	A	M	J	J	A	S	O	N	D
Rain (mm)	20	14	33	53	99	110	119	120	124	93	68	30
Snow (cm)	78	65	51	19	1	0	0	0	0	3	38	82

Places of Interest

The most recognizable symbol of Quebec City is the Chateau Frontenac, an impressive historic hotel which overlooks the St. Lawrence River.

The Mega Parc des Galeries de la Capitale is a large shopping centre, similar to the West Edmonton Mall. It contains a roller coaster, a skating rink, and a climbing wall.

Cultural Events and Festivals

The Carnaval de Quebec is the largest winter carnival in the world. This annual event began in 1955 and features dance parties, dogsled races, and ice sculpture competitions. Envol et Macadam is an annual event that features performances of new and alternative music at various indoor and outdoor venues throughout the city.

Sports

Winter sports—particularly skiing—are a major attraction in the city, so there are many ski resorts in the Quebec City area.

Quebec City's Sports Teams:
• Quebec Radio X (hockey)
• Quebec City Kebekwa (basketball)

Atlantic Canada

Atlantic Canada is the region of Canada made up of New Brunswick, Newfoundland and Labrador, Nova Scotia, and Prince Edward Island.

Halifax

Halifax, Nova Scotia is located on the Atlantic Coast. The city of Halifax is fairly small, although it joined with its surrounding area to become the Halifax Regional Municipality (HRM) in 1996. The HRM is home to almost half of the province's residents.

At a Glance

Population	Average Annual Growth	Population Density	Unemployment Rate	Average Home Price	Average Rent (2 bedroom)
372,679	2.14%	175.9/sq.km	9.2% (Dec. 2005)	$134,286	$762/month

Industry

The city has a strong economy, based mainly on tourism, manufacturing, and fishing. Nova Scotia has the distinction of being the world's largest lobster exporter.

Transportation
In addition to bus service, the transit system in Halifax also provides ferries which cross Halifax Harbour; the trip only takes about 12 minutes. During summer, bus service throughout the downtown area is free.

Climate
Halifax has cool summers, moderate winters, and a lot of fog; the city has an average of 122 days of fog each year. Halifax experiences stormier weather than any other city in Canada, with its winter storms being especially dangerous.

Temperature (°C)

	J	F	M	A	M	J	J	A	S	O	N	D
Maximum	-1	-1	3	8	15	20	23	23	19	13	7	1
Minimum	-9	-10	-5	0	4	9	13	13	9	4	0	-6
Average	-5	-5	-1	4	9	15	18	18	14	9	3	-2

Precipitation

	J	F	M	A	M	J	J	A	S	O	N	D
Rain (mm)	87	62	80	101	107	98	97	110	95	126	141	119
Snow (cm)	64	60	44	22	3	0	0	0	0	3	14	51

Places of Interest
The city's downtown waterfront has many historic buildings to explore, and the Maritime Museum of the Atlantic displays a collection of artifacts salvaged from the Titanic.

Alexander Keith's Brewery is the oldest operating brewery in North America. Actors dress as brewers from 1863 and guide visitors on tours of the brewery.

Cultural Events and Festivals
The annual Atlantic Film Festival is one of the biggest events in Halifax, and offers a series of international and local films. The city also hosts the Halifax Highland Games and Scottish Festival; in addition to the traditional feats of strength displayed in the Highland Games, the festival offers Scottish music and dancing.

Sports

The city's location makes it ideal for paddling and sailing, both popular sports in the area.

Halifax's Sports Teams:
• Halifax Mooseheads (hockey)
• Halifax Rainmen (basketball)

St. John's

Newfoundland and Labrador was the last province to become part of Canada, joining in 1949, and St. John's is the provincial capital.

At a Glance

Population	Average Annual Growth	Population Density	Unemployment Rate	Average Home Price	Average Rent (2 bedroom)
181,113	0.94%	225.1/sq.km	8.5% (Dec. 2005)	$137,471	$635/month

Industry

The economy in St. John's relies heavily on oil, gas, and the fishing industry. Increasingly, the tourism industry is becoming important to the city.

Transportation

Buses provide public transportation in St. John's, although travel by car is more common in this city.

Climate

St. John's has cool summers and mild winters. It also has some extreme weather: it is the foggiest, snowiest, wettest, windiest, and cloudiest city in Canada.

Temperature (°C)

	J	F	M	A	M	J	J	A	S	O	N	D
Maximum	0	0	1	5	10	16	20	20	16	11	6	2
Minimum	-7	-8	-5	-1	1	6	11	11	8	3	0	-4
Average	-3	-4	-2	1	6	11	15	15	12	7	3	-1

Precipitation

	J	F	M	A	M	J	J	A	S	O	N	D
Rain (mm)	69	69	74	80	91	95	78	122	125	147	122	91
Snow (cm)	83	69	54	27	8	1	0	0	0	4	22	55

Places of Interest

The Rooms is a large facility in downtown St. John's that houses the Provincial Museum, the Provincial Art Gallery, and the Provincial Archives. The unique structure was designed to look like the fishing rooms where people used to gather to process their catches for the day. Another popular attraction is St. John's Harbour; tours of the harbour are offered regularly by many different companies.

Cultural Events and Festivals

The Festival du Vent is an annual celebration of French culture and Newfoundland weather. There are other festivals throughout the year, including the Shakespeare by the Sea Festival, featuring outdoor performances of classic plays.

Sports

Rugby is popular in the city, and the local Rugby Canada Super League team is the Newfoundland Rock. St. John's hosts North America's oldest continuing sporting event, the Royal St. John's Regatta, a rowing event dating back to 1816.

St. John's Sports Teams:
• The Rock (rugby)
• St. John's Fog Devils (hockey)

Key Words

amenity: a feature in a place that helps makes it pleasant or easy to be there

average annual growth: the typical increase in population within the period of one year

capital: the town or city where the government of a country or province is

high-tech: using a lot of modern equipment, especially computers

light rail transit: a system of public transportation that uses trains which run on steel rails and are designed for a light volume of traffic

population: a number of people who live in a particular place

population density: the number of people in a place in relation to its area

precipitation: rain, snow, etc. that falls to the ground

public transportation: (the system of) buses, trains, etc. that run according to a schedule and that anybody can use

unemployment rate: a measurement of the percentage of people in the population who are out of work

Note: Entries taken or adapted from the Oxford ESL Dictionary

Creating Your Canadian Experience

If your new city is not in this chapter, research on the Internet and ask people in your community to help you fill in the blanks below.

Your City

_____

_____

_____

_____

At a Glance

Population	Average Annual Growth	Population Density	Unemployment Rate	Average Home Price	Average Rent (2 bedroom)

Industry

_____

_____

_____

_____

Transportation

_____

_____

_____

_____

Climate

_____

_____

_____

_____

_____

Temperature (°C)

	J	F	M	A	M	J	J	A	S	O	N	D
Maximum												
Minimum												
Average												

Precipitation

	J	F	M	A	M	J	J	A	S	O	N	D
Rain (mm)												
Snow (cm)												

Places of Interest

_____

_____

_____

_____

Cultural Events and Festivals

_____

_____

_____

_____

Sports

_____

_____

_____

_____

Your City's Sports Teams:

- _____

- _____

When you have filled in as many of the above answers as possible, or if your city is in this chapter already, answer these questions and complete these tasks to get to know your city better.

1. Look on the Internet to find out the different areas of your city and what they are known for.
   Tip: a municipal website might be a good place to start.

Area	Known For
_____	_____
_____	_____
_____	_____

2. Make a list of three places you would like to visit in your city (either places you read about in this chapter or that you have heard about elsewhere). Set a date that you will visit them.

Place of Interest	Date to Visit
1. _____	_____
2. _____	_____
3. _____	_____

3. Find a public transportation map in your city. Plan your route to each of the places of interest above.
   Tip: you can find a map online by searching "public transportation" and your city, or by asking for one at a bus or train station.

Bus/Train/Subway	to Bus/Train/Subway	to Bus/Train/Subway
1. _____	to _____	to _____
2. _____	to _____	to _____
3. _____	to _____	to _____

4. Do some research on the Internet for cultural events and festivals. Write down two that you would like to attend, and when and where they are held.
   Tip: try looking on the websites of local newspapers for an event calendar.

Event	Date	Location
_____	_____	_____
_____	_____	_____

5. Pick a sports event in your city and plan to go to it.
   Tip: check your local newspaper's sports section to see what games are coming up.

Sport	Date	Ticket Price
_____	_____	_____

Chapter 3

What to Know Before You Go

In This Chapter

- What household items should you bring?
- What documents do you need to gather before you arrive?
- How can you get a licence to practise your trade in Canada?
- How much money will you need to tide you over until you get work?

You now have your landing papers in hand. Congratulations! Before you depart the shores of your beloved homeland, however, there are a number of important steps you should take to ensure a smooth transition into your new life in Canada.

Perhaps the first thing you should consider is how you want to transfer your cash and other investments to Canada. This will be a personal decision and probably something you'll want to discuss with your banker in your home country. You will naturally want to retain some cash, as well as traveller's cheques, and some credit cards to handle your immediate out-of-pocket expenses. Keeping your credit cards from your homeland for identification purposes is a good idea, too. You might also want to begin familiarizing yourself with the value of the Canadian dollar to help you judge costs upon your arrival.

Q: How do I transfer my money to Canada?

A: You can get an international wire transfer using the SWIFT (Society for Worldwide Interbank Financial Telecommunication) system. SWIFT operates a worldwide network which can transfer funds between different financial institutions. Ask for details at your bank.

As an immigrant, you will experience many different emotions before and after moving to a new land. They will range from excitement about your new home to nervousness about the future. Making the decision to move to a foreign country requires enormous courage, determination, and strength. The enormity of what you have done will continue to hit you for days, weeks, and months after you arrive.

Homesickness

Your first few months will be spent settling in, adjusting, and job hunting. You will go through periods of **homesickness**. This won't last long, however, and as soon as you begin meeting new friends, making connections with people from your own country, and introducing yourself to members of the community and ethnic associations in your neighbourhood, you will begin to feel at home.

If you have the feeling of homesickness, you are not alone! Almost every immigrant I know has felt the same way. Memories of relatives and friends make you miss your old country, and this could lead to depression. Add to this the challenges of setting up a new home, and sure—what you left behind does seem a lot better at times.

Upon re-settlement, some immigrants may develop post-traumatic stress disorder (PTSD). PTSD affects people who have experienced extreme trauma, and that may include the difficulty of moving to a strange new country.

PTSD has both physical and psychological symptoms. Some of the physical symptoms include breathing difficulties, headaches, and trouble sleeping. Some of the psychological symptoms include nightmares, feelings of loneliness, and poor concentration.

These symptoms are normal reactions to stress, and many people will display some of these symptoms soon after they have experienced a difficult event. It is only when the symptoms last for more than one month that an individual may have PTSD.

Suggestions for fighting homesickness:

• Stay positive—keep away from complainers!
• Take time out to go and enjoy Canada—the land and the people are what you chose.
• Take time out from chores and go for walks or to **community centres**.
• Attend classes for new Canadians—you will meet more newcomers like yourself and find you are not alone in this journey.

By expanding your knowledge of your new community and building a social circle, you will be better equipped to deal with feelings of homesickness. And, of course, the busier you are, the less time you will have to wonder if moving to a strange new country was the right decision! I highly recommend joining a recreation or community centre and a library.

Recreation and community centres are located in almost every neighbourhood in Canada, providing convenient facilities for swimming, racquetball, basketball, weight lifting, and many other athletic activities. The centres also provide ongoing instruction on a variety of topics, including sports and arts and crafts. Membership fees are generally very reasonable, and will be lower if you choose a quarterly or yearly membership rather than a monthly one.

In 1891, Canadian-born James Naismith wanted to motivate his physical education students. Dividing them into two groups and throwing them a soccer ball, he told each team to try to get the ball and, passing it from one player to another, throw it into a raised peach basket guarded by the other team. Naismith had invented the game of basketball!

There is no cost to join a library. You can access information from your homeland through either newspapers or the library's computers. While most newcomers will naturally want to stay informed of what's happening in the country they've left behind, I suggest that too much emphasis on your homeland will keep you from truly embracing Canada; you'll have one foot in the old country and one in the new.

While everyone will bring his or her own set of expectations, hopes, and goals, it is probably safe to say that things will get easier after the first year. In the brief yet powerful words of my 16-year-old, "Hang in there."

Taking It All With You

As a landed immigrant, you are entitled to bring with you, free of duty and taxes, any personal and household items that you owned before your arrival in Canada. These may include furniture, furnishings, silverware, linens, books, musical instruments, family **heirlooms**, antiques, stamp and coin collections, paintings, boats, power tools, outboard engines—even a private aircraft!

If possible, you should retain the receipts for these goods to prove that they are your personal items and for your personal use. Any valuable jewellery, watches, heirlooms, and artwork must be assessed by professional valuers before you arrive.

As for clothing, don't underestimate how cold Canadian winters can be. In some major cities, such as Winnipeg and Ottawa, it is not uncommon to experience temperatures as low as thirty degrees below freezing (-30° Celsius) accompanied by howling winds. Even the supposedly mild West Coast can get pretty miserable in the winter.

Our first winter in Vancouver in 1998 was one of the wettest, greyest winters on record. My wife was ready to pack up and head south by mid-January, and the wet period lasted until about July. Whether you arrive in summer or in winter, warm clothes are a necessity. When packing for your move, plan to keep enough of these clothes and other necessities with you to live comfortably until all your belongings arrive in Canada.

If your household packing is done by professional movers, they will itemize and label your belongings, making it much easier to unpack at the other end. Ensure that the movers provide you with a detailed packing list as well.

Freight forwarding companies offer either shipping only, or may include an unpacking service. **Insurance** against loss or damage of your possessions while in transit is not necessarily included in your moving bill, so you might want to arrange for coverage before you hand over all your possessions to a moving company. Word-of-mouth recommendations from friends and relatives in your home country will probably lead you to a reliable mover.

Pashmina Balani: First Impressions

"Clean" was one of the first words that popped into Pashmina Balani's head when she and her parents arrived in Mississauga from Pune, India.

Next, Balani was impressed by the friendly greetings she received wherever she went. "We boarded the bus and the driver said, 'Good morning' with a smile. We went to get our SIN numbers and were greeted with a smile; in the bank also. Everywhere we went, everybody wore a smile."

When she started school, her initial impressions were strengthened. "Everything was so clean. The corridors and classes are so wide and uncrowded. I got a locker to myself, something unheard of in India. The teachers were so friendly and approachable," she says.

"Each student gets more individual attention. And boys and girls go to the same class, unlike in India. All in all, I like Canada more than India, especially since there is not as much homework here," Balani adds, with a mischievous **glint** in her eyes.

— *Lachman Balani*

A word of advice about packing the little things: as it could be some time before you will be in a position to buy day-to-day items such as cutlery and dinnerware, you might consider bringing a box or two of such necessities from home. It didn't take me long to regret leaving all our kitchenware behind!

It is probably best to leave your appliances behind. The electrical current used by small appliances like lamps, radios, televisions, and DVD players is 110 volts, 60 cycles in Canada. If your appliances don't conform to this voltage, leave them behind. For a long time, I had an entire room full of useless TVs, VCRs, and other electrical appliances that I had brought from home. Converters burn out too quickly to use for any length of time. Also, your DVDs may not work in Canadian DVD players; check their compatibility before packing them.

Bringing Animals

Dogs and cats younger than three months can be brought into Canada from the United States without **documentation**. Also, Seeing Eye dogs in good health, regardless of their age, can be brought into Canada from any country in the world, as long as they accompany their owner.

Dogs and cats from the United States that are three months old or older can be imported, provided the owner submits a certificate for each pet, signed by a veterinarian. The certificate must show that the animal has been vaccinated against rabies within the last three years. In addition, the certificate has to identify the animal by breed, age, sex, colouring, and any distinguishing marks.

Robert Mayall: Lost and Found

When asked what moving to Canada was like, young Robert Mayall is quick to answer, "Hell."

"My PlayStation left a month before me and arrived a month after me. Two months without my PlayStation was pure hell," he says.

"But the most disastrous part was that when it finally arrived, it didn't work!"

—*Margaret Jetelina*

For all other animals from the United States, and for all animals from other countries, owners should check with Canada Food Inspection Agency's Import Service Centres (ISC).

Endangered Species

Canada has an international agreement restricting the sale, trade, or movement of many animals, birds, reptiles, fish, insects, and certain forms of plant life that are considered endangered. The restrictions include products made from these animals. You should find out in advance what goods you can bring into Canada by contacting the Canadian Wildlife Service's CITES Office.

Importing Firearms

Canada has strict regulations on firearms. Consult the chief firearms officer of the province or territory where you intend to enter the country if you plan to bring a firearm with you.

For more information on the rules governing the importation, possession, and use of firearms, call the Chief Firearms Office.

Important Documents

Long before you leave your home country, make sure you begin to gather the following documents:

- Passport
- Adoption papers
- **Birth certificates** for all family members
- Marriage certificates, separation papers, and divorce papers
- School diplomas and degrees, or trade or professional papers and certificates
- School reports, transfer certificates, college transcripts
- Certified immunization records for all children under 16, required in all school districts before children can be registered to attend school
- Driver's licence, which will usually be valid for up to six months in Canada. You might also want to obtain an international driver's licence before you leave home, as it will be valid for six months.
- If you have a history of safe driving, ask for a letter of reference or history from your insurance company proving your "no claim" status. This could save you money on future car insurance premiums. By doing this, I saved 40 percent on my insurance in the first year.

- Medical records including X-rays, test results, known allergies, and perhaps even a recent history of medication taken by everyone in your family. It is also a good idea to bring a supply of any prescription and over-the-counter drugs you use. Make sure you keep these drugs in their original bottles.
- Dental records and optical prescriptions
- Reference letters from companies for whom you have worked or volunteered
- Two copies of a list of goods to be imported, including full descriptions, serial numbers, makes, and models. For jewellery and heirlooms, you might also want to attach photographs of the items. If you have receipts for the more expensive items, attach them to the list. The list should note which items are being imported at the time of landing and which goods will follow at a later date, or you can make two separate lists.

While all the documents above constitute your "official papers," don't forget to gather the phone numbers, addresses, fax numbers, and email addresses of all your friends and relatives. It is far easier to put this list together before you leave town than to try to do so afterward. It is also advisable to carry one copy of each document with you and have a second copy tucked into your luggage somewhere or have it carried by your spouse. The following immunization schedule will show you which immunizations your child will need, from the ages of 2 months to 16 years. You may have to prove that your child's shots are up-to-date in order to enroll him or her in school.

Immunization Schedule

Publicly Funded Routine Immunization Schedule for Children Beginning Immunization in Early Infancy

Age	2 months	4 months	6 months	12 months	15 months†	18 months	4–6 years	12 years (grade 7)	14–16 years
Diphtheria	✓	✓	✓			✓	✓		✓
Pertussis	✓	✓	✓			✓	✓		✓
Tetanus	✓	✓	✓			✓	✓		✓
Polio	✓	✓	✓			✓	✓		
HIB	✓	✓	✓			✓			
Pneumo-coccal conjugate	✓	✓	✓		✓				
Measles, Mumps Rubella (MMR)*				✓		✓			
Men-C conjugate				✓				✓‡	
Chickenpox (Varicella)					✓		✓**		
Hepatitis B								✓	

* MMR = measles, mumps, and rubella vaccine must be given after the first birthday.

** If your child has not had chickenpox or the vaccine, he/she can receive the chickenpox vaccine at 5 years of age.

† These vaccines can be given as early as 12 months of age.

‡ If your child has not had the meningococcal c-conjugate vaccine (at 1 year of age), he/she can receive the vaccine at 12 years of age in Grade 7.

NOTE: The MMR and varicella vaccines are live virus vaccines. If not given on the same day, they must be given at least 28 days apart.

The following is a copy of a form that you will have to fill out and present upon your arrival, declaring all the items you are bringing into the country.

<table>
<tr><td colspan="2">■◆■ Canada Border Services Agency   Agence des services frontaliers du Canada</td><td>PROTECTED (when completed)   A</td></tr>
<tr><td colspan="2">PERSONAL EFFECTS ACCOUNTING DOCUMENT
(Settler, Former Resident, Seasonal Resident, or Beneficiary)</td><td>Accounting document number</td></tr>
</table>

☐ Shaded areas for CBSA use only

Importer's name	Cargo control number		CBSA stamp
Importer's address	Country of origin	Country of export	
	Landed immigrant / Permanent resident		
	Port of entry	Date of landing	
	IMM 5292 No.		

Item	Description of goods (include serial numbers, if applicable)	Value (CDN Dollars)
1		
2		
3		
4		
5		
6		
7		
8		

▼ All conveyances MUST be eligible for importation in accordance with Transport Canada requirements. Vehicle import registration fees may also apply. ▼

	Conveyances (make, model, serial number of vehicle, vessel, aircraft, or trailer)	Value (CDN Dollars)	K22 / Vehicle import form number
1			
2			
3			

Additional list of goods ▶ ☐ Form B4A ☐ Mover's inventory ☐ Other	Goods to follow ▶ ☐ Yes ☐ No	Form B15 number (if applicable)

CLASSIFICATION TYPE – See information on reverse

☐ **FORMER RESIDENT (tariff item No. 9805.00.00)**

I hereby declare that I have read and qualify for the provisions of tariff item No. 9805.00.00 and that:

1. ☐ I have been a resident of another country for at least one year; or
2. ☐ I have been continuously absent from Canada for at least one year; and
3. I left Canada on _____ ; and
4. I returned to Canada to resume residence on _____ .
5. With the exception of wedding gifts, bride's trousseau, alcoholic beverages and tobacco products or replacement goods described in the *Tariff Item No. 9805.00.00 Exemption Order*, all household and personal effects imported or to be imported by me under this tariff item have been actually owned, possessed, and used abroad by me for at least six months prior to the date of my return to Canada to resume residence.
6. All goods imported are my personal or household effects and were not used abroad for any commercial purpose nor will they be used in Canada for any commercial purpose.
7. If any item is sold or otherwise disposed of in Canada within 12 months of the date of its importation, I will notify a CBSA Office of such fact and pay all duties owing at the time.

☐ **BENEFICIARY (tariff item No. 9806.00.00)**

I hereby declare that I have read and qualify for the provisions of tariff item No. 9806.00.00 and that I am a beneficiary of personal and household effects which were bequeathed to me without remuneration as:

1. ☐ The result of the death of_____ ,
   a resident of _____ ,
   who died on _____ ; or
☐ In anticipation of the death of_____ ,
   who resides in _____ .

I have attached:

1. ☐ A copy of the will, showing that I am a beneficiary of the estate;
2. ☐ A signed statement from the donor outlining the circumstances of the gift; or
3. ☐ A statement from the executor of the estate or other legal representative of the donor outlining the circumstances of the gift.

SEASONAL RESIDENT (tariff item No. 9829.00.00)

I hereby declare that I have read and qualify for the provisions of tariff item No. 9829.00.00 and that:

1. I arrived in Canada to occupy my seasonal residence for the first time

   on _____ .

2. All goods imported or to be imported by me under this tariff item have been in my ownership, possession, and use prior to my first arrival in Canada to occupy my seasonal residence.

3. All goods imported are my personal or household property and they will not be used in Canada for any commercial purpose.

4. If any item is sold or otherwise disposed of in Canada within 12 months of the date of its importation, I will notify a CBSA Office of such fact and pay all duties owing at the time.

5. I have not previously claimed the benefits of tariff item No. 9829.00.00.

SETTLER (tariff item No. 9807.00.00)

I hereby declare that I have read and qualify for the provisions of tariff item No. 9807.00.00 and that:

1. I am entering Canada with the intention of establishing, for the first time, a permanent residence for a period in excess of 12 months and I arrived in

   Canada on _____ .

2. With the exception of wedding gifts, bride's trousseau, alcoholic beverages and tobacco products described in the *Tariff Item No. 9807.00.00 Exemption Order*, all household and personal effects imported or to be imported by me under this tariff item have actually been owned, possessed, and used abroad by me prior to the date of my arrival in Canada.

3. All goods imported are my personal or household property and they will not be used in Canada for any commercial purpose.

4. If any item is sold or otherwise disposed of in Canada within 12 months of the date of its importation, I will notify a CBSA Office of such fact and pay all duties owing at the time.

Signed at _____ on _____

Signature of Importer

B4 E (07)   (Ce formulaire existe en français.)

Canadá

Source: Canada Border Services Agency

Professional Credentials

Before you leave your country, it is crucial to find out as much as you can about the Canadian standards required to practise your profession. Unfortunately, many foreign-trained professionals and skilled tradespeople encounter difficulty obtaining Canadian recognition of their training. The process for getting a licence or certificate to practise any of the regulated occupations varies from province to province and from job to job. Frequently, it seems even highly trained and experienced immigrants have trouble getting licences to practise. Among the many regulated professions are nursing, engineering, teaching, electrical work, and plumbing.

The government's Foreign **Credentials** Referral Office website (www.credentials.gc.ca) features a useful search engine called "Working in Canada." You can type in your occupation and the search engine will bring up a comprehensive report that tells you whether this occupation is regulated in Canada and whether you need to be licensed by a regulatory body. Then it will tell you where in your region you can get licensed.

It is a good idea for you to contact the professional or trade association governing your occupation in your home country to determine if it has any connection with a similar association in Canada. You might also want to check with the Canadian consul in your country to obtain information about your occupation and possible licensing requirements. Most Canadian diplomatic offices stock a publication entitled National Occupational Classification (NOC) that might help you find more information about your occupation in Canada.

Be forewarned that it may take you months, if not years, to obtain the additional training and pass the exams required to receive a licence or certificate to practise your profession in Canada. (See Chapter 10—Looking for and Landing a Job for more information on professional accreditation.)

Q: I hear a lot about getting my qualifications assessed. Could you please tell me something about this?

A: You can have your qualifications assessed by filling out a form and paying the required fee. The forms can be downloaded from the Canadian Information Centre for International Credentials website at www.cicic.ca.

Medical Coverage

Depending on the province in which you plan to take up residence, there will be a waiting period before you qualify for medical insurance (see Chapter 6—Medical Coverage for more information on the Canadian medical system). In British Columbia, for example, the waiting period is three months. It is therefore recommended that you arrange for private medical and hospitalization insurance for your family before you land in Canada. Ensure that the coverage you obtain applies to immigrating families, and not simply families who are visiting on a vacation.

I discovered the importance of this insurance about three weeks after I arrived when my teenage son, Dan, sprained his wrist while rollerblading. A short visit to the emergency room of a nearby hospital, an examination, an X-ray, and a tensor bandage cost me $500. I can only imagine what it would have cost if he had broken his wrist.

How Much Money Do You Require?

Citizenship and Immigration Canada requires you to prove you have settlement funds of at least $10,000 Canadian, plus an additional $2,000 for each dependant who will immigrate with you. Note that the minimum amount of settlement funds may vary according to where you want to move within Canada.

The amount of money that you need to have to support your family is determined by the size of your family.

Funds Required Based on Number of Family Members	
Number of Family Members	Funds Required ($CDN)
1	$10,168
2	$12,659
3	$15,563
4	$18,895
5	$21,431
6	$24,170
7 or more	$26,910

Source: Citizenship and Immigration Canada

You do not have to show that you have these funds if you have arranged employment in Canada.

While every family's needs will be different and every region of Canada has a different cost of living, I suggest the following basic guidelines for a newcomer's **budget** (excluding moving costs and airfares):

- One adult moving alone: $25,000 (Canadian)
- A couple moving together: $30,000
- A couple with one child under 10 years: $33,000
- A couple with a child over 10: $35,000
- For each additional child under 10, add $1,000
- For each additional child over 10, add $2,000

Basically, this sum of money will allow you to live comfortably in your new country until you are able to find a job and start making an income. Anything less than this will make it extremely difficult. This should take care of your basic **living expenses** for four to six months depending on how skilled you are at budgeting.

In the summer of 1987 the Royal Canadian Mint (which produces Canadian coins) introduced a new one-dollar coin to replace the one-dollar bill. Many people called it the "loonie" because of the image of a loon that appears on one side, and the name has stuck. When a new two-dollar coin was introduced nine years later, it was quickly nicknamed the "toonie."

The following is a suggested budget for a family of four. Keep in mind that rent and food costs vary widely across Canada. Even within one city, rent varies greatly from one neighbourhood to another.

Suggested Average Monthly Expenses for a Family of Four (Vancouver Used as an Example)	
Accommodation rental (two bedroom)	$900
Heating or air conditioning (if extra)	$75
Electricity/Hydro (if extra)	$65
Laundry	$35
Basic telephone	$40
Medical insurance (in some provinces)	$100
Cable television	$40
Transportation (bus passes)	$100
Entertainment	$200
Food	$600
Miscellaneous	$200
Total	$2,355

Disclosure of Funds

If you are carrying more than $10,000 when you arrive, you must tell a Canadian official. If you do not tell an official, you may be fined or put in prison. These funds could be in the form of any of the following:

- Cash
- Securities in bearer form (stocks, bonds, debentures, treasury bills)
- Negotiable instruments in bearer form (bank draft, cheques, traveller's cheques, money orders)

Checklist—Things to Do Before Moving to Canada

- [ ] Research the rules for your profession in Canada. Find out if you'll need to be licensed.

- [ ] Gather your family's important documents, including marriage certificates, diplomas, transcripts, and medical records.

- [ ] Apply for an international driver's licence.

- [ ] Purchase private medical insurance.

- [ ] Find out what you need to do to import your pets into Canada.

- [ ] Collect your receipts for the items you plan to import into Canada.

- [ ] Purchase insurance for the items you plan to import.

- [ ] Plan your monthly budget for living in Canada.

- [ ] Purchase traveller's cheques.

- [ ] Transfer your cash and investments to Canadian accounts.

- [ ] Make sure you have clothing that is appropriate for the time of year and area of the country you are moving to.

- [ ] Pack a box of the items you'll need for your first few days in Canada.

- [ ] Get excited about your new life in a new country!

Key Words

birth certificate: an official piece of paper that states the date and place of a person's birth

budget: a plan of how to spend an amount of money over a particular period of time; the amount of money that is mentioned

community centre: a building where local people can take part in classes, meetings, etc.

credentials: the skills, training, and experience that show you are qualified to do something; documents such as letters that prove that you are who you say you are and can therefore be trusted

document (also documentation): an official piece of writing which gives information, proof, or evidence

glint: an expression in somebody's eyes showing a particular emotion

heirloom: something valuable that has belonged to the same family for many years

homesick: sad because you are away from home (n. homesickness)

insurance: a contract in which, in return for regular payment, a company or the state agrees to pay a sum of money if something (e.g. illness, death, loss of or damage to property) happens to somebody

living expenses: money spent on the things needed for living

Note: Entries taken or adapted from the Oxford ESL Dictionary

Creating Your Canadian Experience

1. What is the current currency exchange rate between Canada and your native country? Come up with an easy way to calculate the conversion so that you can do it quickly when you need it.
   Tip: use the Bank of Canada's currency converter at www.bankofcanada.ca/en/rates/converter.html.

   a. $1 = _____

   b. $5 = _____

   c. $10 = _____

   d. $20 = _____

2. Use the Internet or your phone book to search for the location of the nearest

   a. Community Centre:

      Address: _____

      _____

      Hours: _____

b. Library:

Address: _____

_____

Hours: _____

c. Post Office:

Address: _____

_____

Hours: _____

3. The table of monthly expenses in this chapter was based on the cost of living in Vancouver. Do some Internet research to find out the amount of each expense in your city, and determine your monthly budget.

Accommodation rental (two bedroom)	
Heating or air conditioning (if extra)	
Electricity (if extra)	
Laundry	
Basic telephone	
Medical insurance (in some provinces)	
Cable television	
Transportation (bus passes)	
Entertainment	
Food	
Miscellaneous (Other)	
Total	

Chapter 4

First Things First

In This Chapter

- What's this SIN card all about? It sounds bad.
- How can you safeguard your money immediately?
- What do you do if a family member gets sick the first week in Canada?
- How do you get your 10-year-old into school?

As I stepped out of the airport, I couldn't help but think, "Wow, so this is where I am going to spend the rest of my life! I am now officially a landed Canadian immigrant!"

Upon arrival in your new country, the number of details that need to be immediately attended to may overwhelm you. This chapter will help you prioritize these steps and steer you to other chapters that feature more details on each.

Among your first concerns will be finding a place to live, obtaining medical insurance, obtaining a **Social Insurance Number** (SIN) card, enrolling your children in school, opening a bank account, and learning how to move about your new city using public transportation.

One of the first things I'd recommend that you do is obtain a good street map, and a telephone book with a directory of businesses listed by category. These resources will be important tools during the first couple of weeks and months following your arrival.

Q: What are host programs?

A: Their goal is to create friendships between newcomers and volunteers from the local community. You are matched with a Canadian volunteer who will meet with you several times each month for conversation and to help you get to know your new community.

You might also want to find out if your community has a host program, which is a volunteer-based program, usually offered through immigrant service organizations or community centres, that guides immigrants through their first few months in Canada. Your host might be able to answer a multitude of questions about shopping, apartment hunting, and schooling. Most large communities have immigrant service agencies and community centres that can provide you with information on the host program and many other helpful organizations.

The Airport Landing

One of the first people you will meet at your point of arrival in Canada will be a friendly Canada customs agent. You will be required to produce the list of goods you are importing along with your **landing papers**. The list will be divided into goods you are carrying with you and goods to follow by freight or mail. As this will be your only opportunity to import goods duty free, it is important that your list is thorough and includes details such as brand names and serial numbers (as described in Chapter 3—What to Know Before You Go).

The other officials you will meet upon arrival at the airport will be from Immigration Services. You will need to produce your passport and visa papers. After the officials look at your papers, you will be given one copy. Remember to make at least five photocopies of your visa papers, as they will come in handy on many occasions over the next few months, such as when you open a Canadian bank account. You will be given a form for a

John Furlong: Welcome to Canada

John Furlong remembers his first day in Canada like it was a minute ago.

"I remember I got off the plane, walked up to a customs agent and gave him my passport," says Furlong with little hint of his native Irish accent. "He said, 'Welcome to Canada. Make us better.'"

"I had no idea what he was talking about. I wondered, 'Does everyone get told this?'" chuckles Furlong. "I took from it that this is not a place where you come, **enjoy the spoils**, but not do something for your community," he says. "And if you tried hard, you were rewarded for it."

Furlong told this same story to the International Olympic Committee (IOC) in Prague when it was deciding who would host the 2010 Winter Olympic Games. "It gives you an idea of why this country works," he explains. "Canada is almost the biggest country in the world for a very small number of people, but it's successful. There's this sense that if everybody makes a great contribution, you can do impossible things."

—*Margaret Jetelina*

Permanent Resident Card (PR Card), which is proof that you are a legal resident of Canada. After you have submitted your form, the card will be mailed out to you.

Immigration authorities at your point of arrival will give you application forms for a variety of documents that you will need, such as your all-important SIN card, which is an identification card issued by the federal government to every person living in Canada. This is a very important document; you can't work without it.

You will also receive application forms for a driver's licence, for a medical card which will eventually allow you to receive medical treatment and hospitalization, and for a child tax credit, which will be explained later.

You should also be aware that Citizenship and Immigration Canada currently tests all immigrants for **communicable** diseases, and examining doctors have the right to request tests as well.

When Your Goods Arrive

When your personal effects arrive, you will be required to appear at the Canada Border Services Agency (CBSA) office to collect them. This is a simple procedure; if your papers are in order, there should be no delay.

Your Permanent Resident Card

The Permanent Resident (PR) Card is a wallet-sized plastic card. You will need this card whenever you re-enter Canada by airplane, boat, train, or bus. It is proof of your permanent resident status.

Newly arrived permanent residents automatically receive a PR Card as part of the immigration process. If Citizenship and Immigration Canada does not receive your mailing address within 180 days of your entry into Canada, you will need to re-apply for your PR Card and pay the necessary fee.

Once you become a Canadian citizen, you will no longer need a PR Card. You will be provided with a Citizenship certificate instead. As a Canadian citizen, you will need a Canadian passport for international travel.

Your SIN Card

As mentioned, applying for your Social Insurance Number (SIN) should be one of your first steps after arriving. Without this number, you cannot get a job or apply for any government assistance or credit. In fact, without it, you are basically a person without an identity in Canada.

One of the first things any employer will ask you for is your SIN number. Although you will eventually receive a wallet-sized card with this number on it, it is a good idea to memorize it, as you will use it frequently. Every tax dollar you pay, every pension plan you contribute to, and every employment insurance premium you pay is tracked through your SIN number. It is one of the most vital forms of identification used throughout the country.

Applications for a SIN card can be made through a Human Resources and Skills Development Canada (HRSDC) office. You will need to show your original Record of Landing (IMM 1000), as well as your passport or other identification, and any documents showing a change of name, such as a marriage certificate, divorce papers, or adoption papers. While you can make an application for a SIN card by mail, HRSDC prefers that you visit one of its offices in person with all your identification in hand.

For the address of the HRSDC office nearest you, check the **blue pages** of your local telephone book under Government of Canada, Human Resources and Skills Development Canada.

Immigrant Services

There are numerous immigrant service bureaus and offices throughout Canada to help newcomers settle into Canadian society, and many of them provide their services for free. (See Appendix—Useful Websites.)

Most community centres can provide you with a list of immigrant assistance associations operating in your community. Many of these organizations are managed by staff or volunteers who speak your language and are probably familiar with your customs.

In addition to private and charitable organizations, such as churches, community groups, or ethnic associations, all levels of government provide various programs and publications to help newcomers settle in to their new home. These range from English as a Second Language (ESL) classes to information on starting a new business in Canada.

Canada Child Tax Benefit

You may be eligible to receive financial assistance from the Government of Canada if you have children. The Canada Child Tax Benefit (CCTB) is tax-free and is paid monthly to the parent most responsible for caring for any child under the age of 18. Payments are determined by family income and the number of children in a family: the lower the family income, the higher the CCTB. It could be worthwhile to check into this immediately upon your arrival. (See Chapter 5—Assistance Available for more information.)

In order to apply for the benefit, you must file an income tax form, even if you did not receive any income in Canada for the taxation year. You must also show your child's birth certificate and proof of your immigration status. Quebec residents will automatically receive a registration form for the Canada Child Tax Benefit.

Health Card

Although Canada's health care system is, like many health care programs around the world, suffering from lack of funding, it remains one of the best in the world. Hospitalization, clinic visits, and most doctors' services are available free of charge to all residents of Canada registered under the national insurance program, which is often called medicare, although it is important to note that prescription medications are not covered by the Canadian medical system.

Medicare is funded largely by governments through taxes. Although this is a national program, it is administered differently in each province. In most provinces, medicare is totally funded by the province. In some provinces, however, everyone must pay medical insurance premiums to help fund the program. In many cases, employers in these provinces pay the medical insurance premium for their employees as a benefit of employment. Also, seniors or those on income assistance may have their medical premiums covered in these provinces.

Provinces also differ regarding which services are included and which are not included under their health care plans. Basic general physician services as well as basic hospitalization are covered in all provinces. But other services, such as ambulance, chiropractic, and physiotherapy services, may or may not be covered, or there may be a user fee involved. (For more details, see Chapter 6—Medical Coverage.)

One of your first steps will be to apply for your official health card. Since there may be a waiting period involved before you become eligible for medical insurance, don't delay in applying. Application forms for these cards are available from doctors' offices, hospitals, most pharmacies, or by calling the provincial medical services authorities for the province in which you live. Your health card will be accepted throughout Canada. However, you must re-register if you move to another province.

Your health card allows you to get medical services from the licensed medical doctor of your choice, although in the last few years finding a local doctor who is accepting patients is challenging. There is no limit on the number of visits you can make and there is no user fee or service fee. You should get a referral from your general practitioner if you want to see a specialist.

Rules for Refugees

In Canada, government-sponsored refugees are eligible for the Interim Federal Health Program and can apply for government health care and receive it in three months.

Those people who arrive as refugee claimants are eligible for the Interim Federal Health Program, but they will be able to apply for government health care only after they are determined to be refugees or protected persons.

Seeking Medical Attention

Do not hesitate to obtain medical attention if you or any member of your family is sick during the first few days or weeks in Canada, even if you are not yet covered by a medical insurance plan. If you have a condition that is contagious, it is extremely important that you obtain treatment immediately to protect yourself, your family, and other members of the community.

Whenever possible, make an appointment to visit your own doctor at his or her office rather than visiting a hospital. Hospitals are frequently overcrowded and the waiting time in **emergency rooms** can be many hours. It is also much more costly to the health care system to treat a patient at a hospital than at a doctor's office.

Naturally, if you or a family member is seriously injured or suddenly becomes sick, you should go to the emergency room of the nearest hospital whether you have a family doctor or not. If you have taken yourself to the hospital enter through the emergency entrance, which is usually well marked.

If you consider the situation very serious, call your local emergency telephone number for an ambulance. (See "Emergency 911.") Make sure to take your health card to the hospital with you, if you already have it.

If you need to call an ambulance, you may be required to pay some or all of the ambulance service fee, depending on the province in which you live. Also, if your doctor decides that you did not, in fact, require an ambulance, you may be asked to pay the ambulance fee. Of course, the cost is not important if you feel that you or someone in your family is seriously ill. All ambulances are staffed by paramedics and carry useful medical equipment.

If you live in an urban centre, there is a good chance that interpreters will be available at the hospital. It is a good idea, however, to make sure that every member of your family knows enough English or French to call for help in an emergency. (See Chapter 6—Medical Coverage.)

Canadian doctors have made numerous contributions to the world of medicine over the years. In the 1890s, Dr. William Osler wrote one of the first great textbooks of modern medicine; Sir Frederick Banting and Dr. Charles Best, along with two colleagues, physiologist J.J.R. Macleod and biochemist J.P. Collip, discovered insulin in 1921–22; and Dr. Norman Bethune introduced the practice of mobile blood **transfusion** on the battlefields of Spain and China in the 1930s.

Emergency 911

Most regions of Canada use the 911 emergency telephone number to handle all emergencies that require the police, the fire department, or an ambulance.

Once you settle in your new home, you should determine whether 911 is in fact the emergency number used in your community, and then you and your children should memorize it. Do not hesitate to call 911 if you feel your life or the life of someone else is in danger, or if you feel threatened.

It is also the number to call in the event of an automobile accident resulting in injuries, or if you witness someone having a heart attack, even if that person is a stranger. You should also instruct your children on how and when to call 911. There is no fee for calling this number.

If you forget the number 911, dial 0 and ask the operator for help. You might also want to check in the front of your telephone book for the emergency numbers for centres dealing with other kinds of crises or problems. These centres usually include a poison information line, a sexual assault help line, and a crisis line for emotionally disturbed individuals.

Prescription Medicines

If you require any **prescription medicine**, be sure to learn about regulations in Canada as soon as you arrive. Medicine is either controlled by prescriptions from physicians, available on the shelves of pharmacies, or available behind the counter at pharmacies, meaning you have to speak to a pharmacist to purchase these semi-controlled drugs. Many kinds of drugs for minor problems, such as headaches and colds, are available in the self-serve sections of pharmacies. Every pharmacy employs a registered pharmacist who can offer free advice about which medicine you might consider for minor health problems.

The pharmacist cannot prescribe drugs for you, but can fill prescriptions requested by your physician. The pharmacist will give you your prescription and explain how and when to use the drug. You will also be advised to not allow anyone else to use your medicine, even if you believe they have the same symptoms as you. Prescription medicines can be expensive, and medicare generally does not pay for prescription medicines unless you are a senior citizen or are receiving social assistance in some form.

Public Health

Public health laws exist to maintain healthy living standards for all Canadians. For example, they make sure that the food you buy is clean and that it meets approved health standards; that restaurants and grocery stores are inspected and properly maintained; that medicines and drugs are properly tested and approved before they are sold in Canada; and that children are **immunized** against a variety of serious diseases such as polio, diphtheria, mumps, measles, and chicken pox.

Your children must be routinely immunized against serious diseases that can be easily spread from person to person. Your child cannot go to school without an immunization card to prove that his or her immunizations have been kept up to date. You can arrange this through your doctor or through public health clinics. No one with an infectious disease should attend school or work until he or she is out of danger of infecting others.

Getting Around

With your street map in hand, spend some time in your first few days exploring the public transportation system in your city. Buses, trains, and subways are usually cheap, reliable, and safe.

In some cities, bus drivers are not permitted to handle change, so you will need to deposit the exact fare when you board. If you don't know how much it costs, make sure you carry a pocket full of change with you. You will be told how much to drop in the fare box. If you need to change buses along your route, you should ask the driver for a transfer paper, which will allow you to move from one bus to another without paying a second fare, within a certain amount of time.

In most cities, monthly passes are available for a flat fee. Also, lower rates are available for seniors and students, but you must provide identification to prove your status.

Most major cities offer an information and direction service for public transit passengers wanting to know how to use public transportation to reach a particular destination.

I was amazed by the efficiency of the transit system in Vancouver. I used to call the company's telephone number, tell them exactly where I wanted to be and at what time, and they would tell me exact timings for the bus, where to catch it, and where to transfer in order to arrive at my destination on time. Your local public transportation provider should be able to do the same.

Banking

Another priority in your first few days will be finding a safe place for your money. To begin with, select a bank or a credit union near your home or work. You can switch banks later if you find one that is better suited to your needs or is in a more convenient location, but you need to open some kind of an account immediately.

Banks and credit unions provide basic savings accounts and chequing accounts. Most banks charge a monthly fee of $5 to $10 for services such as cheque processing and automatic monthly withdrawals. To open an account, you will need your landed immigrant papers and any other identification you have to prove your place of residence.

You may want to rent a **safety deposit locker** to store such valuables as jewellery and important documents. Most banks offer this service for a fee. Charges vary according to the size of the locker. (See Chapter 9—Banking, Credit, and Insurance for more information.)

Enrolling Your Children in School

Every child between the ages of 5 and 18 is entitled to attend school. Enrollment is generally required for children between these ages, although the exact ages vary slightly from province to province. It is mandatory that you enroll your child in school as soon as possible after arriving in Canada. (See Chapter 11—Education for more information on schools and the school system.)

Schools generally operate on weekdays from 8:30 or 9:00 a.m. to 3:30 or 4:00 p.m., from September through June, with many extracurricular activities such as sports practices and games, as well as school club meetings, taking place immediately following school hours. Schools usually close for one or two weeks over the Christmas and New Year's holidays and also close for a week in March or April for spring break.

All publicly funded schools are co-educational, meaning they accept boys and girls, and most do not require children to wear uniforms.

For information on enrolling your child in the tax-funded public school system, contact the school board in the district in which you live. If there is an elementary school in your neighbourhood, you may even be able to simply go to the school to ask about enrolling your child. If the school is unable to accept your child for whatever reason, you will be directed to the appropriate authority. Generally, elementary school children will be enrolled in the school nearest to their home, although in some regions students may have to take a bus to a farther school.

Secondary school students may be enrolled at the school nearest their home or they may, for a variety of reasons ranging from special sports interests to particular academic interests, want or need to attend a school in another region. Again, the school board responsible for your municipality will be able to assist you in choosing an appropriate school.

The Canadian education system guarantees education to everyone. Children with special needs are either placed in regular classrooms and provided with additional help or are provided with special classes or schools. Your school board will be able to help you find the right school and class for all your children, regardless of their needs and requirements.

Many parents in Canada choose to send their children to private schools. Many private schools are only open to either boys or girls, and they often require students to wear uniforms. The tuition fees paid directly by students' parents largely fund these private schools. Check your phone book for private schooling options.

If your children are out of high school and you want information on enrolling them in post-secondary schools, or education following high school, contact the university or other institute in which you are interested. (See Chapter 11—Education for more information on types of universities and colleges in Canada.)

Milena Stojkovic: Senior Settles in to New Life

Milena Stojkovic remembers well what her mother used to tell her: "If you are venturing into the unknown, be sure to tie your shoelaces well." Stojkovic remembered those words of wisdom when at the ages of 62 and 67 respectively, she and her husband, Rasa, decided to leave their home in Yugoslavia to come to Canada.

"It wasn't an easy decision to leave, especially at our age," she says. "It wasn't a good age for making big life changes." But she tied her shoelaces tight and worked hard to settle in.

She took evening English classes, got her driver's licence, took several computer courses, and got a part-time job in a retail store to socialize and practise her English. She admits the challenges at first were enormous. "Different language, different culture, different lifestyle without friends with whom you can talk openly from the heart about your feelings," she says. "But being a Canadian is a big privilege."

—Margaret Jetelina

Using the Telephone

When you move into your first home, you'll want to arrange for a telephone number right away. Telephone service in Canada is charged to each household on a flat monthly basis, and is based on the number of telephone lines coming into the house and how many optional telephone services you purchase. The number of local calls you make is unrestricted. **Long-distance calls**, however, cost an additional amount.

You can call the telephone company and arrange for a phone connection or hook-up when you move into an apartment or home. Be prepared to provide the phone company with your rental contract and identification if this is the first time you have applied for phone service in Canada.

At a later time, you must also advise the telephone company when you are moving out so that your telephone service can be disconnected.

In recent years, a number of private telephone service providers have begun offering competitive rates for long-distance telephone calls. Once you have your basic telephone service, you can shop around for a long-distance calling service that meets your individual needs. Some even offer unlimited long-distance calls for a flat monthly fee. Note that rates tend to differ for national and international long-distance calling.

Also note that phone numbers starting with 800, 888, 877, or 866 are **toll-free**. Many companies and government offices have such toll-free numbers for the benefit of their customers. Soon, toll-free exchanges will be expanded to include 855, 844, 833, and 822.

Beware of telephone numbers that begin with 1-900. You will be charged not only a long-distance fee, but also a fee for calling the number. These numbers are frequently used for personal services, such as horoscope readers, psychics, or chat lines.

Many businesses and individuals use some sort of **voice mail** or answering machine to handle their incoming calls. Usually, you simply need to listen to the message and follow instructions. You will normally be instructed to wait for a beep and leave a message, listen to some options and make a selection, or enter the **extension number** of the person you want to speak to. When you leave a message on an answering machine, repeat your name and phone number twice and speak slowly. If you are job-hunting, an answering machine may be a valuable investment.

If you're away from home, you can use a pay phone. Local phone calls from pay phones cost anywhere from 25 to 50 cents. If making a long-distance call, you must have enough change to pay for the call. Sometimes you can use a credit card or a long-distance calling card number, which you can get from your telephone company.

Alexander Graham Bell, a Scottish immigrant who came to Canada in 1870, is usually credited as the inventor of the telephone. There were actually many individuals who contributed to the creation of this useful device. However, Bell was the first to apply for a patent for his telephone, and was awarded his patent in 1876.

Directory Assistance

If you do not know the number of the person or business you wish to call, dial 411 for information. In most regions of Canada, this will cost between 75 cents and 1 dollar. Requests for information about telephone numbers are free when made at a pay phone.

All area codes in North America are listed, with their geographic location, at the front of the telephone book. When calling a long-distance number, dial "1," followed by the area code, then the individual phone number.

You can obtain the telephone number for almost anyone living in Canada or in the United States as long as you know the city in which they are living. You simply obtain the three-digit area code for that region from the phone book and dial "1," plus the area code, plus 555-1212, which is the information line. To obtain the phone number of someone in Toronto, for example, you would dial 1+416+555-1212. Of course, Toronto, because of the large number of residents, is divided into three area codes—416, 905, and 647. You may have to try all three to find the correct Toronto phone number. And remember, there is a charge for using this service.

You can also obtain telephone numbers for free, virtually anywhere in the world, through the Internet. Phone numbers for Canadian individuals or businesses are available on sites such as www.canada411.com.

If the number you are looking for is overseas, call the operator by dialing "0."

Telephone Options

There are all kinds of special options available through your phone company to help you handle telephone communications: you can block calls from someone who is harassing you; you can redirect calls from certain numbers to a recorded message; you can trace the origin of the last call on your telephone by dialing *69; and you can prevent someone from tracing your name when you make a call by dialing *67 before you dial the phone number. Check out the extensive descriptions of all these services in the front of your telephone book or call your telephone company for assistance. Most of these services will cost up to 1 dollar per use.

Cell Phones and PDAs

Cell phones have become enormously popular throughout the country. Many Canadians are now choosing cell phones over traditional home phones.

Personal digital assistants (PDAs) like the famous Canadian BlackBerry are very popular and allow you to receive emails, phone calls, and browse the Internet all with one device.

Canadians usually expect cell phone users to exercise some courtesy by turning off these devices in restaurants, theatres, churches, at meetings, and in other places where they could be considered intrusive.

Cell phone companies generally charge a monthly fee plus additional charges for using the phone beyond a set number of minutes, which can cause your bills to add up quickly.

Telephone Book

Everyone is given a telephone book listing the residents and businesses in his or her community.

The telephone book lists the names, addresses, and phone numbers of most individuals with telephones in the region, in alphabetical order. The blue pages in the book list the telephone numbers of all government bodies and departments in that region, including those of the Government of Canada, the provincial government, and the various regional and municipal governments.

The book's **yellow pages** are a directory of businesses and services, listed alphabetically and broken down into categories such as restaurants, pharmacies, and therapists. Depending on the size of the city and the number of telephone listings, these yellow pages may be found in the same book as the **white pages** or in a separate book.

Telephone books also offer a lot of practical general information, such as what to do in the event of an emergency, how to perform CPR, and who to call in the event of a sexual assault. In some cities, the telephone book also contains maps and diagrams of public buildings.

Telemarketing

Telemarketing is a frequent and sometimes irritating marketing method used by some companies to sell their products, promote their business, or ask for charitable donations. Telemarketers work from public telephone lists and call as many people as they can. The best advice police give to the public regarding dealing with telemarketers is that you should not give out your credit card number to someone who calls you.

If you feel the caller is doing something illegal or abusive, you can report him or her to the police or the telephone company.

Special Needs Callers

Various telephone equipment and devices are available to assist persons who have special needs regarding speech, hearing, sight, or other physical disabilities. Your telephone company can give you more information about this equipment.

Using Computers

Computer usage is growing in Canada, both at home and in the workplace. If you do not know how to use a computer, you might consider taking a part-time course to familiarize yourself with them. You do not need to purchase one right away; most major libraries offer members access to a computer, usually for a fixed period of time. Also, computers are available, for a fee, at many Internet coffee houses. They may also be available at community centres, schools, or immigrant services organizations.

If you have enough time and money, I would suggest that you learn how to use a computer, including the Internet and email, and purchase one as soon as possible. Apart from the fact that it will help with finding a job and accommodation, thanks to the many online employment and housing resources, a computer will allow you to keep in touch with the folks back home and keep up with current events in your native country.

Internet

Canada is at the forefront of Internet usage and Canadians are among the world's most enthusiastic users.

Some residential Internet service providers (ISPs) are:
• Telus
• Shaw

- Bell
- Rogers

Fees differ from one provider to another depending on whether you opt for high-speed or dial-up service.

Key Words

blue pages: the blue pages of a telephone book that give a list of government departments, services, and their telephone numbers

emergency room (abbr. ER): the part of a hospital where people who have been injured in accidents or who are very sick are taken for immediate treatment

enjoy the spoils: to take pleasure in the results of hard work

extension (number): a telephone that is connected to a central phone in a house or to a central point in a large office building

immunize: to make somebody immune to a disease, usually by giving an injection of a substance

landing papers: official documents that prove you are a legal immigrant in Canada

local call: a telephone call made to a place near you

long-distance call: a telephone call made between people that are far from each other

prescription medicine: medicine you get from a pharmacy after giving a form on which a doctor has written the name of the medicine that you need

safety deposit locker: a locker or a metal box you rent, usually from a bank, to store your valuables

Social Insurance Number: a number that the Canadian government uses to identify you, and that you use when you fill out official forms, apply for a job, etc.

toll-free: (used about a telephone number or call) that does not cost anything

voice mail: an electronic system that lets you record telephone messages for someone when he/she is not available to answer the telephone

white pages: the white pages of a telephone book that list the names, addresses, and telephone numbers of people living in a particular area

yellow pages: the yellow pages of a telephone book that list all the business companies, etc. in a certain area, in sections according to the products or services they provide

Note: Entries taken or adapted from the Oxford ESL Dictionary

Creating Your Canadian Experience

1. Search the Internet for the Human Resources and Skills Development Canada office nearest to your home where you can apply for your SIN card.
    Tip: type the name of your city and "HRSDC" into a search engine.

    Address: _____

    _____

    Hours: _____

2. Locate the doctor's office closest to your home so that you can pick up your medicare application.
    Tip: search in your local phone book under "Physicians."

    Address: _____

    _____

    Hours: _____

3. Use your phone book to locate the bank closest to your home.

    Address: _____

    _____

    Hours: _____

4. What is the fare for public transportation in your city?
   Tip: you can find this information by typing the name of your city and "Public Transit" into a search engine.

   a. Single ride: _____

   b. Weekly pass: _____

   c. Monthly pass: _____

5. Find out the rates and advantages of some of the local home phone companies.
   Tip: search for the companies by typing your city's name and "Home Phone" into a search engine. Then, either find out information about the companies from their websites or call the companies to ask them about their services.

Company	Rates	Advantages

6. Find out the rates and advantages for some of the local Internet providers in your area. Use the same method you used to learn about phone companies.

Company	Rates	Advantages
Telus		
Shaw		
Bell		
Rogers		

7. Search the Internet for two immigrant assistance organizations, one provided by the government and one provided by a charitable organization. Tip: type the name of your city and "Immigrant Assistance" into a search engine.

Government Organization:

Address: _____

_____

Hours: _____

Charitable Organization:

Address: _____

_____

Hours: _____

Chapter 5

Assistance Available

In This Chapter

- How can you learn English quickly?
- What is employment insurance?
- Are there government programs to help families?
- What's the difference between OAS and CPP?

This chapter is designed to give you some direction on where to find help in your new community, whether you need language assistance, emotional support, basic information, or financial help. There are many resources available and one of the best ways for you to find the right **community group**, **daycare centre**, employment service, or social service agency is to use your local telephone book. I'd suggest you get acquainted with your phone book as soon as possible.

The white pages of the telephone book alphabetically list every person and company that has a telephone in your community and surrounding communities. The blue pages of the telephone book list the contact numbers of all the government departments, ministries and agencies, at the municipal, regional, provincial, and federal level. The yellow pages of the telephone book list companies alphabetically but in categories that describe the service or product they provide. For example, the category "Car Dealers" lists all outlets that sell cars, and under "Computer," you will find companies that sell computers, service computers, and produce software for computers.

In the various pages of those telephone directories, you will find such valuable information as how to contact:

- Food banks
- Daycare centres
- Help centres for non-English-speaking persons
- Help centres for new immigrants
- Help centres for abused women
- Crisis centres
- Help centres for abused children
- Alcohol and drug counselling centres
- Bus, ferry, and train information
- Treatment centres and self-help groups for every kind of medical condition

Alcoholics Anonymous (AA) is an association that was founded in North America in 1935. Its goal is to assist individuals in overcoming their addictions to alcohol. Membership is free and meetings are open to men and women of all backgrounds who come together to support each other.

A friend of ours, whose husband had preceded her to Canada by six months, arrived in this country with her one-year-old son to find her husband already living with another woman. He had simply abandoned his wife and his child. With no money, no family, and few friends, she was in a desperate situation until she connected with a women's help centre. She received much-needed moral support and advice on what to do. Today she has a full-time job, her divorce is complete, and she has settled in to life in Canada.

Canada does provide a large safety net to help those who, for one reason or another, need a helping hand. Some of the services are provided through government agencies, some through charities, and some through volunteer organizations.

Q: Where can I find information about places of worship in my new community?

A: Contact a local ethnocultural organization for this information, or look in your local phone book under "Churches," "Synagogues," or "Mosques."

Language Training

The federal and provincial governments—through a variety of school boards, immigrant associations, and colleges—offer free English or French language lessons to every permanent resident and refugee over the age of 17 who is living in Canada. This instruction is commonly called ESL (English as a Second Language), or FSL (French as a Second Language). You will need to know one of these official languages to become a citizen of Canada.

This free language program is commonly referred to as LINC, or Language Instruction for Newcomers to Canada. In British Columbia, these programs are now referred to as ELSA, or English Language Services for Adults.

English language lessons are a valuable tool for finding a job and fitting into your new community, but they will not make you totally fluent within a few months. They are designed to provide enough English so that you can speak to your child's teacher, buy groceries, and ask directions.

Q: Is it important to improve my language skills if my community speaks my native language?

A: If you do not try to learn English, you will face difficulties in business and social interactions. You will not be able to benefit from all that Canada offers you. Almost all immigrants who have succeeded have moved outside of their ethnic communities and do have above-average English skills.

To find an appropriate ESL class, contact the LINC or ELSA office in your area. You will be asked to visit the centre to have your English language skills assessed. You cannot decide this level yourself; you must take a test to determine what class you should be enrolled in. Do not take the assessment test until you are prepared to attend classes, as the assessment is usually valid for only six months. If six months pass before you are ready to take the classes, you will likely be asked to take the test again.

You will be placed in an appropriate class for your current language ability. Courses range in length from three to nine months per level. Depending on your region and the school in which you enroll, you may be asked to provide some or all of your immigration papers.

LINC or ELSA classes are usually held in the mornings, afternoons, and evenings to accommodate a variety of family situations. Full-time classes usually involve 25 hours of classroom instruction per week, while part-time classes usually consist of 9 to 15 hours per week. Classes are in progress all the time, so you may be asked to join a group of students who have been in session for a few weeks. You will be slotted into an appropriate class for your skill level at a school near you when space is available.

In most situations, students will be expected to attend all classes. Students who don't attend classes could be asked to leave the course, as there are usually other students waiting to get in to the class. Some schools provide daycare facilities so that students with young children do not have to miss classes. If you will have a problem attending all classes, you should speak to your instructor.

ESL classes are categorized by level, with Level One being the most basic level of English. If you start at Level One, you will be permitted to continue on to further levels as long as your English is improving. Some provinces only provide free ESL up to Level Three; some go all the way to Level Seven.

The YMCA is a worldwide organization open to people of all ages, backgrounds, and abilities. It offers a variety of programs on education, literacy, employment, leadership, health, physical education, and community development. It also provides childcare to thousands of its members across the country. In fact, its many branches collectively make the YMCA the largest provider of community-based childcare in Canada.

Employment Insurance

Employment insurance (EI) is a federal program which basically ensures that workers who lose their jobs, through no fault of their own, are paid a percentage of their wages for a period of time until they find employment. Claimants must be actively job-hunting or upgrading their skills by attending courses while collecting EI.

Employees and employers jointly pay to provide funding for employment insurance, with employers paying a larger amount.

EI is also paid to new mothers as maternity leave and to fathers as parental leave when they take time off work to enjoy the first few months of parenthood. Every year, about three million Canadians receive EI **benefits** for one reason or another.

There are a number of qualifying criteria for those claiming EI. One of the first things you must do is obtain a **Record of Employment** from your last employer to submit to your local EI office. By law, your employer must provide this to you within five days of the **termination** of your employment.

In order to claim EI, you must have worked for the required number of insurable hours (generally between 420 and 700 hours) in the last 52 weeks, or since your last EI **claim**. The number of weeks of employment required varies from region to region, depending on the unemployment rates in those areas. Those entering the workforce for the first time will need a minimum of 910 hours of insured employment, as will those who have been absent from the workforce for two years or more.

Those applying for maternity or parental leave will require 600 hours of employment before they are able to qualify for EI benefits. Employment benefit payments equal approximately 55 percent of a worker's average **earnings**, to a maximum of about $435 per week. You could receive a higher benefit rate if you are in a low-income family.

Ratna Omidvar: A Bargaining Leader

When Punjab-born Ratna Omidvar and her Persian-born husband Mehran first applied to immigrate to Canada, they were turned down, but they never gave up trying to get in.

"We spoke English, had education, we didn't understand why we weren't allowed entry."

After being accepted into Canada, with help from Canadian friends like filmmaker Deepa Mehta, Omidvar and her husband arrived in Toronto, but she found that she was not able to work in her trade as a professor, and took up a job as a secretary. Quickly feeling frustrated at not being able to use her skills, Omidvar became a representative for immigrants and the poor at the Toronto-based **not-for-profit** Maytree Foundation.

"What led me to this work was largely accidental. I started to get involved in the world of NGOs [non-governmental organizations] through my daughter's childcare at St. Stephen's Community House." Omidvar eventually earned the title of Director, speaking out on the state of immigrant settlement in Canada.

"I would say that it's a bargain we make with this nation, and that this nation makes with us, and both sides have to live up to the bargain. We will work hard and try to learn your customs and peculiarities, cope with your winter and our children will be Canadian. And you will treat us equally, fairly. You will not treat us differently simply because of our accent, language, or the country we came from."

—*Sarshar Hosseinnia*

Claimants who have children and a **household income** that is less than about $26,000 will qualify for a Family Income **Supplement** which will bring their employment benefit payments up to 80 percent of their insured earnings. Individuals who are receiving regular, parental, or compassionate care benefits are allowed to work and earn an additional $50 per week without affecting their employment benefits.

Qualified claimants will receive benefits for a maximum of 45 weeks or until they find employment, whichever comes first. They will be required to complete and submit a form that shows their earnings each week. In some cases, they may also be required to provide proof that they are seeking employment, such as a list of jobs they have applied for. They must be available for work at all times while collecting EI.

Canada Pension Plan

The Canada **Pension** Plan (CPP) is administered by Human Resources and Skills Development Canada. It pays retirement pensions and **survivor** benefits. Note that all benefits must be applied for, and in the case of retirement benefits, the application should be submitted about six months before retirement. In other words, the above payments will not be sent to you automatically.

Everyone who works in Canada must contribute to the CPP and is accordingly eligible to collect CPP upon retirement. Your monthly **premiums** are withheld by your employer, who matches your **contributions** and submits the total sum to the CPP. Anyone who makes more than $3,500 per year must contribute to the plan.

The CPP contribution is about 10 percent of an employee's insurable earnings, half paid by the employee and half paid by the employer. The plan is fully portable, so no matter whom you work for or where you work in Canada, all your contributions will go into your CPP account.

The Government of Quebec administers its own pension plan, called the QPP, and provides a similar package of benefits to employees.

CPP Retirement Benefits
The size of a monthly retirement benefit payment is based directly on the amount of money the employee (with matching funds from his or her employer) has paid into the fund over a lifetime of employment. You must **retire**, or at least partially retire, before you can begin collecting CPP.

Canada Pension Plan Payment Rates		
Type of Benefit	Average Monthly Benefit (October 2006)	Maximum Monthly Benefit (2007)
Disability benefit	$772.88	$1,053.77
Retirement pension (at age 65)	$473.09	$863.75
Survivors benefit (under age 65)	$347.89	$482.30
Survivors benefit (age 65 and over)	$293.75	$518.25
Children of disabled contributors benefit	$200.47	$204.68
Children of deceased contributors benefit	$200.47	$204.68
Combined survivors & retirement benefit (pension at age 65)	$667.48	$863.75
Combined survivors & disability benefit	$911.00	$1,053.77
Death benefit (max. lump sum)	$2,227.82	$2,500.00

Source: Service Canada

The monthly payment will vary depending on your total lifetime contributions; the average monthly payment is about $470 and the maximum is about $860, as of 2007. The amount is adjusted annually based on the cost-of-living index. Retirees can choose to begin collecting the pension when they are 60, although monthly payments will be less than if they had waited until age 65.

As the CPP is a pension you contribute to, you will be eligible to collect it no matter where in the world you decide to live after retirement.

CPP Disability Pension
CPP also pays monthly installments to disabled workers, dependant children of disabled workers, and surviving spouses of deceased workers who have contributed over the years.

A disability pension is paid to someone who has contributed to CPP in four of the last six years, is under the age of 65, and has a "severe and prolonged disability" as defined by CPP.

CPP Survivor's Benefits
The surviving spouse of a CPP contributor would receive a full monthly **benefit** from CPP, if over the age of 65; a surviving spouse aged 45 to 65 would receive slightly less. Younger surviving spouses who are disabled or have dependant children could also receive some benefit. Any of these benefits should be claimed by the survivor.

Old Age Security

The Old Age Security (OAS) pension is a monthly payment made to every citizen or legal resident of Canada who reaches the age of 65, as long as he or she has lived in Canada for at least 10 years after the age of 18 and doesn't have a high income. The benefit is gradually reduced by Canada Revenue Agency for persons making more than $63,511 per year (as of 2007). Anyone making more than the threshold will have to repay part or all of the benefit. You can apply for this benefit when you turn 65.

Full benefits, which are about $500 and are tied to the cost of living in Canada, are paid to those who have resided in Canada for at least 40 years after the age of 18. Partial benefits are paid to those who have lived in Canada for less than 40 years. Their monthly benefits are reduced by one-fortieth for each year less than 40 that they have resided outside the country.

In order to collect the OAS pension while living abroad, you must have lived in Canada for at least 20 years after the age of 18, or be covered by a **social security** agreement with another country. If neither of these criteria is met, you will receive the pension for only six months after leaving Canada.

Guaranteed Income Supplement

The Guaranteed Income Supplement (GIS) is designed for seniors over the age of 65 who have little or no income. The amount you receive depends on your total family income during the previous year. If you leave Canada to reside elsewhere, you will be able to collect the supplement for only six months after you leave.

Single persons will be eligible for GIS if they make less than about $15,200 per year, apart from their OAP. Couples who make less than about $20,100 will be eligible for GIS. If one person is a pensioner and one is not, the couple would be eligible for some GIS assistance if their total family income is less than approximately $36,500.

A small amount will be paid to the survivor of someone receiving GIS. She or he must be aged 60 to 64, have an income about $20,500 or less, and must have resided in Canada for at least ten years after the age of 18. This benefit must be applied for annually to Human Resources and Skills Development Canada.

Canada Child Tax Benefit

The Canada Child Tax Benefit (CCTB) is a **need-based**, tax-free monthly payment made to lower-income parents to help offset the cost of raising children. Child tax benefits are paid to parents or guardians who live with the child. The parent or guardian must be one of the following:

- A Canadian citizen
- A permanent resident under the *Immigration Act*
- A refugee under the *Immigration Act*
- A visitor to Canada or a holder of a minister's permit under the *Immigration Act* who has lived in Canada throughout the previous 18 months and has a valid permit in the nineteenth month (other than one that states "does not confer status")

If you meet the above requirements, you should apply for the CCTB as soon as your child is born, as soon as the child begins to live with you, or as soon as you enter Canada. **Retroactive** payments may be made for the 11 months preceding the time at which you apply. Even if you don't think you will qualify, you should apply for the benefit. Your claim will be automatically reviewed every June based on your income tax return for that year. Both parents must file an income tax form every year in order to qualify for this benefit.

Applications for the CCTB are available on the Canada Revenue Agency's website at www.cra-arc.gc.ca.

New residents of Canada may have to provide documentation proving their residency and immigration status. During their first year in Canada, they will likely have to show a statement of world income in order to qualify for the benefit, as the CCTB is based on family income. They will also have to show proof of birth for each of the children for which they are applying.

Proof of birth must be in the form of a certified copy of any of the following:

- A birth certificate or a birth registration
- The hospital record of birth, or the record of the physician, nurse, or midwife who attended the birth
- A baptismal or cradle roll certificate

For a child born outside Canada, officials will also accept a certified copy of one of the following documents as proof of birth:

- A Record of Landing issued by Citizenship and Immigration Canada
- A Notice of Decision issued under the *Immigration Act*
- A passport or citizenship certificate

Child Find Canada (CFC) was formed in 1988. One of its main purposes is to search for children who are missing. With offices in approximately 70 communities, and thousands of volunteers who assist with its work, CFC is the largest and most comprehensive missing children's organization in Canada.

CCTB Calculation

The amount of your CCTB payment is based on the number and ages of the children in the family, the province in which you live, your family's total net income, and your family's deductions for childcare expenses.

The CCTB combines a basic benefit with the National **Child Benefit** Supplement (NCBS) for lower-income families.

Basic Benefit

The basic benefit is paid for each child in your family who is under 18 years of age. In addition to the basic benefit, there is an additional supplement if you have three or more children.

Your benefit will be slightly reduced if your family's net income is higher than about $37,000.

National Child Benefit Supplement

The NCBS was introduced by the federal, provincial, and territorial governments to assist low-income families with children. It ensures a fairly consistent level of financial support to these families whether their income comes from social assistance or employment.

NCBS payments vary based on household income and the number of children in the family.

The following tables show the estimated monthly amounts an Ontario family would receive from the CCTB and the NCBS in 2007 and 2008, based on family income and the number of children under 18. Benefit amounts may differ in other provinces.

$20,000 Income	One Child	Two Children	Three Children
CCTB	106.91	213.83	328.25
NCBS	165.66	312.16	451.58
Total	**$272.57**	**$525.99**	**$779.83**

$30,000 Income	One Child	Two Children	Three Children
CCTB	106.91	213.83	328.25
NCBS	72.97	137.42	198.58
Total	**$179.88**	**$351.25**	**$526.83**

$40,000 Income	One Child	Two Children	Three Children
CCTB	102.21	204.42	318.84
NCBS	0.00	0.00	0.00
Total	**$102.21**	**$204.42**	**$318.84**

Source: Canada Revenue Agency

Provincial and Territorial Programs

In addition to the CCTB and the NCBS, individual provinces and territories often offer financial benefits to families with children. Again, the size of your payments will be determined by your household income and the number of children you have.

Immigration Loans Program

Geared specifically toward refugees, the federal government–sponsored Immigrant Loans Program operates like a line of credit, providing loans to pay for travel expenses encountered during the immigration process. These loans were designed primarily for refugees and their **dependants**, as this group of immigrants generally has limited personal financial resources and is unable to access traditional lending institutions.

Immigration loans may be used to pay for medical examinations needed to gain admission to Canada. They may also be used to cover travel costs to Canada, costs related to finding accommodation and gaining employment, as well as the Right of Landing Fee.

Applicants must demonstrate a need for the loan and they must be able to repay the loan, with interest, within a given period of time.

The Immigration Loans Program may provide the following:

- A transportation loan to help people obtain transportation for themselves or their dependants to their final destination in Canada. This can also help pay for living expenses during the journey. It can cover airfare, airport taxes, and land transportation in Canada and overnight accommodation where necessary. This is the most common loan provided by the loans program.
- A Right of Permanent Residence Fee (RPRF) loan to help newcomers pay their RPRF.
- An admissibility loan to help cover the cost of medical services necessary to be admitted into Canada. The loan can be used to pay the medical costs of anyone applying for landing and their dependants.

Lozano Girado: Mentoring Program Success Story

Lozano Girado had an impressive resume. The certified public accountant had been a banker in the Philippines for 20 years, but he took a survival job as a janitor at a shopping centre when he arrived in Canada.

"It was just to augment our needs so we didn't exhaust the finances we brought with us," he says. "I worked at night so that in the morning I could send out applications." He adds that he sent out about ten resumes a day.

He didn't have any luck at first; he knew he needed more information, guidance, and a connection to someone in the banking or accounting field—in other words, a mentor. He turned to a local immigrant services agency for help.

The agency's mentoring program connected Girado with Ken Dhillon, a business development manager with a local credit union. Dhillon, who came to Canada from India as an 18-year-old, recalls what it was like for him as a newcomer. "I remember that whoever would just talk to me—who had five minutes for me—seemed like an angel to me," he says.

"Ken explained to me his experience after immigrating, before he was able to enter banking," says Girado. "It helped me a lot and gave me full insight into banking in Canada."

Thanks to a helpful lead from Dhillon, Girado soon found a position as a bookkeeper and was able to leave his survival job behind him.

—*Margaret Jetelina*

- An assistance loan to help those who have been granted admission to Canada pay for living expenses and the costs of accessing employment. This may include telephone and utility hookup expenses and the purchasing of tools or other work-required equipment. It may also cover the costs of examination fees required to establish work credentials in order to obtain employment in Canada.

Some not-for-profit immigrant service organizations such as the Maytree Foundation in Toronto and Mosaic in Vancouver, also offer immigrant loan programs which are not restricted to refugees.

Social Assistance

Income assistance is a last-resort safety net that can help provide the basic necessities of life to those who cannot afford to do so for themselves. While most people view the program as a temporary aid, it may be a long-term requirement for some applicants.

Administered provincially, income assistance programs are designed somewhat differently in each province, with different criteria established for eligibility.

These programs operate under a variety of departments and names. In Ontario it is known as Ontario Works, in BC it falls under the Ministry of Employment and Income Assistance, and in Alberta it is called Income Support and is provided by Alberta Human Resources and Employment.

While the names and departments vary from province to province, the following statements are true of most income assistance programs in Canada:

- Income assistance is a last resort, to be used when all other avenues of assistance have failed.
- It's a good idea to seek assistance from relatives prior to applying for social assistance.
- You will need to divulge every source of regular income, including salary, child benefits, workers' compensation benefits, and pensions.
- You will also need to report all sources of extraordinary income, such as inheritance or the sale of an automobile or any other possession.
- You should look for work, enlist in a job-training program, or upgrade your education to prepare yourself for moving off income assistance as soon as possible.

- You must report to a social worker or financial assistance worker (FAW) at regular intervals or when requested to do so by an income assistance representative.
- You should be prepared to produce a range of documents supporting your request for assistance, including your Social Insurance Number card, driver's licence, passport, citizenship papers, health card, and recent rent and utility receipts.

In an effort to reduce income assistance fraud, provinces frequently prosecute recipients who fail to provide accurate information regarding their income or assets.

For information on applying for social assistance, contact the provincial ministry of **social services** in your province.

Lilian To: Making a Difference

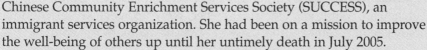

There always seemed to be three questions on the late Lilian To's mind: What are the changes our community needs? What can we do to have these changes met? Where can we can find the resources?

Chinese-born To was the Chief Executive Officer (CEO) of the United Chinese Community Enrichment Services Society (SUCCESS), an immigrant services organization. She had been on a mission to improve the well-being of others up until her untimely death in July 2005.

T.N. Foo, a longtime friend and colleague of To's at SUCCESS, says, "She really had foresight into what can be done for communities." At first, SUCCESS concentrated more on new immigrants, but Lillian's vision was for more human welfare of the whole community, but she understood that we had to start small. The vision she always had in mind was trying to listen, to reach out, and to understand the community needs. At the same time, she found every opportunity to watch out for resources to develop these services to meet all community needs."

Under To's leadership, SUCCESS grew to an impressive size. In a 2004 interview with *Canadian Immigrant* magazine, To said, "We started with a small office, four staff, and a budget of less than $100,000 a year. Now we have 12 offices, 350 staff and 9,000 volunteers, and a budget of $17 million."

—*Margaret Jetelina*

Non-Government Assistance

The following programs are available to everyone, regardless of income.

Welcome Wagon

Welcome Wagon is a business-sponsored welcoming service for people relocating to Canada, moving within Canada, or experiencing some kind of positive change, such as the addition of a new baby or an upcoming wedding.

Welcome Wagon, which is supported by businesses interested in helping the community while also marketing their products to that community, is a member of the Better Business Bureau and the Canadian Chamber of Commerce. Its goal is to greet people who are undergoing lifestyle changes with a friendly visit and provide them with free sample gifts as well as business and civic information about their new community.

Newcomers Club

The Newcomers Club Worldwide Directory is a guide to dozens of organizations that help people adjust to a new community. Many of these groups hold meetings or get-togethers that encourage newcomers to mingle, meet new friends, and make valuable contacts.

The Newcomers Club lists organizations in Alberta, British Columbia, Saskatchewan, Manitoba, Ontario, Quebec, New Brunswick, Newfoundland, and Nova Scotia. You can find these at www.newcomersclub.com.

Key Words

benefit: money that the government gives to people who are sick for a long time, injured at work, unemployed, etc.

child benefit: money that the government gives to families with children up to a certain age

claim: a demand for something that you think you have a right to

community group: a group of people who come together to pursue and further the social, educational, or recreational welfare of their community

contribution: something that you give or do together with others; the act of giving your share

daycare centre: a place that offers the service of taking care of small children while their parents are working

dependant: a person who relies on another person for money, a home, food, etc.

earnings: the money that a person earns by working

employment insurance (abbr. EI): a type of insurance system that is run by the Canadian government, which pays money regularly to people who are out of work

household income: the total amount of money made by all the people who live in one house

income assistance: the money that the government pays to people with no income or a very low income, especially the elderly, the unemployed, and those who are bringing up their children alone

need-based: based on a person's financial needs

not-for-profit (also non-profit): (about a company, organization, etc.) that does not aim to make a profit. Not-for-profit organizations usually offer services to help people.

pension: money that somebody who has stopped working because of old age receives regularly from the government or the company where he/she used to work

premium: an amount of money that you pay regularly to a company for insurance

Record of Employment (also ROE): a form given to someone by past employers to say when they worked and how much they got paid

retire: to leave your job and stop working, usually because you have reached a certain age

retroactive: (used about laws, decisions, payments, etc.) applying to the past, as well as to the present and the future

social security: money that the government pays regularly to people who are poor, unemployed, sick, etc.

social services: a system organized by the government or a charitable organization to help people with money or social problems

supplement: something that is added to something else

survivor: a person who continues to live or exist, in or after a difficult or dangerous situation

termination: (formal) the act of ending something; the end of something

Note: Entries taken or adapted from the Oxford ESL Dictionary

Creating Your Canadian Experience

1. In the phone book, look up daycare centres in your area.

    Name: _____

    Location: _____

    Phone Number: _____

2. In the phone book, look up help centres for non-English speaking persons.

    Name: _____

    Location: _____

    Phone Number: _____

3. Search on the Internet to find free language lessons in your area. Tip: try searching "Free language lessons" and your city.

    Name: _____

    Location: _____

    Phone Number: _____

    Class Times: _____

4. What are the employment insurance requirements in your region? Look on Human Resources and Social Development Canada's website to find this information.

    Required Number of Insurable Hours: _____

Maximum number of weeks you may receive EI:

_____

_____

_____

_____

5. Research some non-government organizations that assist immigrants and find out what programs they offer.
    Tip: type the name of your city and "Newcomer Assistance" into a search engine to find these organizations.

Organization	Programs Offered

Chapter 6

Medical Coverage

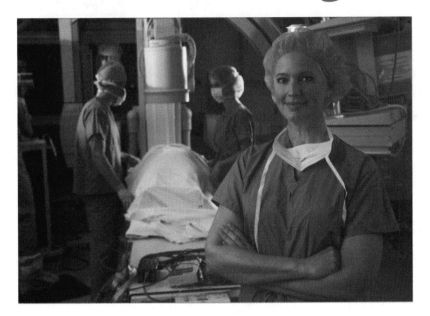

In This Chapter

- What is medicare and what medical services does it cover?
- How can you find a doctor?
- How can you get hospital treatment?
- Do you have to pay for prescription medicines? And what is pharmacare?

Canada's medicare system provides **universal**, comprehensive coverage to Canadians for medically required hospital services, and **in-patient** and **outpatient** services. It is federally funded and administered slightly differently in each of the ten provinces and three territories, despite the fact that it is referred to as a national health care plan.

Each province and territory is responsible for planning, financing, evaluating, and providing hospital care, additional health care services, and some aspects of **prescription drugs** and public health. While this chapter will provide you with some basic understanding of Canada's health care program, it is important to understand that the system is constantly changing throughout the country and varies from region to region. Do not hesitate to ask your health care provider what is and what is not covered by the health care plan in your province.

You will not be asked to pay the clinic, hospital, or physician directly, and there are no **deductibles** or fees charged on any insured service. However, in each province there are some services that are only partially covered and therefore require a fee from the patient. There are also some uninsured services that are not covered at all.

Finding a Physician

A priority for you will be to find a family or primary care doctor for your entire family. It is a good idea to do this before a medical emergency arises.

In Canada, most people choose one general family physician to help them with their regular medical concerns. By continuing to use the same doctor, you will be treated by someone who is familiar with your medical history. This can be an advantage in both emergency and routine situations.

You can select a clinic or physician of your choice in your neighbourhood. There are doctors and dentists of every nationality and language serving in most major cities so you shouldn't have a problem finding one who speaks your native language if this is a priority for you.

When choosing a doctor or a dentist, ask your friends or co-workers to recommend one they know and trust. You can also look in the phone book, which lists the names of doctors and their specialties, and may identify the languages they speak. Agencies that help newcomers will often provide the names of available doctors.

Q: When did Canada get universal medical coverage? Whose idea was it?

A: Tommy Douglas, a Scottish-born Saskatchewan premier, is widely credited with starting universal medical coverage in Canada. His *Saskatchewan Hospitalization Act* led to the federal government introducing the *Hospital Insurance and Diagnostic Services Act* in 1957. By 1961, all ten provinces were included under the act.

Because doctors limit the number of patients they can care for, you may have to call around before you find one who is able to accept you and your family. In most cases, you will need to make an appointment to visit a doctor, although most community health clinics will accept some walk-in patients.

It is your right to choose your own doctor, and you may change doctors at any time. If you disagree with your doctor, you may also seek another physician to obtain a second opinion on a medical problem or treatment. Patients sometimes do this when facing a serious medical condition or possible surgery. It is usually a good idea, however, to find one doctor and stick with him or her.

Specialists

Your primary care physician (also called a general practitioner or family doctor) is usually your first contact with the health care system. These doctors generally control or direct their patients' access to most health care **specialists**, as well as to hospital beds. It is also your doctor who decides which **diagnostic tests** you will need and generally arranges the appointments for these tests. Your doctor will prescribe any necessary **medications**, which you will then pick up at the **pharmacy** of your choice.

In other words, with the exception of a medical emergency—in which case you should head for the emergency room at your nearest hospital—you will need to visit your primary care physician to be treated or referred for treatment for any kind of medical problem.

What Is and Is Not Covered

The health care system covers all medically necessary hospital stays. This includes stays needed for treatment of an illness, **surgical** procedures, and **maternity** services, including childbirth, **prenatal** and **postnatal care**, newborn care, and treatment of complications surrounding a pregnancy.

No provincial health care plan in Canada covers services such as medical examinations requested by a third party (for employment, insurance purposes, or to obtain a driver's licence), cosmetic surgery that is not medically necessary, or preparation of testimony reports for legal purposes. These must be paid for directly by the patient.

Also not covered by medicare are dental care, vision care, artificial limbs, wheelchairs, prescription medication, podiatry, and **chiropractics**. However, certain groups of the population, such as seniors, children, and those on social assistance, may be able to obtain these extended health services through a pharmacare program provided by their province. Canadians in every province can purchase private extended health insurance to cover some of these health services not included in the national health care plan. Most employers provide extended health care benefits to their employees that cover some of these costs. This varies from employer to employer but it can range from about 50 to 100 percent coverage. In some instances, there may be a deductible, or a portion of the expense, which you would pay.

> One of Canadian George Klein's many inventions was the electric wheelchair. It was created in 1952 and was controlled with a lever which allowed its occupant to move about easily.

Prescription drugs provided during hospitalization are included under medicare, but those prescribed outside an institution are generally not paid for by the plan. With the exception of the Yukon Territory, ambulance service in Canada is usually not fully covered by the health insurance plans of any province or territory, except when necessary to transfer patients between hospitals. Some provinces have limited the cost of an ambulance ride, but in other provinces ambulance service can be very expensive.

In Saskatchewan, the cost of ambulance service for seniors has been limited at $250, although there is no limit on the amount that can be charged to

Hedy Fry: Immigrant, Doctor, Politician

Hedy Fry, a Trinidadian immigrant and well-known Vancouver member of Parliament, wasn't always a politician. She graduated from the Royal College of Surgeons in Dublin and became a doctor. Instead of returning to her homeland after graduation, she and her new husband, an English doctor, decided to move to Canada.

After a few years of family practice, Fry found herself pulled into medical politics, with organizations like the BC Medical Association. She became a sought-after spokesperson for the association for eight years. "I spoke on everything from safety helmets, to fetal alcohol syndrome, to nutrition labelling," Fry says.

Then, in 1992, Jean Chrétien, the Liberal party leader at the time, asked her to run as a Liberal candidate. Although she didn't expect to win, she did, and went to Ottawa as a member of Parliament. She has been re-elected several times, including in the 2006 federal election.

—*Margaret Jetelina*

other residents. Ontario residents with a health card pay $45, while others pay $240. In BC, a resident pays $54 for the first 40 kilometres, plus 50 cents for each additional kilometre up to a maximum of $274, and non-residents pay $396.

Medicare: How it Operates

Despite Canada's reputation, it does not offer "socialized medicine" where all doctors are employed by the government and make the same amount of money. Most Canadian doctors operate independently, whether they work by themselves or in a group practice.

Some work in community health centres, clinics, or in hospital-based groups affiliated with outpatient departments. Those in private practice submit their records of the services they have provided to clients directly to the provincial health insurance plan and are paid on a fee-for-service basis. In some situations, physicians may receive a salary rather than a fee-for-service.

Q: Can I use Canada's health care service as soon as I have arrived in the country?

A: No, in most provinces you will have to wait three months or more before being eligible for government medical services, which is why you should purchase private medical insurance upon arrival.

Despite some of the drawbacks and disadvantages of the Canadian health care system, Canada still has one of the highest **life expectancy** rates in the industrialized world. The life expectancy of a Canadian child born in 2001 is about 80 years. Also, **infant mortality** rates in Canada are among the lowest in the world, currently at about five per one thousand live births.

Canadian Hospitals

Generally, Canadian hospitals operate as private, non-profit institutions, each overseen by a community-based board of trustees or a municipality. The regional or provincial health authorities provide funding, with each hospital board deciding how to use that funding.

Fee-based, for-profit hospitals primarily offer long-term care or serve as special centres for the treatment of medical conditions such as drug or alcohol addiction or eating disorders. If you are in need of a private hospital, you can contact the facility directly by looking up its phone number in the telephone book.

General coverage for short-term hospital care provides patients with ward accommodation (two to four people of the same gender stay in the same room); meals; nursing services; laboratory tests and other diagnostic procedures; and the services of **physiotherapists, occupational therapists**, and **dietitians** while in the hospital.

When admitted to a hospital, you will be assigned to a particular ward or area specializing in the kind of treatment you need. Usually there is a patients' lounge where you can spend time meeting other patients or watching TV. If you prefer, you can order a TV to be placed beside your bed for a daily fee. Your meal will be served at your bedside. Depending on your medical condition, you will usually be allowed to have visitors. Some hospitals restrict the number of visitors that patients can have at one time, and some may restrict visits to a particular time. These are questions any nurse at the hospital can answer.

In most cases, patients are referred to a hospital by their family doctor or a specialist. In some cases of elective surgery (surgery that is not immediately necessary) your doctor may place your name on a **waiting list**, which means you will be advised when a bed and a nurse are available in the appropriate area of the hospital where you need treatment. This waiting period has become a point of great debate in virtually every province in Canada, as the length of the wait seems to be getting longer and longer.

In any medical emergency, however, you should head to the nearest hospital's emergency entrance. If possible, try to make sure you have your provincial medical card with you. However, in order to maximize health care service, you should see your family doctor if the medical problem is not urgent.

Canadian Blood Services (CBS) is a non-profit, charitable organization in Canada that oversees the collection of more than 425,000 litres of blood each year. Thousands of Canadians donate blood each day at donor clinics that are held across the country. According to CBS, one blood donation can save up to three lives.

Private Medical Insurance

Some provinces have a three-month waiting period before new residents to the province are eligible for health care coverage, so it's a good idea to obtain private medical insurance coverage before you arrive. You should ensure that your private insurance will cover you as an immigrant, not just as a visitor, to Canada. If any member of your family requires medical attention before you've been in the country for three months, the cost could be quite high. A doctor's consultation fee will likely cost a minimum of $40.

Also, to keep your family's medical expenses down in the first year or two, I recommend you attend to all your family's dental and vision requirements before you leave your home country, where costs for these services may be considerably less than in Canada.

Health Care Premiums

Except for British Columbia and Alberta, health care is financed by provincial and federal taxes. In these two western provinces, however, residents must pay a premium toward basic health coverage. Financial assistance is provided for those living on a low income who cannot afford to pay the premium.

Pregnancy

Women who think they may be pregnant are advised to call their doctor as soon as possible to arrange an examination. Prenatal care is necessary to ensure you have a healthy baby. Most communities and hospitals offer expecting mothers and fathers a wide range of prenatal courses, as well as information on nutrition and maintaining a healthy lifestyle during pregnancy.

Almost all births in Canada take place in hospitals, although home births with the assistance of a midwife are becoming more common among parents and more accepted by medical authorities.

> Pablum is a common cereal for infants that contains many of the vitamins and minerals needed for optimal health. It was developed in 1931 at the Hospital for Sick Children in Toronto, Ontario, by Canadian pediatricians Tisdall, Drake, and Brown.

Mental Illness

If anyone in your family is suffering from any kind of psychiatric or mental illness, your physician can refer you to a professional mental health practitioner for treatment or therapy. Medicare pays for these services.

Death

A licensed physician must officially certify all deaths. Without this certification, it is impossible to process wills, inheritances, **insurance claims**, or proceed with related legal matters. In most parts of Canada, a body must be cremated or buried in a recognized cemetery. You must arrange and pay for funeral services; funeral directors are listed in the phone book. Ask a friend or relative to refer you to a funeral director who knows and understands your religious practices.

Supplemental Health Services

Prescription Drugs

Provincial medical plans do not cover prescription drugs or other medications for most of the adult population. But some form of subsidy or pharmacare is offered in Alberta, British Columbia, Manitoba, Ontario, Quebec, and Saskatchewan for people with high drug costs and modest incomes. Also, a prescription drug plan for seniors operates in Newfoundland, Nova Scotia, Prince Edward Island, New Brunswick, and the Northwest Territories. The drug plans across the country are very complicated and are changing all the time; do not hesitate to ask your doctor or pharmacist what is and what is not covered by your provincial plan when you need a **prescription**. It may be necessary to keep all your medication receipts.

In Quebec, those who are not covered under a prescription drug plan at their place of employment or elsewhere must pay a premium to the Public Prescription Drug Insurance Plan. This will cost between $0 and $538 per adult annually.

The Ontario Trillium Drug Program helps those with high drug costs and modest incomes. There is a deductible of about 4 percent, based on your income. For example, if you have an annual taxable income of $20,000, your deductible will be $800, and you will pay $200 for any prescriptions purchased at the start of each quarter on August 1, November 1, February 1, and May 1. You will receive benefits after your deductible has been paid, and covered prescriptions purchased after this point will cost up to $2 each.

Manitoba Pharmacare sets the prescription deductible based on a percentage of income. For example, a family earning less than $15,000 per year would pay about 2.5 percent of the costs of the prescription, and a family earning more than $15,000 would pay about 4 percent. Pharmacare then pays the balance of the drug costs.

Saskatchewan generally covers the costs of drugs that exceed 3.5 percent of a person's income. A family of three earning $35,000 per year would have to pay the first $1,190 in drug costs, after which the province would pay the balance.

Dr. Godwin Eni: Visionary at Large

Dr. Godwin Eni's whirlwind life in Canada took him to all parts of the country and through many professions before he became an advocate for diversity and multiculturalism.

"When I first came here in 1970, multiculturalism was primarily concerned with the English and French living together and being happy about it. But I've seen a metamorphosis since then."

This transition that Eni went through amazed the Nigerian-born physiotherapist, who had fled his country with a bullet in his armpit. "I was a curiosity to some," claimed Eni, who learned to educate each person he came across. "The more people knew about my background, the more they felt comfortable."

The young-looking 69-year-old is now retired, but continues to work on anti-racism initiatives in an ongoing effort which Eni hopes will prevent marginalizing in Canada.

"We're not there yet. But now is the time to prevent it."

—*Sarshar Hosseinnia*

The British Columbia Fair PharmaCare plan requires BC families to pay their full prescription drug costs until they reach their deductible. Those with net family incomes below $15,000 do not have to pay a deductible. For families with incomes above this amount, the deductible is 2 percent of family income for those earning up to $30,000, and 3 percent for those making over $30,000. Once the deductible is reached, PharmaCare will pay 70 percent of eligible drug costs for the remainder of the year.

Eye Care

In most provinces, standard vision tests are generally only covered for youth and seniors, and usually only once every two years. Newfoundland, Prince Edward Island, New Brunswick, the Northwest Territories, and the Yukon Territory do not insure routine vision testing for anyone.

No government medical plans in Canada cover the cost of eyeglasses, frames, contact lenses, or optical laser surgery. Only private insurance plans will offer this coverage.

Dental Care

Routine dental services for adults are not covered by medicare. However, surgery required to repair dental work due to congenital problems, accident, or infection is covered by provincial and territorial medical plans.

Physiotherapy

Physiotherapy is partially covered by some medical plans, usually for children and seniors. Treatment received while in a hospital is generally completely covered, even for adults. Outside of a hospital setting, however, you will have to pay for all or some of the treatment costs.

Chiropractic Services

Chiropractic treatment, which is the adjustment of joints and the spine to correct certain disorders, is partially covered by some provincial health plans. The provincial governments set the cost to the individual for these services.

Treatments will often be covered by private health care insurers or employee health care benefits programs.

Employer-Subsidized Extended Medical Benefits Plans

Before Sabrina and I began full-time employment, our medical costs for a family of four were pretty high. It didn't help that my doctor put me on medication to lower my cholesterol—at a cost of $70 per month. With various other prescription drugs required by our four-member family, we were spending nearly $180 each month on medication. This changed when Sabrina landed a permanent job that included an extended medical benefits program that covered the whole family.

Q: Should I be willing to take a lower-paying job if the benefits are great?

A: That's a very hard decision to make. While benefits may seem great, you'll need to look over your monthly expenses in order to answer this question. If dental and healthcare costs are regularly a major expense for you, then supplemental health benefits may be a good reason to take a lower-paying job.

Most government and unionized jobs, and many others, will offer some kind of group insurance plan that covers supplemental health services such as medications, although the plans differ a great deal. One plan may pay the entire prescription costs for the whole family, while another may only pay 80 percent. Plans may cover prescription medications, dental work, medical devices such as prostheses, or all of these. Your spouse and children will generally be covered by your benefits, but these plans usually exclude adult dependants.

Special Service Organizations or Charities

Service organizations or charities geared to specific illnesses and disorders are a valuable tool in the care and treatment of persons suffering from various medical conditions. These organizations usually have a large volunteer base and offer their services for free. It is highly recommended

Gerald Raath: Nutrition Guru

It seems that there is something about the Canadian lifestyle that makes immigrants pack on the pounds (gain weight). Adapting to a North American (or fast-food) diet and a sedentary (or "couch potato") lifestyle are the meat of the problem. Gerald Raath, owner of the SureSlim Wellness Clinic franchise in Canada, an immigrant himself, sees this trend swelling.

"I have observed that people who are immigrants, when they come to this country, they start to eat the North American way," says Raath, who was born in Kenya and lived in South Africa before immigrating to Canada. Of course, for every fast-food restaurant in North America, there seems to be a gym or weight-loss clinic, too. Raath's SureSlim franchise is unusual in that its origins were not in North America, but in South Africa.

"I negotiated with the owners to bring SureSlim to Canada in 1999," says Raath. "It wasn't easy; I thought I must be insane to challenge North America on the weight-loss industry," he says. But Raath opened the first location in 2000 and, in 2002, he acquired master franchise rights to sell SureSlim franchises across Canada. Now that's growth that Raath need not try to lose.

—*Margaret Jetelina*

that you or your family contact the appropriate organization should you find yourself facing cancer, diabetes, kidney problems, multiple sclerosis, lung disease, heart problems, or any other serious medical condition.

In most cases, the goal of these organizations is to offer advice on nutrition, mobility, exercise, and to serve as a support system for your entire family. You can look them up in the phone book or ask at your doctor's office for a contact name.

Key Words

chiropractor: a person whose job is to treat pain in people's bodies by pressing on and moving their bones, especially in somebody's back (adj. chiropractic)

deductible: an amount of money that somebody must pay before his/her insurance pays the rest of the cost of something

diagnostic test: a test given to identify a disease

dietitian: a person who gives advice to people on what they should eat to stay healthy

infant mortality: the number of deaths of babies in a certain period of time or in a certain place

in-patient: a person who goes to a hospital for medical treatment and stays in the hospital for at least one night

insurance claim: a request for money that you believe you have a right to from an insurance company

life expectancy: the number of years that a person is likely to live

maternity: connected with women who are going to have or have just had a baby

medication: pills, liquids, etc. that you take in order to treat an illness

occupational therapist: a person who helps people get better after illness or injury by giving them special physical activities to do

outpatient: a person who goes to see a doctor for treatment but who does not stay in the hospital overnight

pharmacy: a place where medicines are prepared and sold

physiotherapist: a person who treats muscle or joint problems by exercises, massage, and the use of heat

postnatal care: care given to a mother or infant after a child's birth

prenatal care: care given to a pregnant woman before a baby is born

prescription drug: medicine you get from a pharmacy after giving a form on which a doctor has written the name of the medicine that you need

prescription: a form on which a doctor has written the name of the medicine that you need

specialist: a doctor with special or deep knowledge of a particular area of medicine

surgical: used in surgery or connected with surgery

universal: connected with, done by, or affecting everybody in the world or everybody in a particular group

waiting list: a list of people who are waiting for something that will be available in the future

will: a legal document in which you write down who should have your money and property after your death

Note: Entries taken or adapted from the Oxford ESL Dictionary

Creating Your Canadian Experience

1. Find out the waiting period before you will qualify for medical coverage in the province where you plan to live.
    Tip: look for this information on your provincial ministry of health's website, which you can find by typing the name of your province and "Health Care" into a search engine.

2. What medical services are covered in your province? Check the appropriate box for each service.
   Tip: use your provincial ministry of health's website to find out which of the following services are or are not covered.

Service	Covered	Not Covered	Partially Covered
Hospital care			
Surgery			
X-rays			
Cosmetic surgery			
Orthopaedics			

Service	Covered	Not Covered	Partially Covered
Services performed by audiologists			
Services performed by podiatrist			
Services performed by osteopath			
Services performed by chiropractor			
Vision tests			
Physiotherapy			

3. Search the Internet for the hospital nearest your home and write down the quickest way to get there.

   Tip: to find your nearest hospital, type the name of your city and "Hospital" into a search engine. Then use a mapping website, such as www.mapquest.ca or maps.google.ca/maps to find out how to get there.

   Address: _____

   Directions: _____

   _____

4. Look for family doctors in your local phone book, under the category "Physicians," and call some to find out which ones are accepting new patients. Make a list of doctors in your area who could become your doctor.

Doctor's Name	Location	Contact Information

Chapter 7

Accommodation

In This Chapter

- What are the advantages and disadvantages of different types of housing?
- How can you find an apartment to rent?
- What's involved in owning a condominium?
- How much money do you need to put a down payment on a house?

Settling in to a secure and safe place in your new country will probably be your first priority after landing.

You may have a relative or friend who can accommodate you for the short term, but unless that person has a really big heart and a big house, you will need to move on fairly quickly. It is always a good idea to live in a new city, get to know the place, and get to know where your friends and relatives live before selecting permanent accommodation.

Housing Costs

Housing is a huge subject area with so many variations that it is difficult to provide sample costs for both rentals and home **purchases** across the country. But, as housing also constitutes your largest monthly **expense**, we wanted to give you some idea of what is fair market pricing.

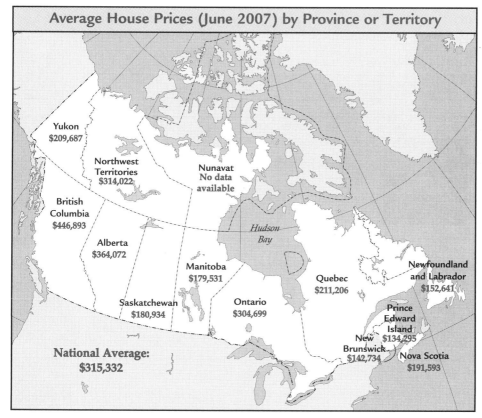

Average House Prices (June 2007) by Province or Territory

Yukon
$209,687

Northwest
Territories
$314,022

Nunavat
No data
available

British
Columbia
$446,893

Hudson
Bay

Alberta
$364,072

Manitoba
$179,531

Quebec
$211,206

Newfoundland
and Labrador
$152,641

Saskatchewan
$180,934

Ontario
$304,699

Prince
Edward
Island
$134,295

New
Brunswick
$142,734

Nova Scotia
$191,593

National Average:
$315,332

Source: Canadian Real Estate Association

The cost of purchasing a standard three-bedroom, detached home in Toronto or Vancouver will be more than $350,000.

In some parts of Canada, you can purchase a perfectly fine house on a large lot for much less. The point here is that location is the key to housing prices in Canada. Naturally, house prices are higher in densely populated areas, such as Toronto and Vancouver, where land is scarce.

Again, prices generally rise as you move toward city centres and popular locations. The same applies for rental accommodation. A fair rule of thumb is that a one-bedroom apartment will cost about $700 to $800, a two-bedroom about $900 to $1,000 and a three-bedroom $1,000 or more, depending on the location. Expect to pay slightly more than these rates in large urban centres.

Types of Housing

Canadian cities and towns offer many different types of housing. Your home may be a house, townhouse, semi-detached house, condominium, rented apartment, basement **suite**, or a room.

Types of Housing		
	Pros	**Cons**
Room	Cheap but still a good amount of space Usually comes with furniture	Must share washroom and kitchen with other people Limited private space
Apartment	Private space Reasonable prices	No return on rent money Landlord and neighbours can be difficult to deal with

Types of Housing

	Pros	Cons
Townhouse	More personal space than room or apartment Can be bought or rented	Noise from neighbours with joint walls can be intrusive Backyard and outside space is limited
Semi-detached House	More personal space than room or apartment Usually owned so money is invested	Can be expensive Attached to neighbour's house on one side
Detached House	Larger buildings and lots Usually owned so money is invested	Can be expensive Usually outside of city centre
Condo	Usually centrally located and have facilities to use (gym, pool) Usually owned so money is invested	High price for small place Condo fees are paid monthly

Do not worry if your first home in Canada is not all you would like it to be. Many Canadians start out with basic housing and then work toward more satisfactory accommodation. In fact, moving and changing accommodation seems to be normal in Canada, as half of all Canadians move every three years.

Rental apartments and homes always include a stove and a refrigerator. Newer or more expensive apartments often come equipped with other appliances, such as a dishwasher, microwave, clothes washer and dryer, and even an air conditioner.

Karim Virani: Immigrant Realtor

Karim Virani was probably a realtor before he even knew it. As a child living in Canada, the Ugandan immigrant looked up to his father, a successful businessperson, and dreamed of being in business himself one day. Virani remembers telling his father about some buildings up for sale on waterfront property. The price? About $250,000.

"I told him to buy it. But my father said, 'These are old shacks,'" says Virani. "And I said, 'But, dad, look at the location!'"

And a realtor was born.

"Real estate always interested me," says Virani.

He obviously has a talent for it. Not only is he one of Re/Max's top producers, he has also won a lifetime achievement award and countless other realty-related awards.

"Thirty percent of clientele are fairly new immigrants—people from Russia, Germany, United Kingdom, Iran, China, and so on," says Virani. Not only does Virani find them a home, but he provides them with information, maps, and school and restaurant guides: "all the information a newcomer needs to make a decision."

—*Margaret Jetelina*

Renting a House or Apartment

Your first task is to clarify in your own mind what kind of accommodation you're looking for—a rental house, an apartment, a townhouse, a duplex— how many bedrooms you need, whether you need to be near public transit, and what neighbourhood you'd like to live in.

Once you've settled on your search criteria, there is no better search engine than the friends and relatives you're already connected to. Let them know what you're looking for, and let them help you in your search.

The following definitions are regularly used to describe various rental accommodations:

- "Apartment" means a separate **unit** in a building, with a number of other units. **Residents** enter the building through one main entrance but have individual units.
- "Rental house" means a detached family dwelling, or at least the main floor or aboveground level of the dwelling. There may or may not be another suite above or below you occupied by other **tenants**.
- "Basement" means below–ground level accommodation in the basement of a home. These are among the cheapest accommodations available.
- "Townhouse" means a two- or three-storey apartment attached to another apartment or a row of apartments. Townhouses usually offer individual street entrances and addresses, as well as a small patio or outdoor space.
- "Bachelor" or "studio apartment" means a unit with no separate bedroom, although it could contain an alcove for a bed.
- "Shared accommodation" means someone with an apartment or house is looking for someone to share that space with. This obviously requires some caution, as you don't know the stranger you are going to live with!

Finding Accommodation

The following list suggests some of the more common means used to find a new home. Whatever you do, make sure you consult a good street map when looking at ads, so you don't waste time following up on a great, cheap apartment two hours from town.

- Nothing beats walking or driving around the neighbourhood you're interested in to look for "Apartment for Rent" signs. Many **landlords** will post a notice outside a building or house advertising the **vacancy** immediately after the suite becomes available or the tenant has given notice. This saves the landlord the costs of advertising the apartment in the newspaper.
- Newspaper classified ads list apartments by municipality and **district**, so you should be familiar with a region before you start browsing.
- Bulletin boards at community centres and laundromats frequently contain ads for rental accommodations in the immediate neighbourhood. They always seem to have postings for shared accommodations, too, which is okay for a single person, but would be a bit crowded for a family.

1 bdrm dntn. Clean, lrg kit, prkg, lndry. Sep entr. $700 incl. Avail Aug 1. Call 555-2211.

Classified ads are paid for by the letter. In order to be more cost efficient, users have developed a short form for many common words. Below are some of these short forms and their meanings.

Bldg = Building	Furn = Furnished
Bdrm = Bedroom	Jr 1 Bdrm = Very small one bedroom
Reno = Renovated	A/c = Air conditioning
Balc = Balcony	Sol = Solarium
Prkg = Parking	Apt = Apartment
UG Prkg = Underground Parking	Sep entr = Separate Entrance
Hrdwd = Hardwood flooring	Kit = Kitchen
Incl = Includes all utilities (Inclusive)	Appls = Appliances
Immed = available immediately	PH = Penthouse
Avail = Available	Dntn = Downtown
Bths = Bathrooms	Bsmt = Basement
Lrg = Large	High ceil = High Ceilings
Flr = Floor	Spac = Spacious (big)
+ hydro = Tenant must pay hydro on top of rent	Lndry = Laundry

---

Once you've noticed an ad for something you're interested in, the standard procedure is to call the landlord to get a few more details. You might ask questions about when it is available, how many bedrooms it has, or whether there are laundry facilities. You may as well tell the landlord over the phone if you smoke or have pets because landlords in most provinces may choose to decline you if you do. If you want to look at the apartment, you can make an appointment to view the suite. If after viewing you don't want it, simply thank the landlord and leave.

If you think you might want the apartment but you need time to think about it, you want your spouse to see it, or you have a few more places to look at, you can't expect the landlord to hold the place for you unless you put a deposit down on it. This will keep the landlord from renting the suite to anyone else for a day or so until you decide. The deposit, which may be $50 or $100, will be deducted from your first month's rent if you take the apartment, but you should clarify whether the deposit will be refunded to you if you decide not to rent the apartment. Make sure you get a receipt and have the landlord specify, in writing, what will happen to the deposit whether you rent the suite or not. It will normally not be returned to you, since the landlord has put off renting the premises to give you time to decide.

If you're interested in the apartment, the landlord might also ask you to complete a rental application. This is basically a form that you will fill out to provide the landlord with your current address, phone number, and employer. You may also need to include references and other relevant information; the form may list the move-in date and the cost of the rent. This is just an application to rent and is not to be confused with a lease or a rental agreement. The landlord might have several prospective tenants from which to choose and naturally wants to select the best tenant to occupy the premises.

Renting: The Legal Side

The laws governing rental accommodation are established by the provinces and territories and are administered slightly differently throughout Canada, although they are all designed to protect tenants from unfair treatment by landlords. Most provinces have an office of the rentalsman or a rental housing tribunal to settle disputes between landlords and tenants. Your chances of encountering a dispute are greatly reduced if you know a few of your basic rights and responsibilities regarding the issue of renting.

Q: What is a lease?

A: A lease is the right to use or occupy personal property, given by the owner to a renter or tenant, for a period of time. The renter obtains exclusive possession of the property in return for paying the owner a fixed payment.

A lease, which sets out a **fixed term of tenancy**—usually a year — is frequently used in some provinces, such as Quebec, but is rarely used in others, such as BC. Tenants don't necessarily have to leave after the one-year period, but the lease establishes the minimum required stay. A tenant who wishes to stay beyond the year should advise the landlord prior to the end of the lease.

If you want to move before your lease has ended, you may sublet the apartment to another tenant if your landlord approves. In this situation, your name will still be on the lease and you will be held responsible if the new tenant does not pay rent.

A **tenancy agreement** may not set a specific term of tenancy, but should clarify the details of the tenancy. This will include the cost of rent and the expected payment date each month, as well as explaining who pays for cable television, who pays for water and electricity, what the arrangement is for parking, and who is responsible for yard work such as cutting the grass. British Columbia and Quebec both require landlords and tenants to complete and sign a tenancy agreement, while New Brunswick and Quebec also offer a standard lease agreement.

A **damage deposit** or security deposit is a common fee paid by the tenant to the landlord as security in case the tenant skips out on the rent or damages anything in the apartment. This deposit is often the cause of disputes between tenants and landlords, so it should be thoroughly understood by everyone. Frequently, the landlord will ask for this deposit, along with the first month's rent, when you agree to rent the suite. In Ontario and Quebec, landlords cannot request a security deposit. The maximum security or damage deposit payable in BC, Newfoundland, Nova Scotia, and Manitoba is half a month's rent. The maximum in other provinces is one month's rent.

All provinces where a security deposit may be charged require that the landlord pay interest on the deposit and return it to the tenant within a certain time period after the end of the tenancy. In some provinces, such as BC, the landlord can retain the deposit only if the tenant agrees in writing to allow the landlord to keep the amount as payment for unpaid rent or damage, or if the landlord applies under the province's tenancy act to settle a dispute regarding damage or non-payment of rent. Some provinces encourage the **landlord** and tenant to complete an inspection report to ensure there are no disagreements regarding the condition of the suite.

Such an inspection report is recommended but not mandatory. It is a written report on the premises before occupancy occurs, describing any pre-existing damage to the walls, carpets, windows, or other areas. It should be signed by the landlord and **tenant** before a tenancy begins, to protect the tenant from being held liable for any pre-existing damage.

Canadians are choosing to live with their parents longer than they have in the past few decades. In Toronto, almost 60 percent of adult children in their twenties still live at home or have returned to live at home after a period on their own. Many of them are staying put for quite some time, often until they are in their mid-thirties.

In most provinces, rent increases can be charged only after one year of tenancy and then can be raised only once per year thereafter. In most provinces, landlords must give tenants three months' written notice of a rent increase; in Nova Scotia the minimum is four months, while in New Brunswick it is only two. The size of the rental increase is also dictated by some provinces, with some setting the increase at 1 to 3 percent of the current rent. In BC, the province requires that rent increases be justified by increased costs. The point is, wherever you live, the landlord cannot raise your rent dramatically or frequently.

A tenant's privacy while living in rental accommodation is protected by law. A landlord cannot enter a rented suite unless there is an emergency, the tenant allows the landlord to enter, the landlord has written permission from the tenant to enter for a given purpose, or the tenant has abandoned the premises.

Repairs to a rental accommodation are the responsibility of the landlord, who must by law provide and maintain the premises in a reasonable state. The landlord must comply with health, safety, and housing standards. If repairs are required, the tenant must advise the landlord, and if the repairs are not made in a reasonable time frame, the tenant should contact the provincial rentalsman or housing committee's office for guidance on how to proceed. In most provinces, tenants are able to arrange for repairs, pay the bills, and deduct these costs from the rent if they provide their landlord with a copy of the bill and an explanation.

The number of people living in a rental property must be considered reasonable by the landlord. If the number of permanent occupants is unreasonable, the landlord may discuss this with the tenant and, if the problem persists, may serve a notice to terminate the tenancy.

Ending a tenancy by a tenant in most provinces simply means providing the landlord with a written letter saying when the tenancy will end. Each province has a minimum period of notice that a tenant must give before moving out.

Subsidized Housing

Some form of subsidized housing exists in all provinces. It is usually adjusted based on the tenant's income and is available through a variety of programs.

The eligibility requirements for subsidized housing vary from province to province, so seniors, low-income families, and single-parent families should contact their local housing authorities for information.

Types of Subsidized Housing	
Public Housing	Owned by provincial government
	Tenants must meet financial eligibility requirements
	All units are priced based on income
Rent Supplements	Owned by private landlords but supplemented by provincial governments
	Supplement makes up difference between rent paid and market value
	Tenants must meet financial eligibility requirements
Non-profit Housing	Owned by private charitable groups or municipalities
	Funding is from donations and government subsidies
	Tenants must meet financial eligibility requirements
Co-op Housing	Owned collectively by co-operative
	Run by a board of directors made up of tenants
	Tenants must join co-op and agree to follow co-op's rules
	Co-op collects monthly fees and is subsidized by the government

Source: Settlement.Org

BC Housing provides assistance, under certain circumstances, to families who are eligible for GAINS, which is the Guaranteed Annual Income Supplement for low-income families. BC Housing also operates a SAFER (Shelter Aid for Elderly Renters) program for lower-income seniors who are paying more than 30 percent of their income for accommodation. BC Housing assistance is generally available to persons who have lived in the province for one year and whose income falls below a level established by Canada Mortgage and Housing Corporation.

Ontario's Ministry of Municipal Affairs and Housing supports thousands of geared-to-income housing units throughout the province. Eligibility is restricted to Canadian citizens, permanent residents of Canada, or refugee claimants, and each household must have at least one person over the age of 16.

Buying a House or Condo

Basically, a real estate transaction progresses along these lines:

- You arrange **financing** with a bank or other lending institution.
- You find a realtor to help you search for your new house.
- You look at many, many houses and select one that suits you.
- You make an offer on the house through your realtor using your province's standard contract of purchase and sale form, often referred to as an interim agreement. Usually, you offer a price lower than the seller's **asking price**, or the listed price.
- The vendor can accept your offer, refuse your offer or—most commonly—make a counter-offer with a price higher than you offered, but usually lower than the original listed price. This offer and counter-offer stage can go on and on.
- Finally, when both parties agree to a price and a closing date, you sign or initial the contract of purchase and sale. You are required to pay a deposit at this point, usually a minimum of 5 percent, but probably more if you are purchasing while living out of the country.
- You remove the subject clauses you have written into the contract. This means that all the **conditions** that needed to be met before the sale of the home, regarding things such as financing and building inspection, are satisfied.
- You hire a lawyer or a **notary** and give him or her a copy of your purchase agreement. The lawyer searches the property records at the local Land Registry Office, contacts your financing institution, and has you sign the appropriate mortgages and other documents.

- You write a cheque for the total amount required to complete the purchase.
- You get the keys.

We will now look at each of the above steps separately to provide you with some fundamentals in this highly complex transaction.

Arranging Financing

Before you even think of browsing for the home of your dreams, it is best to determine what price range you can afford and how much money the banks will lend you.

Generally, the most expensive house you can afford will be about two-and-half times your gross annual household salary. This means that if you have a $50,000 annual income, you can afford a house in the $125,000 range. Of course, your down payment can make a big difference here. The more you have for a down payment, the higher price range you can look at, since your mortgage payments will be lower.

A down payment on a property is usually at least 5 percent. If you can put 20 percent of the purchase price down on the property, you will save a little money in the mortgage costs. If you need to borrow more than 80 percent of the purchase price, your mortgage is called a high-ratio mortgage; if you borrow less than this amount, it is called a conventional mortgage.

Lenders generally consider that your monthly mortgage payment, plus property tax and other related fees, should total no more than one-third of your household monthly income. For example, if your gross monthly income is $5,000, you should be able to pay $1,666 per month on a mortgage payment and property taxes.

Q: What is the difference between a fixed-rate mortgage and a variable-rate mortgage?

A: With a fixed-rate **mortgage**, the **interest rate** remains the same throughout the term of the loan. With a variable-rate mortgage, the interest rate varies to reflect money lending-conditions.

You should consider using the services of a mortgage **broker** to help you find the best mortgage deal. The broker's job is to match a borrower with a lender. And the borrower usually doesn't pay for this service. Most mortgage brokers claim they can get a mortgage for a client who has trouble finding a mortgage company, and get a good interest rate for them as well.

What Is a Realtor?

Buying or selling a house is rather complicated in Canada. Although you don't legally need to hire a professional realtor in order to buy or sell property, a realtor's training and experience in this field can go a long way to ensuring you get a fair deal.

In Canada, the seller, not the purchaser, of a property pays a **commission** to a listing realtor to sell his or her property. Real estate fees are negotiable but generally range from 5 to 10 percent of the selling price, averaging about

Tony Passalacqua: My Canadian Dream

Tony Passalacqua and his family emigrated from South Africa to Canada in 1999. "As with any other immigrant arriving to this beautiful land, we also had our 'Canadian dream,' but we soon realized how competitive the North American job market is and that to survive we would need to be more flexible and creative."

Passalacqua spent a lot of time thinking about his future and what would be best for his family. "My main goal was to work for myself in a career that would allow me to have more time with my family, while at the same time I wanted to be in total control of my own destiny," he says. "I decided to become licensed as a mortgage broker."

He enrolled in a real estate program; this, together with the commerce degree he earned at the University of South Africa, has provided him with the financial background to assist his clients with the best advice when choosing a mortgage.

"This was the correct decision for me and I now enjoy my new career thoroughly."

—*Margaret Jetelina*

7 percent of the selling price up to $100,000, and 2.5 percent on any amount over that.

The seller's realtor is responsible for marketing the property to attract potential buyers. This may include newspaper advertising, advertisements in real estate publications, a For Sale sign on the property, **open houses** at the property, and a fact sheet detailing the specifications of the property. The realtor will also usually post the property on MLS, the Multiple Listings Service, which is a directory of properties for sale in each region across Canada. The realtor then handles any purchasing inquiries made regarding the property. When the property sells, the seller's realtor must share that real estate commission with the real estate agent working for the purchaser, with each receiving half of the commission.

At the very least, the purchaser's realtor should do the following:

- Make notes about the purchaser's needs and desires regarding a home, including the preferred moving or purchase date.
- Establish what kind of financing the buyer has in place. If this has not yet been taken care of, the realtor should direct the buyer to various financing establishments.
- Provide the buyer with an estimate of the costs that will result from the purchase.
- Provide the buyer with a list of available homes matching his or her needs and price range; these lists should contain a photo of the house, its price, size, location, age, and other relevant details. A good realtor will also provide a list of the prices of houses recently sold in the neighbourhood in which the purchaser wants to buy.
- Have enough knowledge about the buyer's needs and the marketplace to recognize when a good deal or a good match comes on the market.
- Arrange with the selling realtor for the buyer to visit any properties in which he or she is interested.
- Be sufficiently articulate and assertive to be able to negotiate with the selling realtor. Negotiations can be stressful and drawn-out, so buyers need to have confidence and trust in their agent.
- Be prepared to transfer documents, keys, and cheques at the conclusion of the transaction.

A selection of photos of the property

This gives you at-a-glance information about the house

The description gives you more detailed information

The name and contact information of the realtor for this property

Source: Canadian Real Estate Association

How to Choose a Realtor

The best method is always word of mouth. Ask your friends and business associates for names and don't hesitate to call the realtors recommended; you'll find out how promptly they return calls as well as getting a sense of their general professional conduct.

You can also determine a lot about an agent, as well as the housing market, by attending open houses. These are standard marketing tools used by selling agents; the realtor posts an "Open House" sign on the lawn and lets you look through the house, allowing you to poke into bathrooms and closets to see if the property appeals to you. Usually, the owner is not present. If you like the way the agent treats you as a prospective buyer, perhaps she or he could handle your purchase as well.

Look for an agent who is familiar with the area in which you want to live. Ask for a list of houses she or he has sold or purchased in that area in the past few years.

Scan all available newspapers to see which realtors are selling the kinds of houses you want in the neighbourhoods in which you are interested.

Jot down the names of realtors listed on the For Sale signs in the area in which you want to live.

Vesselina Chela: Realtor for Newcomers

Bulgarian-born Vesselina Chela went from being a computer engineer in England to a realtor in Canada. She says that after a long career in the technology field, she needed a change.

"I would sit behind a computer screen all day, fixing bugs. It was too dry for me," Chela says. "I needed flavour. I love meeting people."

Her application to come to Canada was processed in nine months, and within one month after their arrival, both Chela and her husband found computer jobs. But she started looking for a different career and decided that real estate was her new calling. "I have no regrets; my real estate business is doing well."

Now, in her role as realtor, Chela wants to help other newcomers in their transition to Canada. "I'd like to help newcomers and help in relocating. That will be my main direction in real estate."

—Margaret Jetelina

Make sure you feel comfortable with your realtor and that she or he really listens to your needs. Verify potential realtors' track records, finding out things such as how long they have been in business and what previous customers think about their performance.

Talk to your realtor. Ask your prospective agent about the housing market and financing options. Ask what he or she will do for you as a client. Also, be sure to ask for references from buyers for whom the realtor previously worked.

Choosing a House or Condo

Although the decision to purchase a particular home is frequently made for emotional rather than practical reasons, you should make a list of all the features you want in your new home, such as number of bedrooms, number of bathrooms, and proximity to schools, shopping, and your workplace.

A number of special considerations are involved if you are purchasing a condominium rather than a single-family detached home. As a condo owner you are subject to the rules imposed by a **strata council** made up of a number of owners from your building. The council is a democratic political group, with elected representatives and majority rulings. Strata council meetings are held regularly; minutes are maintained and meetings are open to every owner.

The strata council can implement rules that govern how many people may live in your suite or whether you can have a pet. It can forbid you to rent your suite to others, dictate what colour of curtains you install, and decide whether or not you can hang your laundry on your balcony. Before you decide to become a condo owner, consider whether you are prepared to live by the rules of the strata council.

According to real estate company Century 21, the most expensive place to buy a condominium in Canada is downtown Vancouver, British Columbia. Prices in this West Coast city have increased by 15 to 20 percent annually for several years now as more and more wealthy people have chosen to settle in this multicultural city with its temperate climate, healthy economy, and beautiful natural surroundings.

Also, condo owners share the expenses and responsibilities of the common areas of the building, such as the parking area, lawn, laundry room, elevators, stairs, lobby, and corridors. All expenses, maintenance, and cleaning of these areas are shared by the condo owners, usually on a scale pro-rated to the size of their condo units. For example, the owner of a 1,000-square-foot suite would pay more than the owner of a 500-square-foot unit. Strata council fees are paid on a monthly basis, with interest penalties levied against condo owners who pay late.

Although strata councils are obligated to collect enough money from condo owners every month to maintain a contingency fund for major repairs to the building, it's fairly common to find the funds insufficiently stocked to pay a large bill for something like a new roof. In this event, the strata council can vote to raise the funds required by charging all owners with a special levy or special assessment, again pro-rated to the size of each owner's suite. There is no way a unit owner can escape this levy, which can be thousands of dollars if there is a major repair bill.

The strata council is also empowered to levy fines for infractions of its rules. These fines, if not paid before the condo is sold, will be collected from the sale proceeds of the condo unit and submitted to the strata council.

Buyer's Checklist

The following checklist is designed to help you categorize and judge the homes you see to determine how closely they match your needs. For each home that you visit, make a copy of this checklist. In the top half, fill out the information for the home you are visiting along with the important contact information. In the second half, write out your home wish list in the first column and what the home actually has in the second. Compare the two columns to get a better idea of what each home has to offer.

Buyer's Checklist	
Location	
Area	
Address	
Realtor	
Phone	
Mortgage Company	
Phone	
Lawyer/Notary	
Phone	
Home Inspector	
Phone	
Costs	
Asking Price	
Likely Selling Price	
Property Taxes	
Utility, Garbage, or Other Municipal Levies	
GST	
Property Transfer Tax (varies provincially)	
Other Costs	
Down Payment	
Mortgage Terms	
Monthly Payments	
Principal and Interest	
Taxes	
Life Insurance on Mortgage	
Household Insurance	

General Condition		
Roof		
Furnace		
Gas or Electrical System		
Appliances		
Landscaping		
House Details	**Wish List**	**House**
Home Type		
Age		
Total Square Feet		
Kitchen (Square Feet)		
Dining Room		
Living Room		
Family Room		
Great Room		
Den		
Master Bedroom		
2nd Bedroom		
3rd Bedroom		
Other Room		
Number of Bathrooms		
Storage Space		
Fireplace: gas or wood-burning		
Garage or Street Parking		
Garage: attached or detached		
Carport		
Front Yard		
Back Yard		
Fence		
Patio		
Driveway		
Special Features		
The Neighbourhood (Distances to:)		
Work		
Schools		
Public Transit		
Shopping		
Parks		
Community Centres		
Sports Facilities		

Additional Notes or Comments on This Home

_____

_____

_____

Making the Offer

If you decide you want the property, you can make a formal offer to purchase, using an interim agreement which your realtor will complete and give to you to sign. Generally, the price you offer will be less than the asking price. Your realtor will present this offer to the owner in the presence of his or her realtor. The owner can accept your offer, refuse your offer, or make a counter-offer that is higher than what you offered. This process can go back and forth for hours or days. If you have a good realtor, she or he will be able to help you determine how high you should go before walking away from the deal.

Once a price is agreed upon, the seller and purchaser sign the contract and the purchaser places a deposit on the property. This deposit is often quite small, but can be high for offshore purchasers.

The deposit is held in trust until the deal closes or collapses. If the deal closes, the deposit amount goes toward the purchase price. If the deal collapses, the deposit may be paid to the courts while legal action is pursued. If the purchaser changes his or her mind and decides not to purchase the property, she or he will likely lose the deposit. In any event, once the deal is "firm," (in other words, once the subject clauses have been removed) either party could be subject to a breach of contract lawsuit should they back out of the deal. But back to the deposit—sometimes the deposit is paid in two installments: the first installment when both parties sign the contract of purchase and sale and the second installment when the subject clauses are removed and the agreement becomes a firm offer.

If the purchaser makes a subject offer, this means that he or she wants to withhold making a final commitment to purchase until after checking on one or more important points. The purchaser may want to look through the strata council minutes for any indication of trouble or possible additional expenses faced by residents of the building, check strata council bylaws for rules affecting all owners, or have a building inspector survey the premises. Another common subject that a purchaser might add to a contract of purchase and sale agreement is one that says the agreement is "subject to purchaser procuring financing."

If you have made your offer subject to a building inspection, your agent can help you arrange for a building inspector to view the property. If the home is approved and you want to proceed with the purchase, you must sign the sale agreement again, confirming your intentions to proceed with the purchase. If you are not happy with the inspection, you can cancel the deal at this point and you will have your deposit returned. Be aware, however, that the more subjects you add to your contract, the less attractive your offer becomes, as there is a greater possibility that the deal will collapse. In other words, an offer that carries no subjects might entice the owner to sell at a slightly lower price than an offer with many subjects.

It is a very good idea for purchasers to obtain the services of a reputable building inspector before proceeding with any real estate purchase. This will cost several hundred dollars, but it is well worth this expense to find out if the house has termites, dry rot, or a cracked foundation, none of which would be obvious to the average homebuyer. As a buyer, you must carefully consider whether you still want the property if the inspector discovers some problems.

If you are purchasing a condominium, another extremely important condition to be included in the contract of purchase and sale agreement is one that allows you to inspect the strata council's minutes covering at least the past year or two. They will indicate any problems with the building such as water leaks, a cockroach infestation, or frequent break-ins, and they will have information about some possible future building expenses such as new hall carpeting or a new roof.

You should also inspect the bylaws of the condo building, as these bylaws will govern much of what you can and cannot do in your condo.

The Legal Finishes

Once you and the seller have concluded negotiations and arrived at an agreed price, all you have to do is pack your bags. Your realtor should take the contract of purchase and sale to your selected lawyer or notary. Your lawyer or notary will determine that the seller is legally entitled to sell the property, obtain documentation from your financial institution regarding your mortgage, and calculate exactly how much you will need to pay for legal fees, mortgage costs, appraisal fees, and document registration at the

Land Registry Office. You will need to tell the lawyer whose name the property will be held in. This person will be required to visit the law firm several days before the closing to sign documents.

You will normally take possession of the property at noon on the date of possession, unless you have negotiated otherwise. Your realtor will give you the key.

Closing Costs

Keep in mind that when it comes to buying, you will have to come up with a large sum of money to pay for lawyers' or notaries' fees, registration of documents at the land titles office, bank appraisal fees, house inspection fees, and, in some provinces, a property purchase tax. Your realtor will provide you with a fairly comprehensive list of the expenses you will face.

Key Words

asking price: the price that the seller wants to sell something for

broker: a person who arranges the buying and selling of things such as property, insurance, etc. for other people

commission: money that a person gets for selling something

condition: something that must happen so that something else can happen or be possible

damage deposit (also security deposit): a sum of money that you pay when you rent something and that you get back when you return it or finish using it without damage

district: an official division of a city, state, country, etc.

financing: providing the money to pay for something

fixed term of tenancy: a set length of time for which a person rents an apartment, a building or a piece of land

interest rate: the money that you have to pay for borrowing money, usually expressed as a percentage of the total sum borrowed, for a stated period of time

landlord: a person or company that rents a house or an apartment to people for money

mortgage: money that you borrow in order to buy a house

notary (also notary public): a person with official authority to say that he/she has seen a person sign a document, which makes that document valid in law

open house: a day when the public can visit a place that is usually closed to them

resident: a person who lives in a place

strata council: a group of unit owners of a condominium who run the day-to-day operations of the strata corporation, which manages the affairs related to the common areas of the condominium

suite: a set of rooms, especially in an apartment or hotel

tenancy agreement: a contract between the tenant and the landlord that contains details about the terms and conditions of the rental arrangements

tenant: a person who pays money to the owner of an apartment, a building or a piece of land so that he/she can live in it or use it

vacancy: a room in a hotel, etc. that is not being used

Note: Entries taken or adapted from the Oxford ESL Dictionary

Creating Your Canadian Experience

1. Find out the average house price in the city where you live.
   Tip: type the name of your city and "Average House Price" into a search engine.

   _____

2. Choose a city or town near where you live and search on the Internet for the average house price there.

   _____

3. Contact friends, look in the phone book, and search on the Internet for realtors in your area.

Name	Company	Contact Information	How Found	Comments

4. Research the mortgage rate at two local banks and compare that to the rate a mortgage broker can offer.
   Tip: look up the names of two banks and a mortgage broker in the phone book. Then type each lender's name into a search engine to find its website.

Bank 1	Rate	Bank 2	Rate	Mortgage Broker	Rate

Chapter 8

Smart Consumerism

In This Chapter

- How much will housing, utilities, and food cost?
- Any shopping tips?
- What's the deal with garage sales?
- How should you dress for Canadian weather?

Adjusting to a new **currency** may be extremely confusing at first. For a while, you will find yourself **converting** prices to your native currency for price **comparisons**. Within a very short time, however, you will treat a dollar as a dollar.

But knowing the **value** of a Canadian dollar is only the beginning of becoming a smart consumer. Generally, smart spending means budgeting—planning what you need to spend to support your family, and putting aside that amount of money every month to cover your **expenses**. This will help you determine how much money you have to spend on additional expenses, such as new towels, shoes, or a car. If you know how much money you can spend before you go shopping, you are more likely to shop wisely.

Some immigrants may be accustomed to seeing **fixed prices** for **merchandise** in their native countries. Not so in Canada. In a free **economy**, individual **retailers** are free to charge whatever they want. In fact, price fixing, where **competitors** agree to charge exactly the same price for the same **product**, is against the law.

The main thing that keeps prices down is the purchasers' unwillingness to pay for a product that is overpriced. Most major stores, recognizing that their shoppers are fairly knowledgeable about prices, will try to keep prices comparable to their competitors to retain their share of the consumers' business. Retailers don't want to lose customers to the store down the street that offers a lower price. Nonetheless, as a shopper you must be aware of what constitutes a fair price. If you're not, you could end up purchasing items that are overpriced by normal standards.

This chapter aims to familiarize you with certain costs and provide you with some tips on how to save money wherever possible.

Utilities

In some provinces, you may have to pay to get your home or apartment connected to electricity and natural gas supplies. At any rate, you'll need to contact your electrical company either before you move in to a new home or immediately upon moving in to arrange for the continuation of electrical service. Similarly, you should advise the electrical company when you are moving out so that they can disconnect your service.

When you rent or buy, you can generally assume the following regarding your accommodation:

- The water from the taps is safe to drink.
- An efficient sewage disposal system will flush waste from bathrooms, kitchens, and laundry rooms.
- The electricity will work in all rooms.
- A heating system powered by natural gas, oil, or electricity will keep the premises warm in winter.
- Telephone lines will be connected to the accommodation, although you will have to arrange for activation.

Electricity

Your electricity costs may be around $75 per month, depending on the size of your premises, the efficiency of its insulation and furnace, and the area of the country in which you live. Some rental accommodations include the heating and electrical costs in the rent. In other situations, landlords will ask tenants to pay a portion, perhaps one-half or one-third, of the monthly costs. This arrangement should be discussed prior to agreeing to rent the premises.

The Telephone

You can buy a telephone or rent one from your telephone company. You may have to pay a deposit on a rented telephone.

You must arrange with the telephone company for a service connection; at that time the company will supply you with a phone number. When you are moving out of a home, make sure you also advise the telephone company so your telephone service can be disconnected on your moving day. If you fail to disconnect after you move, you will be responsible for any telephone costs that build up after you have vacated that home.

As we brought all our phones with us, we didn't need to purchase any, but we still had to arrange for a connection and pay a hookup fee. Long-distance calling tends to be a major expense, particularly for immigrants who want to keep in touch with relatives and friends back home. Many long-distance suppliers in Canada now have extremely competitive rates. Shop around for the company that offers a package that includes the best long-distance rates available to your home country. **Pre-paid** phone cards offer cheap international rates, but beware of connection charges which could be high and "eat up" your air time.

Cable Television

When renting, your cable television costs may or may not be included in your rent. You will need to clarify this with your landlord before you move in. Generally, it is not included because there are so many different levels of service and pricing; most viewers prefer to make their own selections as to what kind of service they want. When you select your service, you will need to discuss with your cable company what package of services you want, and arrange for a connection. The monthly fee for cable television can be $40 or more depending on the package of channels you choose. High definition television (HDTV) costs will vary depending on the channels you choose and your service provider.

Tony Singh: Bringing Produce from Around the World

Tony Singh, who is now the president of the fruit and produce franchise Fruiticana, was an entrepreneur-in-waiting as a young child in Montreal.

"I always wanted to do something at a young age," he says. "In elementary school, I did my first paper route, as many immigrant kids will do. I actually had three paper routes."

In grade nine, he became a stock boy at a grocery store and started to work his way up in the produce industry, eventually to the position of buyer and franchise developer for a chain of produce stores. He moved to Vancouver in 1992 to start a new life and a new business.

"We liked what we saw here," Singh says. "When I came here I wanted to use the knowledge that I learned in Montreal and open a produce business."

He quickly realized that no produce markets in the Vancouver area were specifically serving immigrants. "There was one produce store in Fleetwood, and they had apples, oranges, but they didn't have the okra, the ginger, the garlic, and all the other exotic foods we were used to in Montreal. No mangoes, no limes. That's when I saw the need."

He opened his first store in 1994, and has been expanding the business ever since.

—*Margaret Jetelina*

Internet

Canada has many Internet service providers (ISPs), and you can choose between them depending on your needs and budget. I have often been asked whether immigrants should bring computers from their home countries and the simple answer is this: yes, if it is less than a year old. Laptops and desktops can be inexpensive in Canada, and if you purchase a new computer, you'll get the advantage of sales and technical support. I must also mention that having anti-virus and anti-spyware software is essential.

You should also know that many companies offer phone, cable, and Internet service. If you order your services from the same place you may save money on your total bill.

Putting Food on the Table

Food and cooking in Canada will likely be different from what you were accustomed to in your native country. Like everyone who moves to a new country, you will probably have to make changes in some of the ways you buy, store, and cook food.

Most Canadians shop for food at large supermarkets. In a supermarket, as in most stores, you select what you want from the counters and shelves, stack your selections in a grocery cart and when you are finished, you proceed to the checkout counter to pay for your selections. In most stores, you can pay for your **purchases** by cash, credit card, or debit card.

You will notice that at some large grocery stores, the shopping carts are chained together to prevent customers from walking away with the carts. You'll need to slip a coin, usually a quarter or loonie, into a small coin box located on the front of the cart in order to release the chain and use the cart. When you have finished your shopping and returned the cart, you can get your coin back.

Of course, you can also purchase food at smaller grocery stores and specialty shops. In cities with large immigrant communities, you will undoubtedly find **specialty stores** that sell food from your home country. But you may find that some of your traditional foods may not be available in Canada or may be very expensive here.

Other neighbourhood stores, known as convenience or corner stores, sell such basic items as milk, bread, and snack foods. Convenience stores are usually open longer hours than supermarkets and specialty stores, with some open 24 hours per day, but they are usually more expensive and don't have much variety of merchandise.

Many larger Canadian cities offer **open-air markets**, usually in the summer. These markets, like those around the world, usually sell fresh fruits, vegetables, and other locally grown produce. Keep your eyes open or ask at your local community centre for the location of such markets. They frequently provide very good produce at good prices, as well as crafts and homemade jams, sauces, and baked goods—and the shopping experience can be fun, too.

As virtually every household in Canada has a large refrigerator and many have deep freezers, many Canadians shop for groceries just once a week.

Getting a Good Price

How much you pay for food depends on what you buy and where you shop. Generally, food imported from other countries is more expensive than food grown and produced in Canada. Sometimes you will find that frozen fruits and vegetables cost less than fresh fruit and vegetables.

Canada produces a significant proportion of its fresh fruit and vegetables in the summer. That is the best time, therefore, to stock up on some of the locally grown crops, which include apples, peaches, cherries, potatoes, squash, and tomatoes.

In general, the more **processed** and packaged a food product is, the more it will cost. This means that ready-to-serve food will be more expensive than if you buy fresh ingredients separately and make your own meals. Also, foods that are labelled "**organic**" (meaning they are grown without the assistance of pesticides or fertilizers) are usually more expensive than non-organic foods.

Q: Are processed foods as healthy as freshly made meals?

A: No. **Processed foods** have a long a shelf life and tend to contain preservatives. They do not have all the nutrients you would get in freshly prepared foods.

Most supermarkets have sales on certain foods each week. Many stores sell their own brands of packaged products, such as oatmeal or fruit juice, which is usually less expensive than the popular brands of similar items. In addition, some chain stores offer frequent-buyer programs which allow shoppers to receive slightly **discounted** prices on selected items.

There are also "club" grocery stores across Canada, which frequently require that buyers become members for an annual fee of $25 or more. These stores are generally huge and offer many aisles full of products in large quantities at discounted prices. If you have the room to store large amounts of food and household items, these stores might work for you.

Prices in supermarkets will usually be marked on the shelf below the item or directly on the product. You cannot bargain with salespeople in supermarkets. Canadian retailers also often post the cost per 100 grams of most items, ensuring that consumers can more easily compare the prices of similar goods.

Food Safety

In Canada, there are strict government rules regarding the production, handling, labelling, and selling of food. Government health inspectors ensure that standards are upheld regarding cleanliness, health, and safety throughout the cultivation, manufacturing, transportation, and preparation of food. Health Canada, a federal government department, has set standards for the safety and **nutritional** quality of all food sold in Canada.

The Canadian Food Inspection Agency inspects food produced at federally registered processing plants and slaughterhouses (where animals are killed for their meat). The agency can also recall products that are found to contain toxins or other harmful ingredients.

Generally, the provincial governments are responsible for inspecting food-processing facilities that distribute products across provincial borders. Restaurants and other establishments that serve food are generally inspected municipally.

The federal government prohibits misleading or deceptive labelling of any food, and requires that claims regarding the nutritional content of food products are accurate.

Any packaged or canned food sold in Canada must have a label, in both French and English, listing the ingredients in order of their weight.

Canadians store food in the same manner as you would in your native country. There are, however, certain kinds of common foods here that require special treatment. For example, frozen vegetables, fruit, and meats, and packaged frozen dinners must be kept frozen and well covered until they are ready to be thawed and used. They should never be refrozen once they have been thawed or partially thawed.

You can buy infant formula or milk for your baby and prepare it in advance, but remember that both can easily spoil when left at room temperature. If you choose to use bottles of milk or formula, prepare them with care and refrigerate them promptly. Place enough formula in each bottle for one feeding and dispose of any leftovers. Reheating the same milk in a bottle several times can spoil the milk.

While water from the tap is safe to drink, do not use water from lakes, springs, or rivers for drinking or cooking, no matter how clean the source appears. You have no way of knowing whether there is a dairy farm, logging operation, or landfill site somewhere upstream. Many consumers prefer to purchase bottled water, which can be found at any grocery store.

For public health reasons, it is illegal to raise animals for food anywhere except on a farm or in certain areas permitted by municipal bylaws.

Q: How do I make a consumer complaint?

A: Visit the Consumers' Association of Canada website at www.consumer.ca. It will provide you with step-by-step information on the complaint process.

Dining In

Canadian kitchens are equipped for efficient and safe meal preparation. They usually include an electric or gas stove and oven, a refrigerator, storage cupboards, and a sink with hot and cold water. Many homes also offer a dishwasher and a garborator, which is a device mounted under the kitchen sink to trap and shred waste food particles before sending them down the drain.

A collection of other appliances are frequently found on kitchen counters in Canada: microwaves, blenders, toaster ovens, coffee pots . . . you name it,

Canadians have a small appliance that can handle things electrically. Nobody—especially children—should use kitchen appliances until they know how to operate them.

Alcohol

The legal drinking age in Canada varies among provinces. It is 18 in Alberta, Manitoba, and Quebec, and 19 elsewhere. You are not allowed to drink in a public place, such as a park, on the street, or on the beach anywhere in Canada, except with a municipal permit under special circumstances. It is also forbidden throughout Canada to drink in vehicles. Any alcohol you transport in Canada must be in a sealed bottle and should be in the trunk of the car.

George Cziglan: Slovak with a Bubbly Idea

Although Slovaks are known for their love of beer, George Cziglan knows there's more to a good drink than just barley and hops. This Slovakian immigrant is a partner in a beverage company that produces a sporty alcoholic energy drink called Score.

"It's a fun product," he says. In his own youth, Cziglan didn't have much time for fun. He was a refugee who escaped his homeland of Bratislava, Slovakia (then still Czechoslovakia) in the 1980s. "I spent 18 months in a refugee camp," he says, explaining that a friend of his who was already in Canada encouraged him to come. "That got me going. I wanted to leave my homeland and it seemed like a good place to go," he says.

Although he didn't speak English when he first arrived, Cziglan began working in different trade shops. What he really wanted was to pursue advertising. In the late 1990s, he found work with a large alcohol company. "I learned a lot about the alcohol industry," he says. So when two of his friends from the company asked him to join them in developing Score, he recognized a good product and joined the new business.

Cziglan has certainly scored a great new life in Canada.

—*Margaret Jetelina*

It is illegal to drive in Canada if you have a blood alcohol level of more than .08, which can take as few as one to two drinks. Many factors, of course, come into play here, including your weight, how much alcohol is in the drink you consumed, and how much food you've eaten. Penalties are severe for drinking and driving. (Learn more about drinking and driving in Chapter 12—Driving in Canada.)

Only government-licensed outlets can sell beer, wine, or liquor in closed bottles. One of the exceptions to this rule is in Quebec, where some alcohol can be sold in grocery stores. Alcohol for on-site consumption can be sold only in licensed lounges, bars, or restaurants, or at certain sporting events or at private clubs.

In some provinces, you can purchase a case of beer from a bar or restaurant, a practice that is called "off-sales;" this is beer to be consumed off the premises. Most provinces do not allow consumers to bring their own alcohol to bars or restaurants.

Dressing for the Occasion

Most Canadians wear the same fashions as Western Europeans, although Canadians dress somewhat more casually than Europeans. Business wear is generally considered appropriate for those working in offices, while jeans and runners are standard weekend attire. Canada, of course, has four distinct seasons, with the peculiarities and severity of each season varying across the country. Your clothing requirements change to meet the various climatic needs.

Business suits can be tailor-made or purchased "off the rack," from a store that has different sizes hanging on a rack. Like everywhere else in the world, the more you pay for a suit, the better the quality. Expect to pay at least $200 for a basic man's suit and another $80 to $100 for good shoes.

Women's business attire can cost $50 or more for a jacket or a dress.

Keeping Warm in Winter

To keep warm and safe in winter, you should wear sensible, warm clothes. As some regions of Canada can experience sub-zero temperatures for weeks on end, proper winter clothing is very important whenever you are outside.

For adults and older children living in most parts of Canada, except for the West Coast, winter clothes include warm, lined boots; a thick, windproof coat; a scarf around the neck or across the face; lined or heavy mittens (which are warmer than gloves); and warm socks and undergarments. A hat covering the ears or a toque is an important part of winter clothing because most body heat is lost through the head. If you have no outdoor winter clothing, you should expect to pay several hundred dollars or more for boots, a coat, gloves, and hat. Standard winter gear on the West Coast consists of an umbrella and a raincoat.

Winter clothing for young children usually consists of a snowsuit, which is a zippered, lined garment with a hood that is worn with boots, mittens, and a hat over normal indoor clothing. A snowsuit for a child will cost at least $30. It is, by the way, normal practice for children to be sent outdoors to play in the snow in the winter, as long as they are properly bundled. Common sense must rule here, however: if it's 20 degrees below zero and the wind is howling, don't send your children outside.

Severe cold weather (temperatures below negative 15 degrees Celsius) can cause frostbite to your fingers, toes, nose, and ears before you even realize it is happening. Frostbite is often painless at first, but it feels and acts like a serious burn when you warm up again. Once skin is frostbitten, it may never recover.

Hot Summers
From June through August, many areas of Canada—particularly the inland regions—can experience extreme heat, sometimes reaching 30 degrees Celsius. Virtually all larger office buildings, stores, and shopping malls are air-conditioned, but many homes are not. Summertime business attire may include cotton dresses or lightweight suits, while many Canadians wear shorts, sandals, and T-shirts for recreational or casual activity.

Shopping Tips

Shopping in Canada may seem challenging at first, but you will soon adapt. In fact, exploring new stores and shopping malls and trying new products can be a lot of fun. Many clothing, grocery, and furniture stores advertise their products in newspaper flyers or inserts delivered to your door. These are useful guides for familiarizing yourself with prices, quality, and styles.

A shopping trip often involves heading to a nearby mall or shopping centre. These centres can span several blocks and may be spread over two or more floors, with underground parking, restaurants, cinemas, and video arcades, and often contain two or three large department stores that sell a variety of

Q: What is the taxation system in Canada when buying products at a store?

A: There is GST (a federal Goods and Services Tax) and PST (Provincial Sales Tax). GST is currently 5 percent, while PST varies from province to province, and is sometimes combined with GST into an HST (Harmonized Sale Tax). These taxes are added to the price of most items that you buy.

products, such as women's wear, furniture, appliances, and tools. Malls certainly offer convenient one-stop shopping with plenty of free parking.

Keep in mind that every store or outlet in a mall is an individual business where you can browse to your heart's content. When you select an item to purchase, you must pay for it before leaving that store and heading to another one. Many stores will specialize in one type of product, such as shoes, ties, or baked goods. You may prefer to shop in small, independently owned and operated stores where you will often receive more personal service. You can look up the products you need in the phone book to find the names and addresses of stores that sell the items you are seeking.

In larger cities, such as Toronto, Montreal, Vancouver, and Calgary, you will find neighbourhoods or shopping areas that specialize in various ethnic restaurants, products, and merchandise. Ask around in your community for tips on the various ethnic areas in which to shop.

In 1981, the world's largest indoor shopping centre was built in Edmonton, Alberta. The West Edmonton Mall is now the largest in North America (but no longer the world) and contains over 800 stores and businesses, 100 restaurants, and many exciting attractions including a water park, an ice rink, and the world's largest indoor amusement park.

Savvy Shopping

Savvy shopping means shopping around, choosing carefully, and buying a good product at a fair price. Stores compete with one another to attract customers, so it is wise to visit or call a number of different shops to find the best price, particularly for such expensive items as furniture and large appliances.

One of the ways Canadian stores compete with one another is by offering sales at various times throughout the year on various items. If you know exactly what you are looking for, such as a particular brand name of washing machine, and you know how much it is selling for, you will be ready to purchase it when it goes on sale. Grocery stores also offer lots of sales and discounts on products.

Buying **off-season** at low prices makes good sense. Immediately after Christmas, you may find greeting cards, decorations, and other festive products marked down to about 10 percent of their original prices! Similarly, as winter comes to an end sweaters and pullovers are marked down to bargain levels.

What to Expect in the Store

Many Canadian stores are self-serve, with sales clerks usually available to help you find what you are looking for and to answer questions about products. Consumers are permitted to browse through stores and handle the merchandise without being obligated to buy anything.

Most items in stores will have stickers or tags attached to them with such information as the size and the price. In most cases, the marked price does not include the provincial sales tax (PST) or the federal Goods and Services Tax (GST). PST varies from province to province, while the GST is 5 percent in every province and territory, and covers most merchandise as well as services. There are some exceptions to this, however, such as

Provincial Sales Tax	
BC	7%
Alberta	0%
Saskatchewan	5%
Manitoba	7%
Ontario	8%
Quebec	7.5% (tax on tax)
Newfoundland	13% HST
Nova Scotia	13% HST
New Brunswick	13% HST
PEI	10%
Territories	0%

children's clothing and some school supplies, for which you do not have to pay some taxes. Inquire about this when you are at the cash register.

Items that you select from a store rack or shelf should be paid for at the cash register. The location of the cashier may not always be obvious, especially in larger stores. In some stores, books must be paid for in the book department and shoes paid for in the shoe department. You will be directed to the appropriate cashier if you end up at the wrong one.

Whatever you do, don't leave the store without paying for your goods. Also, until you have paid for your items, don't put them into your purse or bag to carry around the store; this could be viewed as shoplifting, or stealing. In order to discourage people from stealing, any shoplifters who are caught are dealt with very severely. They may have to pay a fine or spend time in jail. Most stores are equipped with alarms and cameras, as well as security personnel, to help identify shoplifters.

Always retain your **receipts** for the goods you purchase. If an item is defective in some way, the receipt will let you return or exchange it. Also, many larger stores will usually allow you to return an item within a few days or weeks from the date of purchase if you simply change your mind about it. Naturally, the product you return must not have been worn or used, and should be returned in its original packaging. **Refunds** are not mandated by law in Canada and are strictly a store policy.

Many smaller stores may be reluctant to refund your purchase, but they may instead offer you a credit toward another purchase. Usually, discounted or "final sale" items cannot be returned. It is important to check the store's refund and exchange policy before you buy anything.

Bargaining

Bargaining, or negotiating prices, is not normally done in Canada, although there are a few exceptions. For example, almost everyone bargains for a better price when buying a car or a house. It is rare, however, for storeowners or managers to lower their marked prices on other goods.

Senior and Student Discounts

If you or a member of your family is a student or a senior over the age of 65, be aware of the variety of discounts available. These cover everything from movie tickets, to museum entrance fees, to airline tickets. Frequently, a children's or a seniors' menu is available at restaurants as well. Don't hesitate to ask if there is a student or senior discount, and be prepared to show proof of age or a student card to qualify for it.

Pre-owned Merchandise

Garage sales and flea markets are Canadian passions. We are hooked! Garage sales provide people with a means of disposing of unwanted clothes, tools, sports equipment, books, and other items—and allows them to make a little money doing it. They simply pack their unwanted goods into their open garage, or onto their front lawn or back alley, put up a "Garage Sale" sign on a sunny weekend, and wait for the customers. I once bought a video cassette recorder for $8! A friend bought a freezer chest for $40!

Most garage sales take place in good weather during the spring and summer, so don't go looking for them in winter. And, of course, everyone expects these sales to include some haggling or bargaining.

Thrift stores, many of which are operated by charity organizations that receive all the merchandise for free, are also interesting places to buy discounted, used goods. The range of products is huge, and may include clothing, appliances, furniture, televisions, microwaves, records, books, and CDs.

Consignment stores are another source of pre-owned goods or another avenue to dispose of your unwanted goods, depending on how you look at them. At these stores, you can hand over your old clothing, tools, or sports equipment; the manager puts a price on it and you get a portion of that price when it sells. Usually, the price is reduced every week until someone purchases the item.

Child Daycare

When both parents in a family work outside the home, they will often pay licensed daycare centres to care for their children. While the rates at these centres vary from region to region and depend on the age of the child and the number of children, the average weekly cost can range from $45 to $90 per child.

Families also frequently employ nannies or babysitters to care for children in the parents' home. Nannies may be live-in or live-out, and their rates will vary substantially.

Before placing your child in any facility or hiring anyone to care for your child, ensure that you check the caregiver's references. It is also a good idea to inspect the home in which a babysitter lives, if he or she plans to take care of your children there. You can also ask friends and relatives for referrals.

Disposing of Garbage

Most urban areas of Canada offer weekly garbage pickup. In rural areas, you may have to take your own garbage to a landfill site or garbage dump. Regular removal of garbage, from your house and from your garbage bins, helps to keep control of insects and rodents. As family pets and wild animals such as raccoons, rats, and birds are often attracted to the smell of trash, garbage bins should have tight-fitting lids.

Trash that is too large to fit into a garbage container, such as an old mattress or a sofa, must be taken to your municipal garbage dump or recycling station for disposal. Disposing of such articles on the street or in a lane could result in a littering fine. In fact, most cities and provinces carry stiff fines for littering of any kind.

The plastic garbage bag was created by three Canadian inventors in the 1950s. Harry Wasylyk, Larry Hanson, and Frank Plomp experimented separately with leftover plastic resin in an attempt to develop a strong bag for waste. They each produced plastic bags which they sold to hospitals, offices, and manufacturing plants in their communities.

Bottle Deposits and Recycling

Every province in Canada deals with waste and recycling in its own way. British Columbia is the most progressive in this field, as it has developed a program of deposits and refunds on the containers of nearly every beverage sold in the province, with the exception of dairy and soy milk products.

What this means is that when you purchase any pop, juice, water, liquor, wine, beer, or other beverage sold in a bottle or can, you will pay a deposit of 5 to 20 cents for the container. After consuming the product, you should rinse the container and return it to any store that sells that beverage, or to a bottle depot, for a refund of that deposit. Some stores may restrict the number of bottles you can return at one time.

This program greatly reduces the amount of waste that ends up in landfills, and most provinces have carried out a bottle deposit and refund system to some degree. Basically, if you are charged a deposit on a container, that means you can obtain a refund when you return it. Check with the stores in your neighbourhood to see which containers can be returned for a refund.

Q: What happens to everything I recycle?

A: Recycling is broken up into various groups—newspapers and magazines, paper and cardboard cartons, cans, glass, and plastics. The recycling is picked up from households and sent to sorting areas where it is processed and reused, so that champagne bottle you discarded could well be part of a jam bottle you buy a year later!

The Mail System

Canada Post is the federal government agency responsible for handling, sorting, and delivering mail. Sub–post offices are located in many pharmacies and stores throughout the country, and are usually at the back of the store, identified by a large red post office sign. Here you can have your mail weighed, purchase stamps and mail orders, as well as arrange for special deliveries and other mail services. Currently, the cost of sending a letter within Canada is 52 cents.

Average Mailing Times	
Within your province	3 business days
Outside your province, within Canada	3–7 business days
United States	5–10 business days
International	Up to 2 weeks

Source: Canada Post

Your mail will come to your home mailbox on a daily basis (except on weekends and holidays). Oversized packages, parcels, or special deliveries may also be delivered to your home, but if you are not there to accept your delivery, a printed notice will be left, announcing that the package can be picked up at the sub–post office nearest your home. The address of that post office will be printed on the notice, as well as its hours of operation. You will need to show that notice, along with identification, in order to claim your delivery.

Call Canada Post for more information. The number will be listed in the blue pages of your telephone book. Also, when addressing an envelope, remember to include the six-character postal code at the bottom of any address.

On August 31, 1527, John Rut mailed the first letter ever from North America, sent from what is now St. John's, Newfoundland. The letter was addressed to King Henry VIII.

To mail letters and small packages that already have stamps on them, place them in one of the red Canada Post mailboxes located on many street corners.

Key Words

budget: a plan of how to spend an amount of money over a particular period of time

comparison: an act of considering people or things in order to find ways in which they are similar or different

competitor: a person, company, product, etc. that is competing with another or others

convert: to change from one form, system, or use to another

currency: the system or type of money that a particular country uses

discount: a reduction in the price or cost of something

economy: the operation of a country's money supply, trade, and industry

expense: the cost of something in time or money

fixed price: a price that is already decided and cannot be changed

merchandise: goods that are for sale

nutrition: the food that you eat and the way that it affects your health

off-season: the time of the year when business is slow or things don't happen

open-air market: an outdoor place where people go to buy and sell things

organic: produced by or using natural materials, not chemicals

pre-paid: paid for ahead of time

processed food: food that has been treated, e.g. with chemicals, before it is sold or used

product: something that is made in a factory or that is formed naturally

purchase: something that you buy

receipt: a piece of paper that is given to show that you have paid for something

refund: a sum of money that is returned to you, for example if you take something back to the store where you bought it

retailer: a person or company that sells products in a store

specialty store: a store that sells a specific range of goods with unique characteristics

supermarket: a large store that sells food, drinks, things for cleaning your house, etc. You choose what you want from the shelves in a supermarket and pay for everything when you leave.

value: the amount of money that something is worth

Note: Entries taken or adapted from the Oxford ESL Dictionary

Creating Your Canadian Experience

1. Walk around your neighbourhood and find the supermarket that is nearest to your home.

   Name: _____

   Location: _____

   Hours: _____

2. Check the prices of the following items at your corner store, two different supermarkets, and a club store. You can go directly to the store or call to ask about their prices.

Item	Corner Store	Supermarket 1	Supermarket 2	Club Store
Toothpaste	$	$	$	$
Box of salt	$	$	$	$
Can of soup	$	$	$	$
A bag of carrots	$	$	$	$

3. Search the Internet for the electric company in your neighbourhood. Tip: type the name of your city and "Electricity" into a search engine. This should help you find the website for your local company.

Name: _____

Contact Number: _____

Hours: _____

4. Search the Internet for a store in your city that specializes in food from your home country.
Tip: type the name of your city, the name of your native country, and "Grocery" into a search engine.

Name: _____

Location: _____

Hours: _____

5. Is there a market near you home that sells fresh fruits, vegetables, and other locally grown products? Take a walk around your neighbourhood or ask your neighbours if there is a local market.

Name: _____

Location: _____

Hours: _____

6. Compare the prices of cheese pizzas delivered from a restaurant, purchased from a supermarket, and made at home.

Delivered pizza from a Restaurant	Premade Pizza from the Supermarket	The Ingredients to Make Pizza at Home
$	$	$ *

*You may have to buy more than you need to make one pizza. For example, if the pizza dough comes in a package of three, then divide the price by three to find out the cost for one pizza.

7. Fill out this checklist to ensure you are ready for winter. Put a check next to everything you currently own.

Boots		Windproof Coat	
Scarf		Mitts/gloves	
Hat		Warm Socks	

8. In your province, what is the percentage of tax that must be paid on items you buy?
   Tip: find out the rate of PST in your province by looking at the chart in the section of this chapter called "Shopping Tips." Add this to the 5 percent GST. (If your province pays HST, you will not need to add GST.)

9. Calculate the price of these items after your provincial sales tax is included.

Tip: using a calculator, multiply the price by the rate of PST. For example, if your province charges 8 percent PST, you'd multiply the price of a book ($19.95) by the tax rate (0.08) to get the total PST charged ($1.596, or $1.60). You'd then add this to the price before tax to find your total ($19.95 + $1.60 =$21.55).

Item	Price before Tax	Price with Tax	Item	Price before Tax	Price with Tax
Pen	$ 0.99		Book	$ 19.95	
Pants	$47.95		Sweater	$64.95	
TV	$199.95		Mattress	$499.00	
Sofa	$1,299.00		Car	$16,999.00	

10. Compare the weekly costs of different types of childcare in your city for two different daycare centres, a live-in nanny, and a live-out nanny.

Tip: to find this information, look in your local phone book under "Daycare" and "Nannies," and choose several to call.

Daycare 1	Daycare 2	Live-out Nanny	Live-in Nanny

11. Ask a neighbour the following questions.

When is garbage pickup day? _____

When is recycling pickup day? _____

Chapter 9

Banking, Credit, and Insurance

In This Chapter

- What's an ATM?
- How do you develop a good credit rating when you can't get credit?
- What do you do if your wallet and ID are stolen?
- Should you buy insurance for the contents of your apartment?

Opening a Bank Account

One of your first priorities will probably be to establish an **account** at a convenient bank to handle your immediate day-to-day banking needs. One secure way to do this is by electronic transfer from your bank in your home country. Always allow for at least a week or ten days for any kind of international banking transfer. If you would like immediate access to your **funds**, use **traveller's cheques** instead.

For convenience, select a bank or a **credit union** near your home or work. Despite all the bank advertising, there is not a whole lot of difference between banks; credit unions differ slightly because depositors become shareholders. Once you get settled and do some investigating on the various merits of your local banks, you can switch accounts at no cost to you. But you'll need to open some kind of **chequing account** immediately. To do this, you will need your landed immigrant papers and identification showing your place of residence.

Basically, all banks and credit unions provide **savings accounts** and chequing accounts, plus many other services. Most banks will charge a monthly fee simply for providing you with a secure account into which you can **deposit** money and from which you can write cheques. Often, however, you won't have to pay this fee if you keep a minimum balance that has been determined by the bank, usually about $1,000.

Monthly banking fees can range from about $5 to $20 per month. Depending on the bank and the kind of account you select, you may also have to pay a small fee for every cheque you write, for every **withdrawal** from an automated teller machine (ATM), and for every pre-authorized or automatic withdrawal. You may be able to avoid paying most of these fees if you set up an account with an on-line bank. While these banks will generally cost less, you will not have access to a neighbourhood branch where you can speak to a teller in person.

Generally, a chequing account provides you with some free chequing and withdrawal services every month but pays little or no **interest** to you on your monthly balance. A savings account generally pays you some form of interest on your monthly balance, but does not allow you to write cheques from that account or will perhaps allow you to write a minimal number of cheques.

Automated Teller Machine

An ATM is an automated machine which dispenses cash and accepts deposits, and is usually located outside any branch of your bank. You can conduct most common banking **transactions** 24 hours per day at an ATM. Most banks will automatically give you a bank card and a **personal identification number** (PIN) which will allow you to access your account at ATMs.

One of the attractive features of ATMs is that you can usually access your account from any ATM at any bank that displays an **INTERAC** sign. You should be very cautious when using an ATM to ensure that no one sees your PIN or sees you withdraw large amounts of cash. This is especially important at night when there are few people around.

Q: Is there a fee to use ATMs?

A: Almost all banks charge a fee to use their ATMs. You can usually sign up for deals through your bank that will bring down the cost of your ATM usage. Some banks will give you free usage if you keep a fixed amount of money in their bank. Recently, some on-line banks have started offering unlimited free ATM banking.

Direct Debit

Direct debit is a method of paying for goods or services using your bank card and password, authorizing your bank to pay the retailer a certain sum of money. Direct debit draws money directly and immediately out of your account. Depending on the type of banking package you have arranged with your bank, you will likely have a maximum number of free bank debits you can make per month, after which you will be charged for each transaction.

Automatic Withdrawals and Pre-authorized Payments

You can arrange for automatic payments or withdrawals from your bank account to pay many of your regular bills. These might include monthly cable television fees, **insurance** for your car or house, utility fees, property taxes, or even regular newspaper delivery. You simply provide the company with a voided cheque (one that you have clearly crossed out) and sign a form giving your creditor the authority to withdraw the amount you owe every month. This is a convenient and secure method of paying your bills. You may want to keep a list of these automatic payments to make sure you have enough money in your account to pay them every month.

Q: Is it safe to do my banking over the Internet?

A: Absolutely! All banks have highly secure software to allow you to do your day-to-day banking with ease. But, if you are at a public computer, such as at a library or Internet cafe, it is important to make sure you sign out.

Safety Deposit Boxes

You can rent a secure, private storage box at your bank in which you can keep important papers or jewellery. Only you or someone to whom you give your key will be able to access it.

Personal Line Of Credit

Once you have established a good credit rating, you may want to acquire a **personal line of credit** (PLC). This can be useful to combine your credit card bills and other major expenses, as the interest on a PLC is generally much lower than on a credit card. However, as a PLC is basically an unsecured **loan**, your bank may be reluctant to provide you with a PLC until you have established a good record with them.

Term Deposit

You can place a sum of money, usually $500 or more, into a bank **term deposit** for a set period ranging from three months to several years. If you agree to a longer-term deposit, you will earn a slightly higher rate of interest on your money. You can still withdraw your money if you need to, but you will then lose that increased interest.

Anne Lippert: Banking for Success

Arriving in Canada in the mid-1960s, German-born Anne Lippert got a job as a teller with the Royal Bank. She didn't know much about the job, so she learned quickly.

By the early 1970s, she had set her sights on becoming a branch manager. "This was unheard of at the time [for women]," she says. "When I mentioned that I would like to be a branch manager, supervisors would smile and nod but not say yes or no. After a few years I finally said, 'Now is this a possibility or not? Because if it's not, then I'll have to look for something else to do.'"

The Royal Bank then introduced a management development program for selected female employees. Lippert was among its first graduates and was appointed as a branch manager in 1974.

Having achieved her goal of becoming a branch manager, Lippert simply aimed higher. "I started saying, 'Well, I want to become vice-president.'" And in 1989, she was appointed vice-president and area manager for 18 of Royal Bank's branches.

"I always felt that, having reached a management position, it was my responsibility to encourage other women to do the same. I would always say to them, "If I can do it, you can do it—you're the master.""

After completing an exceptional 35-year banking career, she is busier than ever as a principal with C3 Corporate Citizenship Consultants, which assists businesses in developing strategies for community involvement and helps not-for-profit organizations in their fundraising and development efforts.

—Ben Roth

Will That Be Cash or Credit Card?

As about 20 million Canadians use credit cards, there must be something attractive about owning and using them.

For most of the last century, cash was king in Canada and elsewhere. Paying with cash was a sign of success and stability. No more. Credit now wears the crown in Canada. Today you need a good credit rating to buy a home or car, and to obtain a preferred rate on your homeowner's or life insurance policy. You need a credit card to rent a hotel room, lease a car, and often even to rent a video. You also need a credit card to purchase anything over the telephone or over the Internet. As well, it has become a standard form of identification in many situations, such as when writing cheques.

You will soon figure out the importance of credit in Canada, and using credit cards is a good step to establishing a credit history, which unfortunately, most new immigrants don't have.

As a newcomer, your credit history in your country of origin really means nothing here; you'll have to start building a Canadian credit history. You may be frustrated many times as you hear, "Sorry, but we need to see a major credit card" or "You don't have a credit history." Be prepared for this.

The early years in your credit life are crucial to building a strong credit foundation. Establishing good credit will give you buying power when you need it, so establishing credit and monitoring your credit rating should be one of the most important early financial goals you set. Fortunately, it's not all that difficult. But it's easy to run into problems if you don't know the rules.

According to the Canadian Bankers Association, there were 61.1 million VISA and MasterCard credit cards in circulation in 2006.

Establishing Credit

One of the first steps to establishing credit is to open a savings and chequing account at your local bank or credit union. The fact that you have these accounts provides other lending institutions with evidence that you have money and are establishing some roots.

If you have a large enough sum of money, the bank will hold it in a fixed deposit and give you a credit card against that amount. For example, I was asked to deposit $3,000 in return for the bank granting me a major credit card with a limit of $1,000. After some negotiation, the bank agreed to accept a $2,000 deposit and grant me a $1,000 credit card limit. A friend of mine also got a credit card this way and in three months he had his **credit**

limit raised to $5,000 and got another three credit cards simultaneously. This is referred to as a secured credit card, which really reduces the lender's risk to nothing, as the cardholder has enough money on deposit as security in case he or she does not pay the credit card bill. This type of card can help you begin to build your credit in Canada.

Another common and relatively easy route to establishing credit is to obtain a credit card at one or more of the major national department stores such as Sears, the Bay, or Canadian Tire. Most major stores have credit card application forms and can process the applications while you wait, so you'll know immediately whether you're approved or not. If approved, you will likely be granted a small **credit limit**, perhaps $1,000. Use the card carefully, and be aware that most store cards charge a higher **interest rate** than regular credit cards, so be sure to pay off your balance each month.

In a short while, you can use your first credit card to obtain more cards. Although you may have the cash to pay for an item, you can begin to build your credit rating by charging the purchase. In most cases you will not have to pay interest charges if you pay the entire balance by the due date on your statement. Most statements are sent out once per month, and they usually give the credit card holder two to four weeks to pay at least the **minimum payment** before interest starts to build on the card's balance.

The major credit cards, American Express, MasterCard, and Visa, will allow you to purchase just about anything anywhere in the world. If your credit card application is rejected, you will be allowed to reapply in six months.

Here's a small warning: once you do get a credit card, you will probably have telemarketers calling you at dinnertime trying to sell you something or telling you "you've won a prize" or "you have been chosen to receive an exclusive card." Politely tell them you are not interested in what they're offering, and hang up the phone. You are not obligated to purchase anything from telemarketers, and you should never tell them your credit card number.

Get an Independent Credit Card

I was delighted when my wife got a credit card through her employer that came with a spousal card for me. We had also accumulated a few department store cards where I was listed as a spouse. I had assumed that I was building up good credit until I discovered the cards provided me with no credit history at all. This was despite having leased a car in my name and making my lease payments on time for many months. So the moral to this

Q: How many credit cards should I get?

A: Getting too many credit cards can damage your credit score as the total available credit on each card is treated as if you have used it even though you may have no balance! This could affect your ability to get a mortgage or other loan. I suggest two cards—one card that will earn you points, and one low-interest card—from different banks, so that if you face a problem with one (especially while travelling) you can use the other.

story is that both you and your spouse need to apply for separate cards to create your own good credit histories.

Interest Rates

Credit cards charge some of the highest interest rates of any lending institution in the world, ranging from 18 to 24 percent per year. As mentioned above, if you pay off the entire amount due before the due date, you pay no interest. If, however, you carry a portion of that sum beyond the due date, the interest monster wakes up and begins to devour your hard-earned cash. You can also borrow cash from your credit card, but if you do this, you are charged interest from the date of the borrowing.

Banks and other financial institutions will all offer one of the major credit cards, but they make independent decisions on how to market those cards. As a consequence, some credit cards will require annual fees and some will not. The interest rates on any unpaid balances may be different as well. Also, some banks will offer other incentives such as travel insurance, life insurance, or "frequent flyer" points for choosing their credit card. Most banks also have low-interest cards available, but don't advertise them. These cards are basic and do not come with insurance or frequent flyer points. Call a customer service representative to get assistance on this, and be sure to shop around.

If, after receiving a card or two, you find a better deal, you might want to get a **debt** consolidation card. Essentially, this means a new lender will take over your entire debt from the first lender, or several lenders, and offer you one larger debt with a lower interest rate. You will then have only one card and one monthly bill.

How Do Companies Make Credit Decisions?

When potential lenders review your credit application, they are basically trying to determine the likelihood that you can—and will—repay the money they lend you.

They do this by examining your "three Cs": character, capacity, and credit.

Character

Credit **grantors** get a sense of your financial and personal character through such factors as the length of time you have lived in one place and the length of time you have held your current and previous jobs. They get this information from your credit application.

If you've moved around a lot, you lose points. If you've moved because of a better-paying job, you can make up some of those points if your salary has increased because of the move. Are you a homeowner? If you are, you get additional points. Renters are considered more transient and less likely to repay their loans.

Lenders like stable borrowers. That's why they assign more points to people who've lived in a particular place for several years or who've worked for a single employer for many years.

Capacity

Capacity refers to the amount of debt you can realistically pay based on your income, other debts, and savings. To estimate your capacity, lenders look at your current living expenses, debts, and the additional payments that the proposed new obligation would require. This information comes from both your credit application and credit report.

Credit

A key factor here is how you have handled your current and past credit relationships. Do you pay your bills on time or are you always late? In the case of a new immigrant, your history of debt repayment in your native country has no relevance in Canada. You are creating a new credit history.

Building and Keeping a Good Credit Rating

Keeping good credit is critical. Having a realistic budget, keeping a moderate credit limit, and paying your entire balance every month are the keys to good credit and low **finance charges**. When you're starting out, credit companies will not give you a large credit limit, but you still have to be careful. Don't use your credit cards if you can't make the payments. Even paying the minimum monthly payment will keep you in good standing, although it is a better idea to pay off your entire balance each month.

If you can't make a payment, contact the creditor immediately. In most cases they will work with you, depending on how much you owe. Try negotiating with your creditors to reduce your minimum monthly payments. Creditors would rather get smaller payments than none at all.

What might get you into trouble, though, is that paying even a few days late puts you into a default category. The same rule applies to a mortgage payment. Most mortgages offer a grace period of 10 or 15 days after the payment due date before your payment is officially late and you're charged a late fee. But, for credit scoring purposes, if you have not paid by your due date, you're late.

If you move, be sure to file a change of address with the post office and provide your creditors with your new address. If creditors can't find you, your account could become past due and this could damage your credit standing.

One way to guard against these oversights is to set up automatic monthly payments from your bank account to some regular creditors, such as the hydro utilities company, the mortgage company, the cable company, or your credit card company. You will avoid the possibility of missing a payment due to a cheque not clearing or being lost in the mail.

Canada's oldest bank is the Bank of Montreal. Founded in Quebec on November 3, 1817, this bank is now the fourth largest in the country. In 2006 it had over 30,000 employees and managed assets of over $300 billion.

Getting a Copy of Your Credit Report

You can see what credit card companies are saying about you by contacting one of the three national credit agencies: TransUnion Canada, Equifax

Canada, or Northern Credit Bureaus. The agencies will advise you how to order a copy of your credit report.

Keep in mind that every time you apply for credit, your **financial history** is closely scrutinized. And any time you are rejected, this rejection appears on your record. A banker once told me to never apply more than three times within a six-month period.

It is very important to ensure that there are no mistakes on your credit report. With more than 20 million Canadians holding at least one major credit card each, it is easy to see how mistakes might be made. If you find an error in your credit report, be sure to contact all of the credit bureaus to correct the error. A friend of mine realized the importance of this when he applied for a mortgage and was refused. His record inaccurately showed he had a large outstanding credit card debt. He had paid it off before applying for the mortgage, but had not reported it to the bureaus.

How Much Is Too Much Debt?

Credit counsellors advise that your debt payments, such as for car or school loans or **credit card** bills, should not total more than 20 percent of your net monthly income. For example, if your monthly take-home pay is $1,000, you should be devoting no more than $200 a month to credit payments. This general rule does not include mortgage payments in the calculation of monthly debts.

Learning how to spend money wisely is the first step to controlling debt. Keeping a spending diary is a good way to see what you're buying and why, and can also help you establish a monthly budget.

While most of this chapter deals with obtaining credit cards, it is also worth noting that it is even more important to learn how to use those cards wisely once you've got them. Strive to pay them off each month. If you find you can't control your spending, cut your cards up.

Finally, become a smart spender. Look for sales, clip coupons, and stick to your budget. For most people, some debt is unavoidable, but keep yours to a minimum. Reducing debt is one of the best avenues to financial security.

RRSPs

Contributing to an RRSP (Registered Retirement Savings Plan) is a common way to save money for retirement. Each year, you make a deposit into your fund and earn interest on the balance. Since your contributions are tax-deductible, the more you put into your RRSP, the less income tax you'll have to pay. When you retire, the money in your RRSP will provide you with an income which can help you maintain your standard of living.

Setting up an RRSP

You can set up an RRSP at any bank or credit union. The rate of interest you earn will be determined by your bank, although the maximum amount you can invest each year is decided by the Canada Revenue Agency and is based on your income for the previous year. If you contribute more than your maximum, you may have to pay a 1 percent tax on the extra amount. When you are ready to retire, you can convert your RRSP to a form of retirement income, such as a Retirement Income Fund (RIF).

Spousal RRSP

If your income is much higher than that of your spouse or common-law partner, you may want to make contributions to a spousal RRSP. You would generally split your annual contribution into two fairly equal amounts so that both you and your spouse have similar savings and will receive similar payments during retirement. By contributing to a spousal RRSP, your spouse will build a retirement fund and you will get a tax break.

Withdrawing Money from Your RRSP

If you withdraw money from your RRSP before you retire, you will lose out on your tax break and have to pay the amount of tax you originally saved by placing your money in an RRSP. The rate you will have to pay will depend on the amount you withdraw.

There are two exceptions to this rule, however. Under the Home Buyers' Plan, first-time home buyers may withdraw up to $20,000 from their RRSPs to use toward the purchase of a house. They will not be charged a penalty as long as they follow the plan's guidelines and repay the borrowed amount within 15 years. The Lifelong Learning Plan is similar, although the withdrawn money is used for tuition and must be repaid within 10 years.

Big Ticket Loans

The two major areas for which you will need credit are buying a vehicle and buying a house.

Let's take the vehicle first. If you need a car, you may want to purchase it on credit to help establish a good credit rating. (See Chapter 12—Driving in Canada for more information on car purchases.) Shop around for your financing and negotiate with the car dealer; in some cases, dealerships may give you the best financing deals of all.

As for buying a house, you should visit several banks or credit unions before you even start to look for a house. Until you know how much you are eligible to borrow, you won't know what price you can pay for a house.

In 2006, Canadian banks donated $136.5 million to charities in Canada and $179 million to causes worldwide.

Banking Tips

- Pay attention to the credit card offers you get in the mail; many of them have very attractive terms, such as low introductory rates or guaranteed maximum interest rates for the entire period of time you are paying off transferred balances.
- If bogus charges show up on your bill, or if your card is lost or stolen, call the credit card issuer immediately. Getting things straightened out takes a little time, but usually doesn't cost you anything. Visa, MasterCard, or American Express take care of the losses, not the customer.
- Don't carry unnecessary credit cards, your social insurance card, your birth certificate, or other personal documents in your purse or wallet.
- Keep records of all your ATM transactions and credit card, debit card, and other receipts. They will be necessary if an error shows up on any of your monthly statements. When you eventually dispose of receipts, be sure to cut them up.
- Cancel any credit card accounts that you do not plan to use. It is difficult to keep track of too many cards.
- Keep a list of your credit card account numbers and the credit card companies' telephone numbers in a safe place so you can cancel the cards quickly and easily in case they are stolen or lost. A handy way of doing this is to photocopy all your cards; just be careful where you leave the copy. If any card is stolen, inform the police immediately and contact your credit card company.
- Protect your social insurance number. Do not give it out to any person or company unless you are familiar with them and you have initiated communication with them.
- Your driver's licence is an important identification document. Treat it like a credit card, because if it is lost, it can be used by dishonest people to obtain credit cards.

Insurance on Your Life and Your Home

Insurance is a basic necessity for everyone, especially families. This is something you should talk to an insurance **broker** or agent about. I do, however, feel it is important enough to be included here.

Basically, the two kinds of life insurance are **term insurance** and **permanent insurance**. The following are fairly standard components of each.

Components of Term and Permanent Insurance		
	Term	**Permanent**
Premiums	Affordable **premiums**	Premiums may be much higher than those of term policies, but a portion goes into savings
Coverage	You must renew at the end of the term to continue coverage	Coverage will continue as long as you pay your premiums
Age Limits	You cannot renew past a specified age, usually 70 or 80	No age cut-off
Use	Used mainly for family's income protection needs	Used mainly for estate preservation, but may also be used for income protection

Property Insurance

If you buy a house or condominium, your mortgage company will insist that you buy **property insurance** to protect its investment. Insuring the contents of your home, including all your belongings, clothes, and computer equipment, is up to you. Property insurance is also available to renters and will cover the contents of the home against fire, water, smoke, or theft. You will have to decide whether you want to insure your possessions; it is a wise decision to do so, particularly if you have expensive appliances or equipment in your home. If you decide to insure your belongings, you'll need to make an inventory of your possessions, take photos of them, and estimate their replacement value. You might be surprised at how much you have.

Shortly after my family had invested in a costly home theatre, a water pipe burst in our living room and flooded the floor. It didn't reach the precious home theatre equipment, but quite easily could have done so. Luckily, we caught it in time so that although the carpets were ruined (in a rented apartment that is the landlord's responsibility), none of our possessions were damaged. Had they been affected, however, our insurance would have paid for their replacement.

Sumit Ray: A New Life

When Sumit Ray arrived in Canada in 2002, his biggest concerns were finding a job and learning to cook.

The soft-spoken financial analyst from New Delhi, India, made the move to Canada on his own, leaving behind family, friends, and a thriving career.

"I came here to make a better life for myself," he says.

Ray discovered that it was easier to find a job than to learn how to cook. With a little bit of research, he enrolled in a course at an adult learning centre that offered him an internship at the Bank of Montreal.

Since the internship was unpaid, Ray worked nights at factory jobs to make ends meet. The hours at the bank were long, but the experience and hard work paid off. When he finished his course, the bank hired him on full-time. Ray has since advanced to the position of assistant branch manager in one of the bank's Mississauga branches.

Although the adjustment to a new culture was difficult at first, Ray made it work through determination and a positive attitude. He encourages newcomers to look into programs that offer internships, even if unpaid.

"It helps you develop Canadian experience and get a foot in the door," he says.

—Margaret Jetelina

Fraud Warning

As the old saying goes, "There is a sucker born every minute." Just because you're in Canada now, don't make the mistake of thinking scams don't exist. Whether you are sold a new roof by a contractor who never completes the work, are asked to donate to a non-existent charity, or send a cheque to a company for a product that never shows up, there are lots of opportunities to be fooled by someone who wants your money.

One wet, miserable evening, I found a card in the mailbox saying, "You have just won $5,000. Call this number to collect your prize." My wife and I did just that with great excitement. We listened to a long-winded message that just wouldn't end. Finally we hung up and left it at that. Then we got our monthly telephone bill. It was a long-distance scam and we had just been tricked out of $70. Not a huge price to pay for being naïve, but it did teach us a lesson: If something sounds too good to be true, it probably is.

We also ran into a problem when we began receiving unrequested magazines and books, which we simply threw out. Then, of course, we got a bill in the mail for all the unwanted material. A bill collector even came to collect money from us. We had to make many phone calls and complaints before we managed to convince the company that we had not ordered the materials.

Better Business Bureaus (BBB) operate in almost every city in Canada and the United States. They are devoted to promoting ethical business practices in advertising and selling. Contact the BBB in your community if you have questions about a company, a charity, questionable advertising, or a telephone offer that sounds very tempting, but suspicious.

Top 10 Fraud Scams

The BBB of Mainland, BC, wrote about Canada's top ten scams in *Canadian Immigrant* magazine in 2006, as follows.

1. **Internet fraud.**
   The Internet provides scam artists with a whole new toolbox for targeting victims. It has spawned numerous online scams and new jargon to describe them.

   Scammers use emails to "fish" the Internet, hoping to hook you into giving up your login, password, and/or credit card information. The phisher sends an email impersonating a legitimate company (this is called "phishing") such as a financial institution or eBay. The email then directs you to a "spoofed," or look-alike, website to update your account information. The bogus site looks almost identical to the legitimate site.

   Then there is "spyware," which is software that covertly gathers your information, such as passwords and credit card numbers, through your Internet connection without your knowledge.

   Do not respond to, forward, or open attachments in unsolicited (phishing) emails. Legitimate financial institutions or government departments will not seek your personal information through unsolicited email. When purchasing or selling online, ensure any services you use have a privacy policy, terms of agreement, and a customer service line.

2. Identity theft.

ID thieves use all sorts of tactics to steal your personal information —rummaging through your trash or recycling bin, pretending you need to provide information to collect a prize, stealing your mail, placing bogus newspaper ads for jobs, phishing, and spoofing on the Internet.

To prevent identity theft, shred any unnecessary information that contains personal details. Make sure to check your credit report annually with Equifax (www.equifax.ca or 1-800-465-7166), TransUnion Canada (www.transunion.ca or 1-866-525-0262), and Northern Credit Bureaus (www.creditbureau.ca or 1-800-532-8784) to ensure that there have been no unauthorized transactions on your report.

If you are a victim of ID theft, contact the Canadian Anti-**Fraud** Call Centre, PhoneBusters (www.phonebusters.com or 1-888-495-8501).

3. Fraudulent telemarketing.

Scam artists continue to use the telephone to defraud consumers with lottery scams and fraudulent cheque/overpayment schemes.

To report fraudulent telemarketing, call PhoneBusters (1-888-485-8501). You can also remove yourself from telephone calling lists of companies that belong to the Canadian Marketing Association (www.the-cma.org or 416-391-2362).

4. Cheque/overpayment schemes.

In this scam, a fraudster contacts an online seller—often an online business—offering to purchase posted goods. The bogus buyer sends a counterfeit cheque in excess of what is owed; the seller is asked to return the excess funds to the purchaser. When the cashed cheque is returned as probably counterfeit, the seller is out of pocket and has shipped the merchandise.

So the message here is never accept a cheque for more than your selling price; and never agree to wire back funds to a buyer —a legitimate buyer will not pressure you to do so. Consider using an online payment service, like PayPal, instead.

5. Home repair scams.

Scam artists may pose as home repair workers and knock on your door claiming to be doing some work in the neighbourhood. They'll persuade unsuspecting homeowners into making renovations and all too often leave a mess of shoddy workmanship while they make a quick profit. The homeowner is left to pay again to get the job fixed.

When hiring a contractor, check out companies first with the Better Business Bureau.

Remember, a ten-day cooling off period may apply to direct sales contracts, [such as] a contract entered into in person at a place other than the supplier's permanent place of business. Don't be pressured into making a decision you may regret later.

6. Unscrupulous moving practices.

Some moving companies tarnish the industry by using unscrupulous practices such as charging hidden fees or providing a low estimate and then charging more at delivery, holding your goods in storage until you pay.

To avoid this, have the moving company provide a detailed estimate in writing and ensure that the mover has an insurance underwriter. Check the company out first with the Better Business Bureau and the Canadian Association of Movers (www.mover.net).

7. Bogus health and wellness claims.

Fraudulent health treatment claims are a growing concern in the marketplace. They target the most vulnerable consumers such as the seriously overweight and the ill. Beware of too-good-to-be-true advertisements promising "rapid and effortless" weight-loss or "miracle cures" and "newly discovered" treatments for disease and illness. These scams are designed to steal your money and potentially put your health at risk if proper medical treatment is delayed.

Before buying any treatment or medication, consult your physician, pharmacist, or other healthcare professional. To learn more about the misleading weight loss scams on the Internet, visit www.fatfoe.ca. Report bogus health and wellness claims to the Competition Bureau of Canada at 1-800-348-5358 or at www.competitionbureau.gc.ca.

8. **Bogus charities.**
Within days of any natural or human-made disaster, some people will attempt to take advantage of others' eagerness to assist victims of the tragedy. Be wary of appeals that are long on emotion but short on what the charity will do to address the specific disaster. Watch out for bogus charities that use legitimate sounding names or those that don't give enough detail about their organization. And note that third-party fundraisers that solicit donations from consumers require licences.

So do not give donations over the phone or at the door. Ask for the organization to mail its information package to you so that you can check it out with the BBB. Check to see if the charity is registered with the Canada Revenue Agency (call 1-800-267-2384 or visit www.cra-arc.gc.ca/tax/charities).

9. **Deceptive vacation schemes.**
By simply filling out a ballot to win a vacation contest, you may be set up for a "sucker list." You may be telephoned by someone claiming you have won a free or low-cost vacation. Often there are hidden costs associated with collecting your prize or you are required to attend a high-pressure timeshare presentation. Nearly always, you will be responsible for either the travel or accommodation portion of the offer and you'll find the vacation isn't such a bargain after all.

Resist the temptation to fill out ballots for "free" vacations. Travel scam operators typically withhold information until you give them a credit card number or a money order. Investigate travel packages thoroughly for hidden charges and always obtain complete details in writing about any trip prior to payment.

10. **Lottery and sweepstakes fraud.**
You are one of the "lucky" cash prize winners and all you have to do to collect is complete a form with your personal information and send a payment processing fee plus shipping and handling. Sound familiar? [Canadian] residents are bombarded with lottery and sweepstake offers all promising fast riches.

Responding to one solicitation opens the door to dozens more. If you've won something, it should be free of all charges. To reduce unsolicited mail from companies that belong to the Canadian Marketing Association, call 416-391-2362 or visit www.the-cma.org.

account: the arrangement by which a bank holds your money for you

broker: a person who arranges the buying and selling of things such as property, insurance, etc. for other people

chequing account: a bank account from which you can pay for things or take out money by writing a cheque

credit: the status of being trusted to return the money to somebody or something that lends it to you

credit limit: the highest amount of money that you are allowed to spend or borrow using your credit card

credit union: an organization similar to a bank, that is owned by the people who keep their money in it, and which lends money to its members at low rates of interest

debt: a sum of money that you owe somebody

deposit: to put money into an account at a bank

direct debit (also direct payment): an instruction to your bank to allow somebody else to take money from your account, usually to pay bills

finance charge: the amount of money you must pay for a loan arrangement

financial history: the series of events or facts that is connected with a person's management of money

fraud: (an act of) deceiving or tricking somebody in order to get money, etc. in a way that is against the law

funds: money that is available and can be spent

grantor: a person or an organization that agrees to give somebody what he/she asks for, such as a line of credit

insurance: a contract in which, in return for regular payment, a company or the state agrees to pay a sum of money if something (e.g. illness, death, loss of or damage to property) happens to somebody

INTERAC: a payment network that allows a person to pay for purchases with money taken electronically from his/her bank account

interest: the money that you earn from investments or that you pay for borrowing money

interest rate: the money that you have to pay for borrowing money, usually expressed as a percentage of the total sum borrowed, for a stated period of time

loan: money, etc. that somebody/something lends you

minimum payment: the smallest amount of money that you must pay

permanent insurance: a type of life insurance that lasts for the insured person's whole life as long as he/she continues to pay the premiums

personal identification number (also PIN): a secret number that you use with a special card to get money from a cash machine

personal line of credit (also PLC): an amount of credit that a person is allowed to borrow (usually from a bank or credit union)

premium: an amount of money that you pay regularly to a company for insurance

property insurance: an insurance policy a person takes out to protect the things that he/she owns against most risks, such as fire, theft, and some weather damage

savings account: a type of bank account where your money earns interest

term deposit: a type of account at a financial institution in which money is left for a fixed period of time with a fixed interest rate. A penalty may have to be paid if the money is withdrawn before the end of the fixed term.

term insurance: a type of life insurance that lasts for a stated period of time and that does not pay money if the insured person dies after the insurance expires

transaction: a piece of business

traveller's cheque: a cheque that you can change into foreign money when you are travelling in other countries, or that you can use instead of cash to pay for things in the US or Canada

withdrawal: the act of taking an amount of money out of a bank account

Note: Entries taken or adapted from the Oxford ESL Dictionary

Creating Your Canadian Experience

1. Go to three different banks, either in your neighbourhood or on-line, and compare the accounts that they offer.

Banking Institution	Account Name	Fees	Balance Needed to Waive Fees

2. Research three different credit cards and compare them.
   Tip: type the name of a bank you listed in question #1 and "Credit Card" into a search engine. You will find lots of information about the cards the bank offers.

Card Type	Annual Fees	Interest Rate	Benefits of This Card

3. Keeping a spending diary is a good way to keep track of the money that is leaving your pocket. Below is a template that you can use to create your own on your computer.

Regular Monthly Payments		Week 1		Week 2		Week 3		Week 4		
Expense	Amount	Expense	Amount	Expense	Amount	Expense	Amount	Expense	Amount	
										Monthly Total
Totals										$

Note: If you want to be even more specific, break up your columns by days.

4. Make a list of your possessions and estimate their value. Add up the amounts and if the total is high, you may want to consider getting insurance.

Possession	Value
_____	_____
_____	_____
_____	_____
_____	_____
_____	_____

5. Research the Better Business Bureau nearest to your home.
Tip: type the name of your city and "Better Business Bureau" into a search engine.

Address: _____

Hours: _____

Contact Information: _____

Chapter 10

Looking for and Landing a Job

In This Chapter

- Where should you start looking for a job?
- How do you prepare a resume?
- What kinds of questions will you have to answer at an interview?
- What hours will you be expected to work?

You *will* find a job. Keep that thought in your mind as you begin your exciting but sometimes discouraging search for meaningful employment. You will need to make use of all your **experiences**, your **communication** skills, your **diplomacy**, your **networking** abilities, your **marketing** skills, and every ounce of your dynamic personality to compete against everyone else who is looking for the same kind of work you are.

Whether you are looking for a job that thrills you or something to help pay next month's rent, you will need to spend a significant amount of time on every step of the process. In fact, if you don't have a job, then looking for work should be your full-time job.

One of the most important things you will need to do is create a resume. Professional resume writers are listed in the phone book and could charge anywhere from $150 to $250.

You will need to ensure you have all your **credentials**, diplomas, certificates of merit, and school completion records, as well as your **licence to practise** your **trade** or **profession** in your home country and several letters of **reference**—from former employers, professional co-workers, or volunteer organizations—attesting to your character.

Non-English documents should be professionally translated and certified. It may be necessary to earn Canadian equivalency credentials for **occupations** ranging from psychiatrist to machinist. This could take some time and it's something you might want to start working on before you even arrive in Canada.

Q: How do I find a mentor?

A: If you find a person who you believe has experiences and achievements that are worth learning from, ask this person for advice about your own education or **career** path. This may continue into an ongoing relationship, with the person acting as your mentor.

Professional and Trade Credentials

The Canadian Information Centre for International Credentials (CICIC) can help you obtain the credentials and licences you need to find work in your occupational field. Unfortunately, in Canada problems can arise for those trying to obtain recognition and **accreditation** of their **training** abroad. Certification and licensing varies from province to province, and from profession to profession.

The CICIC does not assess anyone's qualifications or grant certification, but does provide guidance from its library of contacts in education, professional occupations, and **skilled labour**.

If you are in a **non-regulated occupation**, you have nothing to worry about. You don't need a licence to perform your job in Canada, although there may be an **association** or professional body related to your profession that offers voluntary membership, training, and support services. This category covers most occupations, including bus driver (although you do need a special driver's licence to drive a public transit vehicle), sales clerk, bookkeeper, journalist, and restaurant worker. Of course, you will still have to satisfy potential employers that you are trained and competent, but you won't need a certificate to prove it.

Difficulties can arise, however, for individuals in the regulated occupations. This covers everyone who needs to obtain recognition of their profession or trade by a provincial or federal **regulatory body** and a relevant trade association before they can obtain a licence or certificate to practise. Regulated occupations are controlled by provincial or territorial law, and are governed by their own trade or professional organization.

These trade and professional organizations set the **standards of practice** required for anyone working in that profession and also establish a format for assessing qualifications. In most professions and trades, **requirements** will vary from province to province, and in some provinces certain occupations may not even be classified as regulated.

However, if your trade or profession is regulated, you will generally need to do the following:

- Demonstrate knowledge of English or French;
- Obtain further training;
- Appear before the regulatory body for an exam.

This process can cost lots of money and take many months or even years to complete. People in regulated professions include engineers, physicians, physiotherapists, chiropractors, nurses, lawyers, social workers, and teachers. Individuals in regulated trades include plumbers, electricians, and many others.

Contact your occupation's professional or trade association in the country where you practised to find out if it has any affiliation with a similar association in Canada. You might also want to check with the Canadian consul in your country to obtain information about your occupation and possible licensing requirements. Most Canadian diplomatic offices stock a publication entitled *National Occupational Classification* that might help you with this.

Contact the Canadian regulatory body for your profession to obtain the specific requirements and costs for licensing, certification, or registration, as well as the procedure for obtaining an assessment.

Also, there are several associations popping up specifically for immigrants in professional occupations. These associations are working to represent those immigrants who are facing barriers to getting licences to practise in their chosen fields, such as medicine and engineering.

Amir Ravesh: Doctor from Iran

When Dr. Amir Ravesh left Iran for Canada, he came with a top, Western-based medical education. But once on Canadian soil, he spent months just trying to find the information he needed to help him begin practising medicine in his new country.

"[International doctors] don't have basic knowledge of what they should do. They don't know where to go," Ravesh says. "It took me six months to find information about the situation and where to go."

He finally learned from the College of Physicians and Surgeons about the three exams he needed to take to qualify for a Canadian medical licence, but he says the help stopped there. "Nobody told me what kind of book to read [to prepare for the exams]," he says.

After successfully completing his exams, Ravesh worked as a trainee with a local Canadian doctor while waiting for his residency to begin. It has been a long process to get where he is, but Ravesh can finally practise his profession in Canada.

—Margaret Jetelina

Looking for a Job

You should gather your credentials together with your resume, several file folders, and some notebooks, and designate a desk in your home as "Job Action Central." Ideally, there should be a phone nearby, and if you have a fax machine or computer, keep them at the desk too. A fax machine that can be plugged into your residential phone line can be purchased for less than $150. It could be a valuable investment, as many job advertisements ask you to submit your resume by fax.

You will need to evaluate your skills, experiences, strengths, and weaknesses before you start looking for any job. Don't forget to include your interests and hobbies. Since you've made a leap to a brand new country, you might decide to choose a whole new career path as well—you may want to forget teaching high school to take a junior job in a photo studio since you've always been interested in photography.

Whatever your job focus, you will need to be clear on the qualities you can bring to that job in order to sell yourself to a prospective employer. Make a list of your skills and analyze all the jobs you've performed in previous placements. Think about all the jobs you've liked and those you never want to perform again. Also list any training or courses you've taken and any **volunteer work** you've done, as employers will value this experience.

While **job hunting**, it might also be helpful to take training courses or offer your services at a volunteer organization, as long as these activities do not take away from your job search. If you can fit in a few hours of training or volunteering per week, you will find it helps in a number of ways: you will improve your English skills if necessary; it will force you to create a structure in your life that includes job search time plus time for other activities; it will introduce you to a wider range of people, which may include possible employers; it will demonstrate to prospective employers that you are energetic and active, as well as interested in getting ahead in life and contributing to your community; and it will teach you more about your new city.

Temporary Work

There is no doubt that the job market is changing, and one of the most noticeable changes is in the number of companies using **contract workers**, or **outsourcing** some projects.

Before you discard any such offers, consider the benefits of a temporary job. You can work while continuing to search for a permanent placement; the company might decide to keep you on as a permanent employee; you will learn new job skills; and you could meet many prospective employers while you're working.

Preparing a Resume

Once you have your documents and you know what kind of job you are seeking, it is time to prepare a resume, which is known in some countries as a ***curriculum vitae***. Although there are many formats for resumes, they all should contain the following:

- Your full name, address, telephone number, fax number, and email if available

- The **position** being sought or your overall career objective, which many people omit from their resumes
- A summary of your education, including the names of any schools or institutions you've attended, the name of diplomas or certificates you've received, and the dates they were granted
- A summary of your job history. (If you have had many jobs, you might want to limit this list to only those that directly relate to the **position** for which you are currently applying.)
- A list of any skills and talents you have that will help you do the job you're applying for. (Because Canadian employers may not be able to relate to your foreign work experience and education, a breakdown of what you are capable of doing is helpful.)

You should not include your age, gender, race, or marital status on your resume.

In addition to organizing your resume properly and ensuring that it contains no grammatical errors or spelling mistakes, it is extremely important that the document looks professional from a design viewpoint. When faced with a stack of resumes, a prospective employer may judge a potential candidate based on the physical appearance of his or her resume. One spelling mistake could mean your resume is going right into the recycling box. If your English skills are not perfect, ask someone to proofread your resume, not only for typos, but also for awkward phrasing.

Think of your resume as a personal advertisement. It must be visually pleasing in order to make someone want to read it. Structure it so that you place the most important details about you and your work history in a prominent location. Remember, it should not provide details on your entire life, only the experiences related to the job for which you are applying.

If you have access to a computer, customizing your resume for each employer will be fairly easy. But even if you don't own a computer, you might want to prepare two or three different versions of your resume for different employers.

Keep it brief; your resume should be a maximum of two pages. Again, you may want to create two different resumes, one that is one or two pages in length and another that is three or so pages in length, providing additional details. If you get called in for an interview, bring along the more detailed resume and your letters of reference and ask if the employer would like to see them.

The Mechanics of Resume Preparation

- Always use a computer to prepare your resume; never handwrite it. If you don't have the necessary equipment, you can hire someone to prepare your resume or you can ask a friend to do it for you. Also, most employment centres have computers and printers, as well as Internet access, available for job seekers.
- Stick to one typeface or type style, using **bold face** or *italics* only to indicate section headings. Avoid underlining altogether.
- Use evenly spaced margins and leave even line spacing between headings so the material is easy to read and doesn't look crowded.
- Use good-quality paper, either white, cream, or beige.
- Edit and proofread your resume for grammar and spelling, and ask someone else to read it through as well.
- Keep your statements short and dynamic.

A completed resume might look something like the one below.

Adeel Ahmad
30 Main Street
Townsville, Manitoba
A1B 2C3
(204) 555-5555
adeel@email.com

> Make sure that your contact information is clear and correct. If employers cannot get in touch with you easily, they will not contact you for an interview.

Objective
To obtain a position in the field of electrical engineering

Special Skills
- Construction supervision and equipment-testing experience gained on international projects
- Breadboarding, hardware troubleshooting, software troubleshooting
- Telecomm OSP and ISP, CADD 2D and 3D, IC layout design

> Read the wording of the job description carefully. Your resume should include what is important to the company you are applying to.

Management Skills
- Experienced in designing, budgeting, and mentoring project teams
- Six years of administrative experience at Company X

Professional Experience
Engineering Manager, Company X
May 2002—February 2008
- Made engineering calculations in connection with field and office assignments
- Prepared requests for proposals and evaluated bids
- Supervised the modification and layout of Printed Circuit boards and was able to increase production by 12 percent

> Describe your most recent work experience first and work backwards from there. Try to include the results of your actions, as this will give employers a better understanding of your work.

Electrical Engineer, Company Y
July 2000—April 2002
- Added new features to assembly line testers using C in LabWindows/CVI environment, improving productivity by 16 percent
- Built strong in-house electrical design capability for wireless facilities, greatly reducing outsourcing, which saved over $25,000
- Wrote several technical manuals and operating procedures for hardware and software systems

Education
2000
Bachelor of Science in Electrical Engineering, University of Lahore, Pakistan

Highlights
Senior Engineering Award, 2000
Outstanding Student Achievement Scholarship, 1998

References available upon request

You should know that the example given is only one type of resume. Many professions have their own way of presenting the information based on what is important to that industry. Even within an industry there are many different ways to create a resume. Search the Internet to find many different examples and choose the one that best suits your needs.

Cover Letters

Every resume you submit should be accompanied by a cover letter. The letter should be addressed to a specific person and should be tailored to a specific job. Call the company you are applying to and ask for the name of the personnel director or **supervisor**. Always ask how to spell his or her name; never assume that the spelling is obvious.

Your letter should be no more than one page long. Start by stating which job you are applying for and how you learned about it, such as through someone who works at the company or through an advertisement.

Don't repeat all the points in your resume, but instead focus on one or two of your achievements, such as "With my 15 years experience in this field I could be an asset to your company." Focus the cover letter more on demonstrating your knowledge of the company and how well you'll fit in, rather than just summarizing your past experience.

Many books are available to help you write cover letters. A good letter should read something like the following example.

Your Name
Your Address

Company Contact Name and Title
Company Address

May 15, 2009

Dear Mr. Adams,

In response to your advertisement in the May 12 issue of the Daily Post, I am enclosing my resume for consideration regarding the position of electrical engineer.

I recently moved to Canada from Pakistan, and would be very interested in beginning my Canadian career with your company. My dedication to the field of electrical engineering earned me a GPA of 4.0 in my program at the University of Lahore, and I have made a successful career for myself as an engineer over the past eight years. This experience makes me the ideal choice for a company like yours that is a leader in its field.

Your organization has grown twofold in the last decade and I want to help you continue that growth. I supervised a team of engineers at Company X on many successful projects, and was responsible for evaluating new proposals, based on the company's goals. Over the six years I was at Company X, my department achieved a 32 percent increase in productivity.

I am confident I would be an asset to your organization. Thank you for considering my resume. I have also attached an independent assessment of my education and credentials from the International Credential Evaluation Service. This assessment explains how my credentials measure up to those earned in Canada. I look forward to hearing from you.

Sincerely,

Adeel Ahmad

The Job Search

Employment Centres

For most job seekers, a good place to start is the nearest employment centre. This is a great resource for finding job leads and tips, and provides training and workshops geared to helping people obtain employment. Because they are so popular, the offices are usually packed with other job seekers and lineups are generally long, but it is still a good place to start.

Statistics Canada data show that the average weekly earnings of people employed in Canadian industries increased steadily in recent years. In 2002, the average weekly income was $679, in 2003 it was $688, in 2004 it was $703, in 2005 it was $726, and in 2006 it had reached $747.

Don't forget to pick up some of the helpful brochures available for job seekers at these centres. They outline all the services available though the centre, such as resume preparation, job search planning, and organizational help.

The employment centres have job postings, including a computerized job bank of local and national positions. There are workshops on how to search for a job and information on ESL (English as a Second Language) courses.

Classified Advertisements

Search the **classifieds** section daily, not only in your local daily newspapers, but also in the local weekly newspaper if one is published in your community or region.

The classifieds section conveniently categorizes jobs so they are easy to find. When you see a suitable position, you must act quickly. If an ad asks applicants to fax their resumes to the employer, send your resume that same day. If the ad says "please no phone calls," do not call, or the employer will think you either can't read or can't follow instructions.

If you are looking for a career in business, pick up copies of the local business journals for job offerings, as well as for articles on new companies and companies that are expanding. Read the **trade journals** or business magazines related to your job category, as they will tell you about company expansions, mergers, acquisitions, and new companies moving into your city, all of which may be looking for someone with your skills and experience.

The Library

All major cities and many smaller ones have libraries with a wealth of information for job seekers. A library can be a valuable resource in helping you find out as much as possible about the job field or industry in which you are interested. Search out articles about your chosen industry in old issues of the local newspapers. They will be indexed and easy to find. These articles will give you a good idea of the changes that are occurring in your industry, perhaps relating to the government, new trade opportunities, or new management personnel.

You can also search for one or more specific companies in the newspaper or periodical section. Find out everything you can about the company and the industry before you even start applying for jobs.

The library can also provide you with reference material on the current labour market and job market trends. If you are thinking of starting a new career or a business, the business section at the library is a good place to start. Many libraries also provide workshops that can teach you how to maximize the services of a library.

A good library can provide the following:

- Current and back copies of local daily newspapers, as well as smaller regional newspapers
- Trade journals and newsletters about your job field, featuring articles on companies and people, as well as their promotions and retirements — which lead to job vacancies
- Job search books and reference materials explaining resumes and cover letters
- Business directories listing companies and their descriptions, and in some cases their annual reports
- Descriptions and educational requirements for various occupations
- Information about job training programs or schools

Internet Job Sites

Check out the Internet when searching for a job. Not only can you find the online versions of many newspaper classifieds, there are also many job search websites like Monster.ca, Working.com, and government job banks like the Government of Canada's job bank at jb-ge.hrdc-drhc.gc.ca.

Also, many companies with websites will have a Careers section with listings of job openings. If you know of a company you'd like to work for, keep checking its website to see if there are new openings.

If you're interested in working for the federal or provincial government, their websites often advertise job opportunities that are open to the public. Note that some government job postings are only open to those who already work for the government, not to the general public.

If you don't have an Internet connection set up at home yet, you can access it at libraries, community and immigrant agencies, or Internet cafes.

Submit Unsolicited Applications

The truth is that most jobs are filled without being advertised. You can always send your cover letter and resume to companies that you'd like to work for, even if they haven't advertised an open position. These companies or offices in your area of expertise will be listed in the phone book. Perhaps someone has just given two weeks' notice, has been promoted, has been transferred, has been fired, or is taking **maternity leave**, and a decision has not yet been made on how or where to post the job opening. Or perhaps the company is planning to expand but has yet to make a move in that direction. Any of these situations could lead to a job vacancy.

Also, when one position becomes vacant, several positions are frequently affected. If someone within the company is promoted to that vacated position, then his or her former position becomes available. More often than you can imagine, jobs are landed simply by pure luck and good timing.

Network Your Job Search

Tell everyone you know that you are in the market for a job, what you're interested in, and what your skills are. Don't be shy about asking people to keep their eyes open for potential jobs. You can even ask them to ask their friends and colleagues to help. Many job leads come along this way, so the more people you meet, the greater your chances of meeting someone who knows someone who's looking for an employee with your skills. You might even consider having business cards printed with your name and contact information on it along with your desired job description, such as "Alice Smolten—Bookkeeper" and hand them out to acquaintances.

Q: A lot of people suggest networking as part of job hunting. What is this?

A: Networking means developing a broad list of contacts—people you've met through various social and business functions—and using them to your advantage when you look for a job. They may be able to give you job leads, offer you advice and information about a particular company or industry, and introduce you to others so that you can expand your network.

Employment Agencies

It is a good idea to submit your resume to private **employment agencies**, or "head hunters" as they are called. Their job is to find qualified staff for companies, so you are generally not charged a fee. Rather, the employer pays the agency when it fills the position with someone like you. These agencies are listed in the telephone book under "Employment" and "Personnel."

Cold Calling

If you hear about a possible job opening, you should act immediately by calling the personnel manager or general manager to inquire about the opening. That cold call is, for most people, an uncomfortable step to make, but it is often necessary if you want to be proactive in your job search.

You should practise what you are going to say and have someone listen to you to help you fine-tune your presentation, but don't prepare a script that sounds rehearsed and rigid.

Be brief: state your name, explain where you heard about the job opening, and provide one or two short statements that support your claim to being qualified for the job, such as "I have two years of experience in banking in Hong Kong." Then ask the employer if you can submit a resume.

At some point when you are **cold calling**, you might feel as though you have been rejected. If this happens, you may want to take a small break or take a walk around the block. If you feel rejected, your next cold call contact will be able to sense your negative mood. Keep in mind that most prospective employers will want to hear from you, many will invite you to an interview, and one of them will hire you.

You can use the cold call technique even if you haven't heard that the company might be hiring. Many job searchers interested in a particular company will call the company to arrange an information interview. You can mention that you are an immigrant with a background in this field, but want to learn more about how things are done in Canada. Ask if you could take 20 minutes of the employer's time in the near future to ask some questions about the industry and the company. This is a good way for you to learn and network at the same time. Who knows? Maybe the person you speak with will remember you in the future when the company has a job opening.

Mariana Gerenska: Putting Her Skills to Work

Mariana Gerenska had been living in Canada for less than a year when she began working in the field of her choice. Gerenska has four master's degrees from various European universities and was a training manager and organizational development consultant in Bulgaria. She came to Canada with the hopes of becoming a university professor, an organizational development consultant, or a coach, as well as pursuing her Ph.D.

Fulfilling one of her goals, she found a job as a college business instructor. "I just applied for the job and I got it," she says. "I am lucky to have immediately started doing what I was well-educated for and I think this is appreciated by both my students and the college."

Despite her good fortune, Gerenska says she still can't stop thinking about how much immigrant potential is wasted. "If Canada wants to attract high-calibre immigrants, it should have a system to maximize their potential once they arrive. Why go through such an elaborate screening procedure if this is not the case?"

Gerenska's success is proof that skilled immigrants have what it takes to contribute to Canada; they just need an employer to give them their first chance.

—*Margaret Jetelina*

Upgrading and Retraining

There is probably no better way to **upgrade** your skills these days than to become more skilled in computer technology. An employment centre, your local college, or your local library can provide information on the kinds of jobs that are in demand in your city and where to obtain training for them. You will likely notice them just by looking at the classified section in the newspaper. While it is always important to pursue a career that interests you, it's also a good idea to pursue a career that has job potential.

Many private business schools offer computer courses, as well as courses in virtually every career area. Before you enroll and pay a school any fee, check out its credentials with the Better Business Bureau and ask for references from former students. (See Chapter 11—Education for details on different types of colleges and universities.)

The Interview

If you make it to the interview stage, you're doing well. Keep in mind that every interview, even those that don't result in a job offer, provides an opportunity to practise your interview skills. In fact, it is a good idea to conduct practice job interviews with a friend before you launch your job search.

Keep in mind that you should arrive for an interview about ten minutes early, as many companies will ask you to complete an official job application form before your interview. This is always the case with agencies.

Prior to any interview, review the advertised job description so you know precisely what the employer is looking for. Practise a number of brief presentations outlining your experience, education, training, and skills, and how they will contribute to the job and the company.

Tell the interviewer everything about yourself that relates to the job: your volunteer experience, your hobbies, your travelling experience, the books you read, and the clubs or associations you belong to. But, again, keep your comments focused and to the point.

Research the company on the Internet. Find out as much about the company ahead of time as possible, such as its products, services, size, departments, and the location of its offices. Before the interview, ask the receptionist for brochures, company literature, or even a copy of the annual report if it is a public company.

You should also prepare some answers to the questions the employer may ask you. The following questions are fairly standard in most interviewing situations, so you should be ready to answer them.

- **"Why did you leave your last job?"**
  No matter how you feel about your last employer or your last position, never speak negatively about the company or anyone in it. Speak honestly about your desire to expand your horizons or your need for a career change.
- **"Tell me about yourself."**
  Provide a review of your experience in this field, your achievements, your education, and related training.

- **"What do you feel you have to offer to the job?"**
  Talk about your experience and skills that will be of direct benefit to the job.
- **"Why do you want to work for our company?"**
  You must show that you are particularly interested in this company's success in the marketplace, its innovative plans for the future, or the opportunity for advancement.
- **"What are your greatest strengths and weaknesses?"**
  If you have great organizational abilities or leadership strengths, this is the place to recite them. As for weaknesses, you obviously don't want to give a list here, but perhaps you might mention something like, "I'm a bit of a perfectionist. So I guess I need to lighten up a bit!"
- **"What starting salary do you expect?"**
  A good response I have used is, "What does this position pay?" You can then tell them what you hope to earn. Leave the bottom end open so you have some flexibility. You might want to add that you would be willing to start at a lower salary if a salary review could be guaranteed in three or six months.
- **"Do you have any questions for us?"**
  Your questions, while designed to provide you with answers, will also provide the interviewer with some valuable information about you: how much homework you've done on the company; how well you understand the company and the position; how well developed your oral communication skills are; how comfortable you are thinking and communicating in a stressful situation; and how curious or interested you are overall. Remember, however, that any questions you ask should sound natural and sincere. And make sure you don't ask a question that has already been answered. You may want to ask what plans the company has for expanding or where the company ranks against its major competitors. Or you might inquire how recent events, such as tax changes, trade pacts, or a company merger, will affect the company and its market. It is also important that you know what not to ask. Never ask when you will get a raise, if you have to work weekends or evenings, how long lunch breaks are, if you can smoke on the job (you can't), or how much vacation time you'll get. These questions can be asked when you are offered the job.

Creating a Good Impression

While the following points may seem obvious to some, I believe that they are so vital to a successful interview, I have included them.

- **Dress appropriately.**
  While your wardrobe is a personal matter during your leisure time, at a job interview your clothes and grooming say much about who you are. At the risk of making myself sound like an overbearing, conservative parent, I think you should cut your hair, shine your shoes, iron your shirt, put on deodorant, avoid chewing gum, cut down on the perfume, not wear any big jewellery, and avoid wearing anything too short, too tight, or too revealing.
- **Dress for the job.**
  If the job is in an office, you should dress for business. If it is in a clothing store, you could wear something flashier. If it is at a courier service, you can get away with something more casual.
- **Demonstrate confidence and self-esteem.**
  Sit and stand up straight, speak firmly, and look directly at the person asking the questions. Practise a firm handshake without squeezing too hard.
- **Make small talk.**
  A bit of small talk at the beginning of the interview—about the weather, some major news story, or sports event, but never about religion or politics—can sometimes relax both parties.
- **Thank the interviewer.**
  A short note of thanks to the employer following the interview might set you apart from the other candidates. Even if you don't get the job, the employer might remember your good manners when another job comes up.

Your Rights as a Worker

On the subject of getting a job in Canada, it is helpful to know a few things about Canada's human rights legislation, which was designed to ensure equal opportunities for everyone in all areas of life in Canada.

Employers may not discriminate against anyone on the basis of race, colour, national or ethnic origin, religion, age, family or marital status, sexual orientation, disability, or pardoned conviction. If you feel that you are being discriminated against by your employer, take your claim to your provincial or territorial Human Rights Commission or the Labour Relations Board in your city.

Employment Standards

Canadian employment laws are designed to ensure fair treatment and compensation for workers. Every province has employment standards that govern work hours, overtime pay, holidays, minimum wage, and termination of employment.

Every province has also established a set of regulations governing farm workers, domestic help, live-in help, commissioned salespeople, and working students. For specific information on any of these areas, check out the Employment Standards Branch or the Ministry of Labour in your province.

Fairly standard work guidelines across Canada have established that the average workweek is around 40 hours and that employees are entitled to at least one half-hour eating break for every five consecutive hours worked. Employees who are asked to work longer hours are generally paid overtime.

Also, employers must withhold deductions from all paycheques for income tax, Canada Pension Plan, and Employment Insurance premiums. These must be sent to the government monthly. There may be other deductions for union dues or medical insurance. Generally, however, employers cannot withhold money from paycheques for any other reason without their employees' written permission.

Employers should give employees a statement with every paycheque, showing the employees' gross earnings less deductions. And every February, employers must present employees with T4 slips certifying the total amount of these deductions that were withheld and submitted to the government for the employees.

Employees who become **unemployed** because of a layoff, termination of employment, sickness, or birth or adoption of a child may be entitled to receive Employment Insurance (EI) benefits for a limited time. This is a temporary payment made to unemployed individuals based on their prior earnings, and paid for by regular contributions made by workers through mandatory payroll deductions and by employers. For more information, contact your nearest employment centre (also see Chapter 5—Assistance Available).

```
┌─────────────────────────────────────────────────────────────────┐
│  ABC                    INDIVIDUAL PAY RECORD                     │
│  Company                                                          │
│                         DATE                                      │
│  123 Main Street                                                  │
│  Toronto, Ontario       EMPLOYEE NO.          DEPARTMENT NO.      │
│  ████ SALARY PARTICULARS ███████████████    CURRENT    YTD        │
│                                             ┌─────────┬─────────┐ │
│                                             │         │         │ │
│                                             │         │         │ │
│  ████████████████ GROSS PAY █████████████   │         │         │ │
│            TOTAL DEDUCTIONS                 │         │         │ │
│            NET PAY                          └─────────┴─────────┘ │
│  will be credited to account                                     │
│  at the                                                          │
│  Salary year-to-date (YTD) since 1 July All other YTD(s) since 1 January │
│                                                                   │
│  ████ DEDUCTIONS ████    CURRENT    YTD    ┌────────────────────┐ │
│  Income Tax                                │                    │ │
│  Canada Pension                            │                    │ │
│  CUPE                                      │        A           │ │
│  Employment Insurance                      │       C B          │ │
│  Parking Fees                              │                    │ │
│                                            │                    │ │
│  ┌──────────────────────────┐             └────────────────────┘ │
│  │                          │                                    │
└─────────────────────────────────────────────────────────────────┘
```

Annual Vacations

After one year of employment, an employee is entitled to a paid vacation of one or two weeks annually, depending on the province, with payment for this period equaling about 4 percent of the employee's annual wages.

General Holidays

Employees are generally entitled to nine paid statutory holidays each year. These holidays consist of New Year's Day, Good Friday, Victoria Day, Canada Day, Labour Day, Thanksgiving Day, Remembrance Day, Christmas Day, and Boxing Day. With some exceptions, workers who are asked to work on these holidays should receive overtime pay of one-and-a-half times to two-and-a-half times their regular pay.

Maternity and Parental Leave

A female employee who has worked for 600 hours in the last 52 weeks is entitled to 15 weeks of maternity leave to have her child. In addition, an employee, male or female, who assumes the care of a newborn or newly adopted child is entitled to **parental leave** of up to 35 weeks. The total duration of the maternity and the parental leaves must not exceed 52 weeks.

Statutory Holidays		
Holiday	**Date**	
New Year's Day	January 1	The first day of the calendar year.
Good Friday	Friday before Easter Sunday	Observation of the day when Christ was crucified.
Victoria Day	Monday on or before May 21	Celebration of both Queen Victoria's and the ruling monarch's birthdays. Victoria Day is not a statutory holiday in Atlantic Canada.
Canada Day	July 1	Celebration of Canada's formation in 1867.
Labour Day	First Monday in September	Celebration of the efforts of workers.
Thanksgiving Day	Second Monday in October	A day to give thanks for everything one has. Thanksgiving Day is not a statutory holiday in Atlantic Canada.
Remembrance Day	November 11	A day to honour those who have died in war. Marks the anniversary of the end of World War I. Remembrance Day is not a statutory holiday in Ontario, Quebec, or Newfoundland and Labrador.
Christmas Day	December 25	Celebration of the birth of Christ.
Boxing Day	December 26	The day after Christmas.

Termination of Employment

Employees are generally entitled to one or two weeks' written notice of termination, or pay instead of notice in the case of an abrupt termination, when their employer wants to end their employment. The exception is when the employee is dismissed for just cause, meaning that the employee has done something for which he or she can be fired.

Within five days of termination of employment, employers must provide employees with a Record of Employment, which is required by employees in order to obtain Employment Insurance benefits.

Unjust Dismissal

Employees who believe they have been unjustly dismissed may submit written complaints of unjust dismissal with their provincial Ministry of Labour.

The Canadian Union of Public Employees or CUPE (pronounced "CUE-pee") is Canada's largest union. It represents more than 500,000 workers in Canada who are employed in a wide range of fields including health care, education, municipal government, transportation, and the airline industry.

Wage Recovery

If an employer has not paid an employee wages or other amounts to which the employee is entitled, that employee should take his or her claim to the local Labour Relations Board, and the board will attempt to get payment for the employee from the employer. Unionized workers should talk to their union office.

Workers' Compensation Benefits

Workers' compensation boards and commissions are provincially- and territorially-operated programs that offer no-fault insurance for workers injured in work-related accidents at insured companies in Canada. "No-fault" means that workers are compensated for injuries received regardless of how or why the accident occurred or who caused it. Workers' compensation benefits entitle injured workers to some or all of their lost wages while unable to work, although by accepting the benefits, workers give up any right to sue an employer for providing unsafe working conditions, if this was indeed the case.

Workers' compensation premiums are paid by employers based on the type of work performed by their employees and the number of employees they have. Employees must obtain medical attention and advise their employer as soon as possible after getting injured.

Employees will receive wages, occupational therapy, and **retraining** or vocational counselling if necessary.

Key Words

accreditation: the official approval that says a school, etc. meets certain requirements

association: a group of people or organizations who join or work together for a particular purpose

career: a job or profession for which you are trained and which you do for a long time, often with the chance to move to a higher position

classified advertisements (also classifieds): the section in a newspaper with small advertisements grouped together based on their subject, for people or small companies that want to buy or sell something, offer or find a job, etc.

cold calling: the practice of telephoning somebody that you do not know, in order to sell him/her something

communication: the act of making information or your opinions, feelings, etc. known to somebody

contract worker: a person hired on an official written agreement between the person and his/her employer for a fixed period of time

credentials: the skills, training, and experience that show you are qualified to do something; documents such as letters that prove that you are who you say you are, and can therefore be trusted

curriculum vitae (also CV): a written record of your education, qualifications and employment, which you send when you are applying for a job

diplomacy: skill in dealing with people

employment agency: a business or an organization that helps people find jobs and employers find workers

experience: the things that you have done; the knowledge or skill that you get from seeing or doing something

job hunting: the act of looking for a job

licence to practise: an official paper, card, etc. that shows you are allowed to do something

marketing: deciding how something can be sold most easily, e.g. what price it should be or how it should be advertised

maternity leave: a period of time when a woman leaves her job temporarily to give birth and care for a baby

networking: trying to meet and talk to people who may be able to help you advance in your work

non-regulated occupation: an occupation that does not need a special licence and that may need little or extensive education and training

occupation: a job

outsourcing: the act of arranging for somebody outside a company to do work or provide goods for that company

parental leave: a period of time when a parent leaves his/her job temporarily to care for a baby

position: (formal) a job

profession: a job that requires a lot of training and that is respected by other people

reference: a person who gives a statement or writes a letter describing a person's character and ability to do a job, etc.

regulatory body: a group of people that control a business or industry to ensure it is operating fairly

requirement: something that you need or that is demanded

retraining: learning, or teaching somebody, a new type of work, a new skill, etc.

skilled labour: work, especially of a hard, physical kind, that requires skill or skills

standards of practice: a set of rules against which professional practices can be measured

supervisor: a person who oversees somebody or something to make sure that work, etc. is being done correctly or that behaviour is appropriate

trade: a job for which you need special skill, especially with your hands

trade journal: a magazine, especially one in which all the articles are about a particular area of business and the people or companies that are connected with it

training: preparation for a sport or job, or learning new skills

unemployed: not having a job; out of work

upgrading: changing something so that it is of a higher standard

volunteer work: work done by a person who offers or agrees to do it without being forced or paid to do it

Note: Entries taken or adapted from the Oxford ESL Dictionary

Creating Your Canadian Experience

1. On the Canadian Information Centre for International Credentials (CICIC) website (www.cicic.ca) find out if your profession is regulated.

   Regulated _____   Non-regulated _____

2. If your profession is regulated, find out what the regulatory body in your province is. This information should be on the CICIC website.

   Name: _____

   Contact Information: _____

3. If your profession is regulated, find out what steps need to be taken in order to be recognized.
   Tip: type the name of the regulatory body from Question #2 into a search engine to find its website, which should have the information you need.

   Step 1: _____

   Step 2: _____

   Step 3: _____

   Step 4: _____

4. Create the following lists to help in your career planning.

Skills	Experiences	Strengths	Weaknesses
_____	_____	_____	_____
_____	_____	_____	_____
_____	_____	_____	_____
_____	_____	_____	_____
_____	_____	_____	_____

5. List three places where you could do volunteer work to give you Canadian experience in your field.
Tip: type the name of your city, the name of your occupation, and "Volunteer" into a search engine.

a. _____

b. _____

c, _____

6. In order to better understand what type of career might be good for you, list the jobs and tasks that you have done in the past. Divide them into two categories: those you liked and those you disliked.

Jobs You Liked	Jobs You Disliked
_____	_____
_____	_____
_____	_____
_____	_____
_____	_____
_____	_____

7. Research the employment centre nearest your home. Look under "Employment" in your local phone book.

Address: _____

_____

Hours: _____

8. List three different publications whose classified sections you could search through. Try to pick at least one newspaper and at least one magazine.
Tip: look for these publications at the library, where you can look through magazines and newspapers for free.

a. _____

b. _____

c. _____

9. Using the publications you found in Question #8, find out which companies are hiring people in your job field. Create a contact list of these companies. Once you have finished the list, you can send them a letter and resume.

Organization	Contact Person	Mailing Address	Email Address

10. Below are some common interview questions that you might be asked. Write down your answers.

Possible Interview Question	Your Answer
Tell me about yourself.	
Why did you leave your last job?	
What do you feel you have to offer to the job?	
Why do you want to work for our company?	
What are your greatest strengths and weaknesses?	
What starting salary do you expect?	

11. Write down a few questions that you could ask potential employers in an interview. (It is good to have a lot since some will get answered during the interview.)

_____

_____

_____

_____

_____

12. Look up the employment standards for your province.
Tip: type the name of your province and "Employment Standards" into a search engine. What are the rules in the following areas?

Work hours per week	
Overtime pay	
Holidays	
Minimum wage	
Termination of employment	

Chapter 11

Education

In This Chapter

- How do you enroll your children in school?
- What education options are available after high school?
- How do you get a student loan or scholarship?
- What's the environment like for retraining as an adult?

The School System

Every child between the ages of 5 and 18 is entitled to attend school. Approximately 95 percent of students attend government-funded schools, where attendance is free up to the end of grade 12. At some of these schools, parents may be required to pay extra for some supplies and equipment, as well as for field trips or excursions.

About 5 percent of the students in Canada attend private schools, which are partially funded by the government, but also charge parents **tuition fees** for each student. Many require students to wear uniforms. You can find private schools listed in your phone book.

Children attending elementary or **secondary school** in Quebec will receive instruction in French unless they have been **enrolled** in an English school elsewhere in Canada, or one of their parents was educated in English in Canada. Otherwise, all newcomers to Quebec, with the exception of those residing in the province temporarily, must attend a French-language school.

There are progressive levels in the Canadian education system for children beginning at age five, when they enter kindergarten. This first level of education extends from kindergarten to the end of grade 6 or 8, depending on the province. Students then graduate to secondary education or high school. In some provinces, students move into junior high school for grades 7, 8, and 9 before moving to senior high school for grades 10, 11, and 12. At the end of grade 12, they graduate from high school. Most students at this stage, aged 17 or 18, will enter the workforce or proceed to some form of post-secondary education.

High school is an important stepping stone to **higher education**, as students need to take the **required courses** in high school to qualify for certain programs at the university or college level. The high school curriculum covers core subjects such as English, French, and sciences. While some programs are designed to prepare students who plan to work immediately upon graduation from high school, other programs lead students to college or university.

Outline of the Canadian Education System

Province	Kindergarten	Grade 1	Grade 2	Grade 3	Grade 4	Grade 5	Grade 6	Grade 7	Grade 8	Grade 9	Grade 10	Grade 11	Grade 12
BC	Elementary								Secondary School				
AB	Elementary							Junior High			Senior High		
SK	Kindergarten	Elementary					Middle Level				Secondary Level		
MB	Early Years					Middle Years				Senior Years			
ON	JK/SK	Elementary								Secondary			
QC	Garderie/Maternelle	École Primaire						Sec I	Sec II	Sec III	Sec IV	Sec V	CEGEP
NS	Elementary							Junior High			Senior High		
NB	Elementary						Middle Level			High School			
NF	Kindergarten	Primary			Elementary			Junior High			Senior High		
PEI	Kindergarten	Elementary						Intermediate			Senior High		

Source: Council of Ministers of Education, Canada

Parent Involvement

It is, therefore, important that parents take an active role in their child's schooling beginning at the primary level. Most schools in Canada offer parents an opportunity to get involved in their child's education through a **Parent Advisory Council** or some similar school group. Whether you get involved at this level or on a more informal level, you should consider discussing your child's education and career goals to ensure they are taking the appropriate courses long before they begin high school.

School **counsellors** can also help when it comes to discussing your child's future. A student's **academic standing** in high school may also determine which **institution** and programs he or she will be admitted to at the post-secondary level. You might, therefore, want to talk to a teacher or a counsellor to learn how much homework your child should be completing every night while in high school.

Jinny Sims: Schoolteacher and Beyond

Indian-born Jinny Sims is the former president of the BC Teachers' Federation, but she started out as a schoolteacher herself, first in England and then in Canada.

"We're in Canada by accident, really," Sims says. "My husband and I were looking to go overseas for a year or two, and Quebec was advertising for teachers."

They applied immediately. After working in Quebec, the couple decided to head out west, and they have never left.

When BC teachers began the drive to unionize, Sims decided to get involved and after a few years she became president of the BC Teachers' Federation in Vancouver. She was only the sixth woman to hold the top post of the union group since it began in 1917.

"In Canada, education is the great equalizer. It's also the cornerstone of democracy. With public education, you have an informed citizenship, no matter what your background. Everyone should have equal access to resources."

—Margaret Jetelina

No matter what grade your child is in, you should not hesitate to get involved in your child's education. It is not unusual to call his or her teacher with questions regarding school-related problems, whether they are academic or personal. Should you want to speak to your child's teacher, it is probably best to call and make an appointment, or send a note to the school requesting a meeting, rather than just showing up and expecting to talk.

Enrolling in School

Elementary Schools

For information on enrolling your child in the public school system, contact your local **school board** or simply go to the school nearest your residence. If the school is unable to accept your child for any reason, you will be directed to someone who can help you find an appropriate school. Generally, **elementary school** children—those attending kindergarten to grade 7 or 8— will be enrolled in the school nearest to their home, although in some regions students may have to take a bus to school.

It may be necessary for your child to be tested for his or her language and math skills before being placed in a class. Feel free to discuss the placement with your child's teacher or guidance counsellor.

Children who do not speak English fluently can be placed in English as a Second Language (ESL) classes. These are usually taught in small groups that meet both during and after regular class time. ESL students may attend regular classes for most of the day, then move to a different classroom for language instruction with other new Canadians. Elementary teachers tend to nurture the children when teaching ESL by playing games, using artwork, film, dance, and music, as it is less challenging and easier for the students to grasp.

The ESL difficulty levels rise depending on the learning growth of the child, and also the advancement of schools. As they progress, children learning ESL will begin to engage in more everyday use of English, including using computers and reading newspapers.

The following documents may be required to enroll your child in school and to ensure he or she is placed in the appropriate class:

- Birth certificate
- Immigration landing papers
- Passport

Q: What school supplies do I need to buy for my children?

A: The supplies your children need will vary depending on what grades they are in. For the first day of school, make sure that your children have backpacks, notebooks, pens or pencils, and pencil cases; their teachers will tell them what additional supplies they will need. If your children are in elementary school, their school may provide some items that students will use on a daily basis.

- Medical and immunization records
- All previous school records and transcripts

The Canadian education system guarantees an education to all children, including children with disabilities, such as sight and hearing impairments. These children are frequently referred to as students with special needs. Depending on their individual needs, children are either integrated into regular classrooms and provided with additional help or provided with special classes or schools.

Your school board will be able to help you find the right school and class to accommodate your children and their needs.

Secondary Schools

Secondary school students may be enrolled at the school nearest their home or they may want or need to attend a school in another region. The school board responsible for your municipality will be able to provide you with direction to the most appropriate school.

Some school districts split the secondary school grades into grades 8 to 10, called junior high, and grades 11 to 12, called senior high.

Parent-teacher Interviews

Your child's school in your country of origin may have had parent-teacher interviews, although some immigrants I have met have not been exposed to these meetings. You do not need to get stressed out about parent-teacher interviews. They will definitely help you and your children! The first thing I would suggest is that you talk to your child's teacher, well before your first parent-teacher interview, about the fact that you and your family are new Canadians. Teachers today are very aware of the pressures children face during the immigration process and will try to make the transition an easy one for your child.

Parent-teacher interviews are arranged by your child's school, usually once or twice each school year, and they tend to be scheduled around the same time that students get their report cards. You will receive a notice from the school that will let you know when the interviews will take place. An afternoon or evening will be set aside for interviews, with each parent booking a period of 10 to 15 minutes to speak with the teacher.

Before meeting with your child's teacher, think about what you want to discuss during the interview. Since you will only have a short period of time for the parent-teacher interview, you should know exactly what you want to accomplish. Review your child's report card and recent school work, and ask your child if he or she has any school-related concerns. Make a list of any questions you want to ask the teacher.

You will generally meet with your child's teacher in a classroom or the school's gym. Make sure you arrive by your scheduled time; other parents will be waiting to discuss their children's progress and will not want to give up any of their time with the teacher.

During the interview, ask your questions and listen to what the teacher has to say about your child. Children spend many hours at school each day, so their teachers get to know them fairly well and may have some important observations about them. Be prepared to discuss your child's strengths as well as weaknesses: teachers try to identify areas where your child needs improvement in order to help your child have the best possible experience in school.

You do not need to limit the discussion to your child's school work. Feel free to ask the teacher how your child gets along with other students, both in the classroom and on the schoolyard. Social relationships can have a huge effect on how students feel about school, so if they are not getting along with their classmates, their school work may suffer.

Any time you discuss your child's progress with his or her teacher, you should then talk to your child about the same topic. After all, there's no point in you and the teacher agreeing that your child needs to improve on a particular subject if you never actually encourage your child to do so.

After the parent-teacher interview, you can maintain ongoing communication with you child's teacher through emails, letters, or phone calls. Teachers want to work with parents to make sure that all students do as well as possible in school, so they will be happy to discuss any concerns with you. Keep in mind, however, that teachers have busy schedules and many students, so be respectful of their time.

Post-Secondary Education

After graduating from high school, students can pursue their studies through any of a variety of post-secondary institutions.

About 44 percent of Canada's working-age population aged 25 to 64 has a college or university **degree**–making Canada the highest ranked of all 21 OECD (Organization for Economic Cooperation and Development) countries.

Formal **vocational** or career training prepares students for skilled trades. Training programs can range in duration from a few months to several years. They can include courses in subjects such as food services, hairdressing, computer technology, practical nursing, car mechanics, and architectural drafting. Before obtaining a licence to practise some trades, you may need to complete formal training followed by a term of **apprenticeship**. Since this process is determined provincially, you may have to re-qualify to practise your trade if you move to a new province.

Community colleges offer diploma and certificate programs in technical and academic subjects. These programs, which can be completed in one to three years, often include first- and second-year arts and science programs and career programs for those interested in subjects such as criminology, accounting, food services, journalism, or forestry. This category of schools can also include art colleges or institutions dealing with computer programming, airplane mechanics, or the construction trade. These institutions may be called colleges of applied arts and technology, institutes of applied arts and sciences, community colleges, vocational colleges, university-oriented colleges, or technical institutes. In Quebec, these colleges are known as collèges d'enseignement général et professionnel, or CEGEPs.

Some colleges offer university transfer courses, which means a student can complete the first and second years of a university program and then transfer to a university for the third and fourth years. Many students choose to attend college before they go to university for a number of reasons, such as the smaller class sizes, a smaller campus that is often closer to home, and cheaper tuition. Students should check to ensure that their college courses are **transferable** to a university program, if their goal is to attend university.

Universities offer multi-year degree and **post-degree** programs in arts, sciences, business, and other academic and professional fields. A three- or four-year undergraduate degree is required for acceptance into professional programs such as law or medicine. A law degree usually takes an additional three years of study, followed by a year articling with a law firm, followed by the successful completion of bar examinations. Degrees in medicine (MD) require three to four years beyond a bachelor's degree, then a one- or two-year internship, after which students obtain a licence to practise. A master's degree can generally be completed in two years following an undergraduate degree, while a further three to six years is required to complete a doctorate (PhD).

The University of King's College, founded in Windsor, Nova Scotia in 1789, is Canada's oldest university. When a fire destroyed its main building in 1920, King's College moved to Halifax and began an affiliation with Dalhousie University; its approximately 1,100 students can now study at both schools.

While colleges and universities require students to possess a high school diploma or equivalent, many do permit mature students, who may have been out of school for several years, to enroll without the necessary high school courses, provided they have shown ability in the subject. Also, many post-secondary institutions allow students to audit courses—that is, the students may attend the class, but cannot participate in **exams** or receive **credits** for attending.

As the demand for university courses is usually greater than the number of available spaces, students should apply to the institution of their choice as far in advance as possible. In fact, students should apply to several schools of their choice. Many programs restrict entrance only to those students who have obtained above-average grades at the secondary school level. Most post-secondary schools operate on a **trimester** or **semester** system, meaning courses require three months or six months, respectively, to complete.

Students earn credits for all school courses successfully completed, with each program requiring a specific number of total credits in order to graduate. In most programs, students must complete certain **core courses**, but are also given some choice in the subjects they take. A great deal of reading and research is required to complete most of these courses. It is a good idea for you and your child to discuss with a school counsellor how many hours per week your child will need to spend on schoolwork outside the classroom to successfully complete the course.

Area	Average Earnings (2000)			
	High School or Less	College or Trades	University	Total Level of Schooling
Canada	$34,631	$41,072	$61,156	$43,298
Newfoundland and Labrador	$29,495	$35,807	$54,115	$37,910
Prince Edward Island	$27,167	$31,819	$48,198	$33,511
Nova Scotia	$30,787	$34,630	$52,982	$37,872
New Brunswick	$29,734	$34,946	$50,587	$36,094
Quebec	$31,329	$36,693	$55,975	$39,217
Ontario	$37,434	$44,321	$66,900	$47,299
Manitoba	$30,227	$36,150	$52,363	$36,729
Saskatchewan	$29,358	$35,140	$51,014	$35,461
Alberta	$35,037	$43,302	$63,473	$44,130
British Columbia	$36,807	$43,045	$58,057	$44,307
Yukon Territory	$36,641	$43,835	$57,248	$44,605
Northwest Territories	$42,015	$52,751	$66,953	$51,869
Nunavut	$38,254	$50,084	$67,941	$48,078

Source: Statistics Canada

You should then discuss with your child how much time he or she is willing to devote to the program, as well as to sports activities, employment, and social activities, in order to ensure the student is aware of the responsibilities and commitment required by an undergraduate program. It is a waste of your money and everyone's time if your child is not prepared for the demands of post-secondary schooling.

All post-secondary courses successfully completed will earn students **credits** toward a **degree**, diploma, or **certificate**. A bachelor's degree in arts, science, or business administration generally takes three or four academic years of eight months each. An honours degree usually requires four academic years. Some universities offer courses throughout the calendar year, which allows students to complete a degree more quickly.

While the cost of attending post-secondary learning institutions is about 75 percent covered by taxes, students must also pay tuition fees to attend.

Viet Le: One Immigrant's Post-Secondary Perspective

Viet Le came to Canada as a four-year-old refugee from Vietnam. Educated entirely in Canada, with two degrees, in biology and computer science, Le has some interesting points about choosing the right post-secondary education.

"I think college would have prepared me so much better than going straight to university, for I struggled in my first two years. Not to mention it would have saved me a few thousand dollars," he says, noting that colleges may charge half the price for tuition, as compared to universities.

Another tip: do not take a full course load. "Post-secondary work loads are very heavy," says Le. "Take only four courses per term until you can adjust to the pace. Some professors like to assign two chapters of reading on the first day of classes."

For those whose grades aren't quite high enough to enter university directly from high school, Le says that going to college first and then transferring to university is much easier, even with less-than-perfect grades. But make sure you take college courses that are transferable; not all courses will be recognized by universities.

—*Margaret Jetelina*

Tuition fees can range from $3,000 to $9,000 for an eight-month term, depending on the institution and the program. Generally, medical, science, and business programs cost more than arts programs. And generally, the tuition paid by the 130,000 or so international students who study here each year is about double the fees paid by Canadian residents. Of course, living expenses, books, and equipment are additional costs.

University and college calendars provide a wealth of information regarding entrance requirements, student services, housing, tuition fees, **scholarships**, and a variety of other subjects of interest to prospective students. You can obtain a calendar by writing to the university's or college's office of admissions.

For more information on education or on a specific school, check out the blue pages in the telephone book.

Financial Assistance for Students

A number of programs are available to help students who need assistance in financing their education. These include scholarships, **bursaries**, awards, and loans.

Generally, scholarships are financial awards given to students for outstanding academic achievement; bursaries are awarded on the basis of financial need. Students may also qualify for numerous other awards that acknowledge outstanding achievements or contributions to the school or larger community.

Scholarships are frequently provided by private corporations, unions, religious institutions, service groups, and foundations. Some employers offer scholarships or bursaries to children of their employees.

Students interested in applying for any of the above should check with the college or university administration to obtain a list of available scholarships and bursaries. You might also want to check at your local library and on the Internet. Hundreds of scholarships and bursaries are available every year, and many are not paid out simply because no one applies to receive the funds. Students can check out the **qualifications** necessary for various scholarships and obtain application forms through their student counselling office or **school administration**. Some scholarships need to be applied for months before school begins.

Maclean's 16th Annual Rankings (2006 Nov.)		
Medical Doctor Ranking	Comprehensive Ranking	Primary Undergraduate Ranking
1 McGill	Guelph	St. Francis Xavier
2 Queen's	Waterloo	Mount Allison
3 Toronto	Victoria	Acadia
4 UBC	Simon Fraser	UNBC
5 Western	Memorial	UPEI

In 2006, 26 schools refused to participate in *Maclean's* ranking of universities and did not complete questionnaires.

Source: Maclean's *magazine*

Most post-secondary institutions have established policies regarding scholarships, awards, and bursaries. These define who is eligible to apply, how scholarships are awarded, and what penalties can be levied for making false statements on an application.

Student Loans

The purpose of the Canada Student Loans program and the provincial student loan assistance programs is to assist students who might otherwise not be able to attend school full-time because of a lack of financial resources. Generally, funds are granted only when students have used up other sources of financing, such as their parents and their income from employment, and still have insufficient funds to meet the estimated costs of post-secondary education. Normally, the funds provided under these programs are disbursed through a combination of the Canada Student Loans program and the provincial student assistance program.

Canada Student Loans generally cover about 60 percent of students' expenses during their study period, with the maximum Canada Student Loans assistance available for full-time students currently set at about $165 for each week of study. Provincial funding and private resources are expected to make up the balance required, about another $100 per week.

The exact amount you can borrow will depend on your individual needs and on such expenses as tuition, textbooks, supplies, transportation to school, and childcare expenses during class time.

$10,000 Loan Over 5, 7, and 10 Years

Loan Repayment Calculator	Your Loan at Graduation	Interest Rate	Number of Monthly Payments	Amount of Each Monthly Payment	Total Interest Payable	Total Amount Payable
Option 1	$10,000	6.0%	60	$217.42	$3,045.45	$13,045.45
Option 2	$10,000	6.0%	84	$171.22	$4,382.85	$14,382.85
Option 3	$10,000	6.0%	120	$137.75	$6,530.00	$16,530.00

$25,000 Loan Over 5, 7, and 10 Years

Loan Repayment Calculator	Your Loan at Graduation	Interest Rate	Number of Monthly Payments	Amount of Each Monthly Payment	Total Interest Payable	Total Amount Payable
Option 1	$25,000	6.0%	60	$543.56	$ 7,613.63	$32,613.63
Option 2	$25,000	6.0%	84	$428.06	$10,957.12	$35,957.12
Option 3	$25,000	6.0%	120	$344.38	$15,325.00	$41,325.00

Source: Human Resources and Social Development Canada

Interest on your student loan will be paid by the federal or provincial government for as long as you are registered as a full-time student. Under some circumstances, you may apply to delay paying interest for up to 30 months after leaving school. Normally, however, a borrower must begin repaying the loan, with interest, six months after completing or quitting school. A portion of that interest payment is tax deductible. Generally, the interest paid by the government on a student's behalf during four years of education will amount to about $4,000 on a $25,000 student loan.

Applications for loans are available from the admissions offices or financial aid offices at most colleges and universities. In general, student loans are available to Canadian citizens or permanent residents who are enrolled in full-time studies. Students from the United States may be able to apply for funding through the US Department of Education Student Financial Assistance Program, and use the loan toward tuition at most post-secondary institutions in Canada.

Students who are not Canadian citizens or permanent residents are generally not entitled to Canadian student loans, although they are generally entitled to scholarships and bursaries. They should arrange for financial assistance in their country of origin before arriving in Canada. Also, note that there are restrictions for foreign students finding employment while in Canada.

Under special circumstances, part-time students with demonstrated financial need, as well as students with disabilities or those with dependants, may qualify for a small federal study **grant** or a loan.

Q: Are marks the only factor that determine acceptance into university or are there other things my children can do to improve their chances?

A: The majority of admissions are still based on grades, but some universities are starting to look for other qualities in students as well. They look for participation in extracurricular activities like sports, work on student council, and volunteering experience.

Work-Study Programs

Some institutions may also offer a work-study program that provides employment to students while they are attending classes.

Youth Link is a publication that lists work, study, scholarship, and travel programs for youth funded by the Government of Canada. You can read the publication on HRSDC's website at www.youth.gc.ca, or call 1-800-935-5555 to request a paper copy.

Grants for Students with Disabilities

Students with permanent disabilities, such as blindness or deafness, may be eligible for a Canada Study Grant of up to $8,000 to cover exceptional education-related costs associated with that disability. Such grants may be used to pay for tutoring, interpreting, or special equipment required for education. You will be able to find details through your school's administration and financial aid officers.

Adult Education in Canada

Canada's economic value depends on the training and education of its workforce. The current Canadian population is aging—and aging fast. In order for Canada to continue to grow and be competitive, its current and future citizens must be educated and trained to reach their full potential. This potential can be reached by adults who are in the workforce returning to school to take either academic or skills-based courses.

Currently in Canada, it is apparent that adult workers are not keeping up with increasing skill demands, and cities such as Vancouver, Calgary, and Toronto are facing a worse critical skills shortage than has ever been seen before. For more than a decade, Canadians have known that this shortage would occur at some point. Well, that point is now upon us, and we are further behind than we thought. There are numerous reasons people have not taken part in training and educational upgrades, and the main one is probably the absence of motivation to study. There are also numerous barriers in the system, ranging from lack of access to training, to lack of funds, to working adults' busy schedules.

In Canada, participation rates in adult education training programs vary widely from Newfoundland, where 9 percent of the adult population take these courses, to British Columbia, where 18 percent take them, but what is obvious is that many adults participate in workforce training if it is employer-sponsored. It is also apparent that larger companies, which have more than one hundred employees and human resources departments, offer more training, and have a higher percentage of employees involved in training, than smaller companies without HR departments or company-sponsored training programs. Since most businesses in Canada are small businesses, a lot of effort is going to be necessary to increase the participation rates in education and training across the country.

In Canada, public-sector employees are more likely than private-sector employees to have their education funded by their employers (35 percent versus 20 percent), and full-time workers receive more benefits in terms of employer-sponsored education and training than part-time workers (27 percent versus 20 percent), according to *A Report on Adult Education and Training in Canada*.

Generally, participation rates are higher for males across Canada because many women participate in the economy as part-time workers, due to family commitments. Some of the sectors where employer-sponsored adult education and training are most supported include utilities; public administration; finance, insurance, and real estate; education, health, and welfare; and transportation. So, as a new Canadian, you may want to consider looking for jobs in these fields because they tend to support training and education programs.

While finding employers to fund training and education is possible, it is likely that for longer programs, employees will have to self-finance their education. So, if you are coming to Canada, be prepared to pay for some of your required training using your own resources, especially if you find work in a sector of the economy that is outside those mentioned above.

While there are barriers to education and training in Canada, such as high tuition fees, lack of evening courses, strict entrance requirements, limited course offerings, busy work schedules, and family responsibilities, there are lots of opportunities to participate. This training is valuable and it will help you find a job, improve your language, networking, and business skills, and help you feel more confident about your abilities. The knowledge you gain can probably be transferred from one career to another since many skills are portable and necessary in many careers.

Many working adults in Canada report that the training and education they received while on the job have definitely helped them to find more meaningful employment, become more productive, earn higher incomes, and integrate more quickly into Canadian society. These are things we want for all of our citizens in Canada.

Key Words

academic standing: the position or reputation of somebody in school

apprenticeship: the state or time of being an apprentice

certificate: an official piece of paper that says that something is true or correct

community college: a college that is mainly for students from the local community and that offers programs that are two years long. Some students go to another college or university after they have finished studying at a community college

core course (also required course): a course students must take to complete a program

counsellor: a person whose job is to give advice

credit: a unit of study at a school, college or university

degree: a qualification gained by successfully completing a program at a university

elementary school (also informal grade school): a school for children usually between the ages of 4 and 13

enroll: become or to make somebody a member of a club, school, etc.

examination (also exam): a written, spoken or practical test of what you know or can do, especially at the end of a course

grant: money that is given (by the government, etc.) for a particular purpose

higher education: education at a college or university

institution: a large organization such as a bank, a university, etc.

Parent Advisory Council (also PAC): a group of people chosen to represent parents and guardians of school children who give advice and to encourage parental involvement

post-degree: (of a course of study) carried on after completing a bachelor's degree in order to get a higher degree, diploma or certificate

qualification: a skill or quality that makes you suitable to do something, such as a job

required course: a course that students must take to complete a program

scholarship: an amount of money that is given to a person by an organization or a school or college, in order to help pay for his/her studies or for travel or research connected with his/her studies

school administration: the group of people who organize or control a school

school board: a group of people who have been elected to be in charge of the public schools in a city or an area

secondary school: a school for young people usually between the ages of 11 and 18

semester: one of two periods of time into which a school, college or university year is divided

transferable: that can be moved from one place or person to another

trimester: each of three terms of a school year at some high schools, colleges, etc.

tuition fee: the money that a student must pay in order to take classes at a college, university, or private school

vocational: connected with the skills or qualifications that you need to do a particular job, especially a job that involves working with tools

Note: Entries taken or adapted from the Oxford ESL Dictionary

Creating Your Canadian Experience

1. Research the school progression in your province. For each age, fill in the grade and the type of school (Kindergarten, Elementary, Junior High School/Middle School, High School).
Tip: type the name of your province and "Education" into a search engine to find your provincial ministry of education. The ministry's website should have the information you are looking for.

Age	Grade	School	Age	Grade	School
4			12		
5			13		
6			14		
7			15		
8			16		
9			17		
10			18		
11			19		

2. Search the Internet or your local phone book for the school nearest your home.
   Tip: if you are searching online, type the name of your city and "Education" into a search engine.

   Address: _____

   _____

3. What is the start time and end time for children in the school nearest your home? You may need to call the school to find out.

   Start: _____ am   End: _____ pm

4. Contact your local school board and find out what documentation is necessary to enroll children in school.
   Tip: to find the phone number for your school board, type the name of your city and "School Board" into a search engine.

   a. _____

   b. _____

   c. _____

   d. _____

5. Search the Internet for schools that offer continuing education near your home.
   Tip: type the name of your city and "Continuing Education" into a search engine.

   Address: _____

   _____

6. What courses could you take there? The school's website should have a listing of the programs it offers. If it doesn't, call the school to find out what courses are available.

   a. _____

   b. _____

   c. _____

Chapter 12

Driving in Canada

In This Chapter

- How do you get a driver's licence?
- Can you bring your car to Canada?
- What's involved in buying a car?
- How do you get car insurance?

Putting yourself in the driver's seat can be a complicated and costly process in Canada.

First, you need a driver's licence. Your foreign driver's licence may be valid for only three to six months, so it is a good idea to get an international driver's licence before you leave your home country.

In Ontario, there are different guidelines than there are in the rest of Canada. For example, drivers from another country may drive for 60 days after they arrive in Canada after which they are required to take an Ontario driving test to remain licensed.

However, if you are a licensed driver from the US, Japan, Korea, Switzerland, Germany, France, Great Britain, or Austria, and have been driving for two years or more, you may get your Ontario licence without taking a knowledge or **road test**.

Sooner or later, however, you will most likely need to take a driving test to obtain a Canadian driver's licence. Because it displays your photograph, signature, and address, a driver's licence also serves as one of the best pieces of **identification** you can carry.

Q: Can I transfer a driver's licence from another country?

A: Some countries have mutual driver licence agreements with individual Canadian provinces or territories. To see which countries participate visit the Canadian Council of Motor Transport Administrators' website at www.ccmta.ca.

Driving Instruction

Pamphlets explaining the rules in each province are available from your **provincial ministry** of transportation. Be sure to familiarize yourself with these rules.

You must be at least 16 years old before you can take your driving test. Some provinces have implemented a graduated licensing system that restricts young drivers to driving only during daylight hours throughout their probation period.

In order to help drivers merge into the driving scene, new drivers are provided with a beginner's licence that allows them to operate a vehicle only when a licensed driver is in the car with them. A wise new driver might want to consider taking private driving lessons at this point.

In most regions of Canada, heavy snowfall or freezing rain can turn a highway into an ice rink within minutes. A few practice sessions that include driving in these conditions might save your life some day. Look in the phone book under "Driving Instruction."

Your Driver's Licence

You are legally required to carry your driver's licence with you whenever you drive. In the event that the police stop you, for whatever reason, they will ask to see your driver's licence, the **vehicle registration** for the car you are operating, and your car insurance certificate. Failure to produce any of these could result in a ticket and a **fine**.

Source: Ontario Ministry of Transportation

Your licence will be issued by the province or territory in which you live. In order to receive a licence, you must pass both a written examination and a road test. In order to pass these tests, you need to learn the rules of the road in your province. In some provinces, a minimum of 30 days is required between writing the knowledge test and taking the road test.

Once you obtain a licence, you will have to **renew** it on a regular basis as determined by your provincial ministry in charge of transportation. If you move, you are obligated to inform the ministry of your new address.

The major roadway that crosses Canada from east to west, linking its ten provinces, is the Trans-Canada Highway. Over 7,300 km in length, this highway is longer than any other national highway on the planet.

Importing a Car

Bringing your car to Canada from overseas is not necessarily a good idea. You might be better off selling your vehicle—yes, even your Mercedes—before you leave home. It will most likely cost you more to ship it to Canada, once you calculate freight and other costs, than to buy a new one. It could also cost thousands of dollars to bring your car up to the safety standards required in Canada.

In recent years as the Canadian dollar has gotten stronger, Canadians have been looking to buy cars in the US. Deals can be found, but getting through the legal paperwork can be difficult. Luckily websites and businesses have started to help people. If you are thinking of trying to save some money by buying a car in the US, search them out on the Internet and keep an eye on the Canadian dollar.

If you do plan to import a vehicle from the United States or any other country, you can generally bring it to Canada free of import duties. To do so, you will have to satisfy several conditions, one being that you must have owned and used the car for your personal use before entering the country.

You will also have to check with Transport Canada to see if your vehicle meets the approved standards for a motor vehicle in this country. Even vehicles manufactured in the US don't automatically meet the Canadian standards.

Call Transport Canada's Registrar of Imported Vehicles at 1-888-848-8240 or check out www.riv.ca for more information on whether your vehicle is eligible for importation. You can also find out what modifications, if any, can be made to your vehicle to make it eligible for driving in Canada.

You will need to check with the transportation ministry in your region to see if there is any special **provincial sales tax** payable on imported vehicles.

Also, check with the motor vehicle department in the country you are leaving to ensure that you can export your vehicle.

Buying a Car

You might want to postpone buying a car until you become familiar with the roads and rules in your new city. My advice is to park your money in a bank account and take public transit, at least at first. Eventually, though, you will likely want a set of wheels to begin exploring your new environment.

Car buyers can check out one of the many guidebooks that compare the prices, performance, and serviceability of cars. These guidebooks can often be found at the library.

For a variety of reasons, you may choose to lease a vehicle instead of buying one. At the end of the term, you may return the car or buy it, depending on the lease agreement you have signed. Most leases carry a mileage limit, meaning you may be charged extra if you rack up more mileage than is allowed. Make sure you ask what kind of penalty you will face if you want to terminate the lease before the lease period is up.

If you choose to buy a vehicle, be aware that interest on a car loan for newcomers can reach 24 percent. Many car dealers will offer you a loan as an incentive to purchase one of their cars, but it would be best to shop around (both for a car and financing) before you commit to an offer. Also, check on the penalty you might face if you were to pay off the loan early.

When purchasing a used car, try to obtain an extended **warranty** from the dealer that covers the cost of parts and labour for repairs on the vehicle for a set period of time.

If you buy from a private seller, it would be wise to have the car checked by the Canadian Automobile Association (CAA). For a small fee, CAA will verify the ownership and **accident** history of the vehicle. It is also advisable to check with the motor vehicle office to see if there is a lien against the car. If there is, this means that the vehicle's owner owes money to a creditor and if you purchase the vehicle, you will be responsible for that debt. While a private deal might provide you with a good price, be aware that stolen vehicles in Canada are often sold by private sale. If you accidentally purchase such a vehicle, the authorities could **confiscate** the car and you may even face some tough questioning by the police for possessing stolen goods. Heck, you could even end up in jail!

Car Purchasing Options		
Type of Purchase	**Advantages**	**Disadvantages**
New Car	Car is under warranty and doesn't have a history of problems Price is very high	New cars lose a great deal of value once purchased
Used Car (from Dealer)	Lower price than a new car; car retains more of its value Car's condition depends on the previous owner	Sometimes limited warranty is included Repairs and extra costs are more likely to be needed
Used Car (Private Sale)	Can be cheapest way to buy a car No warranty, so buyer needs to be very knowledgeable about cars or risk getting a bad one	May be able to find great deals Buyer needs to be very knowledgeable about the market for cars or risks paying too much
Lease	Lower monthly payments, but still get a new car When lease period is over, have nothing to show for money spent	Fewer issues with maintenance and repairs Penalties (for damage or putting too many kilometres on the car) may be high

The operation and **upkeep** of a car, whether new or used, will cost a lot of money. Even if you are lucky enough to end up with a trouble-free vehicle, the expense of regular maintenance, upkeep, fuel, monthly payments, and costs of registering and insuring can be thousands of dollars per year.

Transferring title or ownership of a vehicle is straightforward. If you are purchasing from a car dealership, transfer documents will be handled for you. In a private purchase, the buyer and seller must go to an insurance company to arrange the transfer, the insurance, payment of the provincial tax, and pickup of a new licence plate.

Insurance

All vehicles must be registered with the transportation ministry in the province in which the owner lives, and all vehicles need to be insured. There are many different kinds of insurance and many different companies

Christian Chia: Race to the Top

Christian Chia's vision as an entrepreneur is undeniable. He immigrated to Canada from Indonesia as a child, and years later decided to move back to Asia. He ended up in Tokyo, where he got a trainee job with Toyota. "I had this early urge to look into the car business," he says.

After some time working at Toyota, Chia says, "I started to get all sorts of crazy ideas." He realized that there were no Toyota-specific dealerships in China, where the car was quite popular. "I said, 'This can't be true.'"

"There was no network, no service, no business with Toyota. They were being imported by large trading companies only," he says. "So I quit my job, drew on some connections to raise money, and moved to Hong Kong."

"It was a booming success. I modelled it after North American dealerships," he says. In 1998, he moved back to Canada and took over a car dealership here that he and his family had a share in.

—*Margaret Jetelina*

offering it. Insurance companies are highly competitive in both price and service. Call around to find the best price. Private insurance companies are listed in the phone book under "Insurance." In some provinces, insurance is obtained through provincial insurance corporations. You can get more information from the Insurance Bureau of Canada at www.ibc.ca.

In order to receive the best price on insurance, you should try to get a letter from your previous insurance company showing your driving record or history of insurance claims over the past five years. An authenticated translation may be required if your document is in a language other than English or French. This letter could save you up to 40 percent on insurance costs if you can prove you are a **claims-free** driver. Your insurance costs will depend not only on your driving record, but also the make of your car, your age and gender, and the level of insurance you select. If you plan to rent a vehicle, you will normally receive all the required insurance protection with the rental agreement.

Basically, car insurance pays the costs that arise from an accident, no matter who is at fault. Your deductible—the amount of money that your insurer expects you to pay toward these costs—changes depending on the fault aspect: if it is your fault, you will pay a higher deductible.

In British Columbia, Saskatchewan, and Manitoba, vehicle registration is tied in to basic insurance—you can't get one without the other. Also, in British Columbia, cars older than two years need to pass an annual air pollution test administered by a provincial AirCare inspection centre before they are eligible for insurance. If the car fails the test, it will have to be repaired or brought up to pollution emission standards before it can qualify for insurance.

You must carry at least $200,000 in liability insurance everywhere in Canada except in Quebec, where the minimum is $50,000, although this amount is deemed insufficient by many insurers. Liability insurance covers you in the event that you cause injury to a person or to someone's property.

Insurance against theft and vandalism is also available. Your insurance broker or agent will tell you what you need.

Q: How should I prepare for winter driving emergencies?

A: Invest in a winter driving survival kit. This includes an ice scraper or brush, a shovel, booster cables, a fuel line de-icer, a map of the area, tools, a compass, a tow chain, a warning light (that flashes), a fire extinguisher, extra clothing (including winter boots or rain boots), a first aid kit, blankets (special survival blankets are the best), matches, food and water (if driving in remote areas), and a roll of paper towels.

Purchasing Car Insurance

In Alberta, Yukon, Northwest Territories, Nunavut, Ontario, Newfoundland, New Brunswick, Nova Scotia, and Prince Edward Island, you can check the phone book to find a nearby insurance company or broker. Insurance can also be purchased on the Internet. Insurance agents can provide advice on the amount of insurance you need and can help arrange for the purchase or renewal of a **policy**, or can change an existing policy. They can also help when you are making a claim.

In British Columbia, Saskatchewan, and Manitoba, the provincial governments are involved in providing the basic mandatory insurance. Optional additional insurance coverage is available through the government-operated insurance companies as well as through private insurers. The government insurance agencies for these three provinces are the Insurance Corporation of British Columbia (ICBC), Saskatchewan Government Insurance (SGI), and Manitoba Public Insurance (MPI).

Failure to Insure

If you dare to drive in Canada without insurance, you could be charged for doing so. Also, if you are involved in an accident, you could be **sued** for thousands, if not millions, of dollars in damages.

If you are uninsured and cannot pay for the damage from an accident, the person who makes a claim against you will be paid from special funds administered by the government or from the uninsured automobile coverage of the claimant's policy. Your driver's licence may then be suspended until you arrange to repay the amount that was paid on your behalf.

Gabrielle Loren: Accountant's Car Tips

Born in Berlin, Germany, Gabrielle Loren immigrated to Canada as a child in 1965. Today, she is a certified general accountant and a columnist with *Canadian Immigrant* magazine.

"One of the most common questions I get asked by clients is whether to buy or lease their next car," she says. "The simple answer is 'It depends.'"

Loren says that if you own your own business, you can deduct a portion of your car purchase if it costs $30,000 or less. If you lease, you can deduct your lease payments if they don't exceed $800 a month.

Of course, before making your decision, Loren recommends talking to your accountant.

—Margaret Jetelina

Important Driving Rules

The **demerit point** system allocates a certain number of points to drivers convicted of various driving offences. If these start adding up, you can expect penalties ranging from a warning letter to a suspension of your licence or increased motor vehicle insurance.

Among the road rules that seem to confuse newcomers to Canada is the courtesy stop at an uncontrolled **intersection**. At such an intersection, when neither of two drivers has a stop sign or stoplight to control traffic, the law says that the driver who reaches the intersection first has the right of way to proceed through the intersection first. If two drivers approach at the same time, the driver on the right has the right of way.

Four-way stops also involve courtesy. At an intersection controlled by stop signs on all four corners, the driver who arrives at the intersection first should proceed through the intersection after making a complete stop. If two or more vehicles arrive at the same time, it is again the driver on the right who should proceed first.

Another road rule in some Canadian provinces allows drivers to make right turns on a red light, after the driver makes a complete stop and ensures that the turn will not interrupt the flow of traffic.

Common Offences and Points Lost in Each Province										
Offence	BC	AB	SK	MB	ON	QC	NB	NS	PE	NF
Failing to obey a sign	2	2	3-4	2	2	3	3	2	3	2
Not stopping at a pedestrian crossing	2	4	3	2	2	2	3	4	3	2
Improper turn	2	2	3	2	2	3	3	2	3	2
Speeding 16 to 29 over the limit	3	3	4	2	3	1-2	3	3	3	2-3
Speeding 30 to 49 over the limit	3	4	4	2	4	3-5	5	4	6	3-4
Following too closely	3	4	4	2	4	4	3	2	3	2
Not stopping for a school bus	3	6	4	2	6	9	10	6	8	6
Speeding 50 or more over the limit	3	6	4	8	6	5	3	4	6	4
Leaving the scene of an accident	3	7	20	15	7	9	5	6	12	12

There is also a law that requires drivers to stop for pedestrians who are crossing the street, no matter which lane the pedestrian happens to be in. This law, however, is often ignored by drivers. Pedestrians need to exercise extreme caution when crossing the street, whether crossing on green lights or at uncontrolled intersections. It is against the law to jaywalk, or cross the street at any location other than at an intersection, anywhere in Canada.

New drivers in Canada should also be aware that they are required to pull safely toward the curb whenever they hear the siren, or see the flashing lights, of an emergency vehicle approaching from either direction.

Mandatory Seat Belts

By law, the driver and all passengers must wear seat belts at all times when travelling in a vehicle in Canada. As a driver, you can be fined if you or a passenger in your car is not wearing a seat belt. You can also be ticketed for carrying more passengers in your vehicle than the number of available seat belts in the car.

Babies and children who are too small to wear seat belts safely must be placed in car seats appropriate for their age and weight. For example, infants must be placed in special seats that face the rear of the car. There are very strict rules in Canada that apply to children riding in motor vehicles. Check with your local ministry of transportation to determine which ones apply in your region. It is illegal to hold a child or baby on your lap if you are a passenger in a car, as the child could be crushed or thrown out of your arms in the event of an accident.

If any person in your car is not wearing a seat belt and is injured because of an accident, any insurance claims you make could be affected, as she or he could be deemed to be partially responsible for injuries.

Car Seats for Children	
Child's Age or Weight	**Type of Car Seat**
Birth to 1 year	Rear-facing infant seat
1 to 4^1/$_2$ years or 10 to 18 kilograms (22 to 40 pounds)	Forward-facing child seat
4^1/$_2$ to 8 years or 18 kilograms (40 pounds) or heavier	Booster seat
8 years and older or when child outgrows booster seat	Seat belt

Drinking and Driving

Criminal Code penalties are severe for driving while under the influence of alcohol and can include a prison sentence and the loss or suspension of your driver's licence. In Ontario, for example, those convicted of drinking and driving face an automatic 90-day suspension of driving privileges. Those caught driving while under suspension often receive a jail sentence and a criminal record.

Police establish surprise roadblocks throughout the country—particularly during the Christmas season—to check for drunk drivers. A police officer may stop you, poke his head in your window, ask you for your driver's licence, or ask you to take a Breathalyzer test to measure the amount of alcohol in your blood.

This blood alcohol concentration (BAC) indicates the concentration of alcohol in a given volume of blood. Canadian law specifies that the maximum allowable amount of alcohol in the bloodstream of a driver is

Theoretical Blood-Alcohol Content, Based on Your Body Weight, Number of Drinks, and Time Elapsed from Your First Drink						
	3	4	5	6	7	8	9
150 lb.	.075	.100	.125	.151	.176	.201	.226
160 lb.	.070	.094	.117	.141	.164	.188	.211
170 lb.	.066	.088	.110	.132	.155	.178	.200
180 lb.	.063	.083	.104	.125	.146	.167	.188
190 lb.	.059	.079	.099	.119	.138	.158	.179
200 lb.	.056	.075	.094	.113	.131	.150	.169
210 lb.	.053	.071	.090	.107	.125	.143	.161
220 lb.	.051	.068	.085	.102	.119	.136	.153

Step 1: Count your drinks (1 drink equals 1 ounce of liquor, 1 glass of wine or 1 regular sized bottle of beer).
Step 2: On the chart, find the number opposite your body weight and under the number of drinks you had.
Step 3: Subtract from this number the amount of alcohol "burned up" by your metabolism since your first drink. This figure is .015 percent per hour.
Example: A 180 lb. man consumed 6 drinks in four hours.
$$.125 - (.015 \times 4) = .065$$

80 milligrams per 100 millilitres of blood—or .08. Hence, if you drink and drive, you may be charged with driving a motor vehicle with a BAC over .08. If you decline to provide a breath sample when requested to do so by a police officer, you could be charged with "refusing to blow," an equally serious offence. Take your pick.

The more you drink, and to some degree the smaller you are, the higher your BAC will be and the more physically and mentally impaired you will become.

Designated Drivers

If you go to a social event where you will be drinking alcohol, you should choose a designated driver. Designated drivers (or DDs) plan not to drink alcohol so that they can safely drive others home at the end of the night. This is important because drinking and driving is extremely dangerous and can also get you into a lot of trouble with the law. If you are unable to find a friend who is willing to stay sober, you should volunteer to do it yourself.

Most provinces have a service called Operation Red Nose (ORN), which is usually available from late November until the end of December. If you have been drinking and do not have a designated driver, you can call ORN volunteers to pick you up and drive you home in your car. If this service does not exist in your area, consider calling a cab, then find a way to pick up your car the following day.

Parking

Most cities and towns in Canada restrict parking by installing **parking meters** along the streets. In order to park, you must drop coins, or insert a credit card, into the meter designated for your parking space. Parking costs can range from one dime to several dollars. It's a good idea to carry coins just for parking purposes.

As a driver, you must also look for parking signs posted on the street where you want to park. The signs may restrict or forbid parking at certain times of the day and on certain days of the week. Private parking lots also post signs explaining where you can and cannot park. You may be fined for disobeying these signs and in some cases your car may be **towed** away. You will then have to find out where it has been towed—you can usually do this by calling the police. You will have to pay a fine plus towing charges, which are frequently more than $50, to get your car back. It can be a huge inconvenience to find out where your car has been taken and to make your way there to pick it up. To avoid having to do this, make sure to read and obey any nearby parking signs.

Speeding

Police across Canada use **photo radar** to catch speeders. Speeding violations are subject to fines and in some instances drivers will accumulate demerit points for such violations. As points accumulate, your car insurance could rise. In most cities in Canada, the speed limit is 50 kilometres per hour, but you should always be looking for road signs that indicate a decrease or increase in this limit. It is also a rule of thumb in Canada that the speed limit is significantly lowered near parks and schools. Signs will be posted to advise you what the speed is.

On February 14, 1910, Lady Laurier, the wife of Canada's eighth Prime Minister, Sir Wilfred Laurier, was issued a speeding ticket for going 16 kilometres (10 miles) per hour. This was considered much too fast in those very early days of motor vehicles!

Winter Driving

Canadian winters can result in some fairly challenging driving situations. If you are planning to drive across any mountain pass in the winter, it is advisable to check with the province's department of highways first to ensure the pass is open to vehicles. If you are travelling in the more remote areas of the country in winter, you should also keep emergency supplies in your car, including a shovel and perhaps even survival products such as candles, matches, and heavy blankets.

In some situations, the police or the highways department could require vehicles using a particular section of highway to carry winter chains or be equipped with snow tires. It is also worth noting that vehicle handling is optimized when identical tires are installed on all four wheels.

Many drivers in Canada operate their vehicles with **all-season radial tires**, which are marked "M/S" indicating they are mud and snow tires. While they provide safe performance in most weather, they may not be suitable for severe snow conditions. If you intend to drive in severe winter conditions, you should install winter tires. They are marked with a picture of a peaked mountain with a snowflake.

When Accidents Happen

Canadian law requires that if you are involved in a motor vehicle accident, you must provide assistance to anyone injured in the accident. If there is serious damage to a vehicle or if there is any personal injury, you should call 911 or the local emergency number immediately. You must specify whether you need the police, fire department, or ambulance to attend at the scene. In some cases, if the collision is minor and there are no injuries, the police may not go to the scene, but will instead ask you to report the incident at a police station. If possible, you should obtain a copy of the police report, or at least the police incident number, in order to proceed with an insurance claim.

Cars involved in minor accidents should be moved off the road and out of the way of traffic, if possible, to avoid further accidents. If you are involved in an accident, do not leave the scene of the accident until you have exchanged names, addresses, licence plate numbers, telephone numbers, as well as insurance particulars, with all other drivers involved in the accident. It is also recommended that you obtain the names and phone numbers of witnesses to the accident. If you leave the scene of an accident in which you are involved before providing your name and other particulars, you could be charged with leaving the scene of an accident, an offence more commonly known as a "hit and run."

If you need to have your car towed away from the scene, make sure you know where it is being taken and how much towing it will cost before you

Q: What happens in the case of a car accident?

A: Many things happen in the case of a car accident, depending on its severity. Most importantly, you should call 911 and get medical attention. If this is not needed, you should exchange insurance information with any other drivers and write down their licence plate numbers, driving licence numbers, addresses, and phone numbers. Then report the accident to the police and your insurance company. Also, try to find a witness to the accident and get his or her contact information, as this will help to determine fault.

agree to have it removed. Do not sign any blank form that authorizes unspecified repairs to your vehicle. As soon as possible, notify your insurance company and provide them with the incident number from the police, as well as the names and contact numbers of the other drivers and witnesses involved. It is also helpful to draw a diagram of the scene showing all vehicles and street names. This will help you remember the details of the accident in case you are questioned about it at a later time.

For further details on driving in Canada, contact the provincial ministries of transportation, motor vehicle licensing offices, or insurance associations listed in the phone book.

Key Words

accident: an unpleasant event that happens unexpectedly and causes damage, injury, or death

all-season radial tire: a car tire specially designed and manufactured to make the tire stronger and safer for drivers to use in all types of weather

claims-free: without an insurance claim

confiscate: to take something away from somebody as a punishment

demerit point: a mark on a person's driving record to show he/she has made a mistake

fine: to make somebody pay a sum of money because he/she has broken a law or rule

identification (also informal ID): an official card, paper, etc. that proves who you are

intersection: the place where two or more roads, lines, etc. meet and cross each other

parking meter: a metal post that you put coins into to pay for parking a car in the space beside it

photo radar: a computer-operated radar system that photographs the license plate of a speeding car

policy: a document that shows an agreement that you have made with an insurance company

provincial ministry: a division of the provincial government responsible for a particular subject

provincial sales tax: (abbr. PST) a tax that is added to the price of goods in some Canadian provinces

renew: to make something valid for a further period of time

road test (also driving test): a test that a person must pass before he/she is qualified to drive a car, etc.

sue: to go to a court of law and ask for money from somebody because he/she has done something bad to you, or said something bad about you

tow: to pull a car, etc. along by a rope or chain

upkeep: the cost or process of keeping something in a good condition

vehicle registration: an official piece of paper with information about a car, truck, etc. and the name of its owner

warranty: a written statement that you get when you buy something, which promises to repair or replace it if it breaks or stops working within a certain period of time

Note: Entries taken or adapted from the Oxford ESL Dictionary

Creating Your Canadian Experience

1. Research the location of the nearest provincial ministry of transportation. Tip: type the name of your province and "Transportation" into a search engine to find your ministry's website.

   Address: _____

   _____

   Hours: _____

2. Does your new province have a graduated licensing system? What are the steps and restrictions? You should be able to find this information on your province's ministry of transportation website.

Level 1: _____

_____

Level 2: _____

_____

Level 3: _____

_____

Level 4: _____

_____

3. Research four places where you could get a car loan (try to find different types of lenders: two banks, a dealership, and one other lender). On the chart, compare the interest rates, the penalties, and other considerations. Tip: type the name of your city and "Auto Loan" into a search engine.

Lender	Interest Rate	Penalties	Other Considerations

4. Research four auto insurance providers in your area. On the chart, compare their premium, average, and basic coverage.
Tip: type the name of your city and "Auto Insurance" into a search engine.

Insurer	Premium Coverage	Average Coverage	Basic Coverage

5. In your new province, are you allowed to turn right on a red light? You can find this information on your ministry of transportation's website or in the driving manual that the ministry produces.

_____

6. What are the laws regarding driving with children in the car in your new province? Your ministry of transportation's website should have this information, as should your provincial driving manual.

_____

_____

_____

Chapter 13

The Law

In This Chapter

- How should you deal with a robbery?
- What rights do you have if you are arrested?
- What if you can't afford a lawyer?
- Who should you call if a building contractor you hire doesn't finish the job?

Although you are not expected to know everything about the legal system, it is your responsibility to keep on the right side of the law. In other words, ignorance of the law is no excuse for breaking it. This means you can be **charged** with and **convicted** of an **offence** even though you claim you didn't know your action was against the law.

So how do you find out what is and what is not against the law? Well, to begin with, you can read newspapers, pick up pamphlets on all aspects of the law from your local **courthouse**, attend night school courses, and ask at your local community centre and immigrant services society.

While some laws are obvious—such as those that say you cannot walk away with your neighbour's shiny bicycle—other laws are much more complex. For example, you may not add a new room to the back of your house without a building permit from city hall, you may not sell cigarettes to a 15-year-old, you may not ride a motorcycle without a helmet, and you may not enter your tenant's apartment and take his television set because he hasn't paid his last two months' rent. These are all against the law in Canada.

These are just a sample of the numerous municipal, motor vehicle, provincial, and federal laws, as well as hundreds of others in this country that place limits on your actions to protect individuals and the community as a whole.

Many of the laws you might encounter will likely fall under municipal **bylaws**. These vary from city to city, but generally deal with such day-to-day nuisances as your neighbour's annoying barking dog (this is the number one complaint levied at city halls across the nation), someone dumping garbage in the lane behind your house, or even your landlord cutting down a large tree in your backyard (yes, in some municipalities, that is illegal).

If you believe someone has broken a municipal law, do not hesitate to call city hall to see what the bylaw says and how you can proceed to solve the problem. Usually, those who break municipal laws end up paying a fine. For information on more serious crimes, read on.

Public and Private Law

The Canadian legal system ensures that the rule of law applies to everyone, including politicians, members of the police, and high-ranking members of the community. The law protects individual **rights** and **freedoms**, such as

liberty and **equality**. It also ensures that those who want to change the laws can speak out about them, in a lawful manner, without fear of punishment.

Two different sets of laws govern Canadian conduct: **public law** and **private law**.

Public law deals with legal matters that affect society.

This means that **criminal acts**, such as robbery or murder, are viewed as wrongs against society as a whole. Offenders can be charged without anyone having to file a complaint against them. A person found **guilty** of a criminal act could face **jail**, be sentenced to pay a fine, be put on **probation**, be discharged, or face a combination of fines and jail time. Constitutional and administrative law also fall into the category of public law.

Private law deals with private disputes between individuals in society.

This includes matters dealing with contracts, property ownership, libel, family disputes, and other areas where two or more people are in disagreement. Persons who are found to be at fault could be ordered to pay **compensation** to the person who sued them, and their property or salaries may be seized if they refuse to pay.

Criminal Law

You certainly don't want to come into conflict with the *Criminal Code of Canada*, which outlines most of the criminal offences for which you could be charged and jailed. These offences range from unlawfully owning a handgun, to committing assault, to criminal negligence causing death. Of course, there are also many other codes or acts under which you could be charged, such as the *Controlled Drugs and Substances Act*, the provincial motor vehicle acts, and numerous other acts that regulate acceptable behaviour in Canada.

Criminal charges fall under two types: summary and **indictable offences**.

Summary offences tend to be less serious and include crimes such as shoplifting. Indictable offences are more serious, and include murder and robbery. A charge is laid when someone, usually a police officer, files information with a **judge** or **justice of the peace**, claiming a crime has been committed. If the judge decides the accused should have to answer the complaint, he or she issues a summons or a warrant for an arrest. This document tells the accused what the charge is and when to appear in court.

The accused may be taken to jail at this time, but that will usually not be necessary if she or he has a job, family, and home in the community.

Dealing with the Police

If you find yourself in trouble, as a victim of assault, robbery, or rape, or if you **witness** any of the above taking place, don't hesitate to call the police at 911. This is the emergency phone number used across most of Canada to summon the police, fire, or ambulance. Upon your arrival in Canada, check whether this, or another emergency number, is used in your area.

If someone is threatening or harassing you or a member of your family, call the police. In all dealings with the police, whether you are a victim, a witness, or a suspect, try to remain calm, speak clearly, and tell them your name, address, and phone number. Looking at other people, such as police officers, when you are talking to them shows respect and is considered a sign of good manners.

Q: If I call 911 for an emergency, but it turns out that it wasn't one, will I get in trouble?

A: If you explain your situation to the dispatcher, he or she will let you know whether or not it is a real emergency. Don't worry if you are told that your case is not an emergency—the dispatchers can be very understanding. I remember when I had just arrived I was calling New Delhi, and the area code is 911! I had forgotten to dial the prefix and immediately got a call back from the dispatcher. A quick explanation was all it took to resolve this.

If you are **arrested** or stopped by the police for any reason, do not try to escape. Canadian law recognizes that you are **presumed innocent** until you are proven guilty. You will likely be asked to produce some form of identification, which you are required to show to the police.

If you are stopped while driving a car, you will likely be asked to provide your driver's licence, proof of insurance, and vehicle registration. This is standard practice; within minutes the officer can determine if the car you are driving is stolen, if you have a criminal record, and even how many unpaid parking tickets you may have.

Arash Seyedalikhani: Police on Patrol

Like many children of immigrants, Arash Seyedalikhani knew his parents had high expectations of him. After all, his family had come to Canada from Iran to give him more opportunities. Although his parents had expected him to go into the medical profession, he decided to go into policing, an idea he had been toying with since he was 15.

"I highly respected the characteristics of police officers and literally saw them as superheroes," he says. "I was very impressed by the level of bravery, integrity, pride, honour, and professionalism that I had observed."

So after getting his bachelor's degree, Seyedalikhani went for it. "Thankfully, my parents have been very proud and supportive throughout this entire process."

He adds that many Iranians in Canada do recognize that the police in Canada are different from those in Iran. "I constantly strive to improve police relations between the police and the Iranian community, and to correct any misperceptions they have of the police," he says. "I cannot describe the feeling I get after positively affecting people's lives on a daily basis. We are the ones that people trust and turn to. At the end of the day, I feel a great sense of satisfaction and pride."

—Margaret Jetelina

It's a good idea to address any member of the police force as "officer," and whatever you do, don't offer the police money, gifts, or any other kind of favour to let you go. To do so is a serious crime in Canada.

Generally speaking, the police in Canada will treat you fairly if you don't become unruly or attempt to evade them. They are quite decent, honest, and fair, particularly considering what and who they have to deal with most of the time.

If you feel you have been mistreated by the police, there is a procedure for making a complaint. Make sure you know his or her name or badge number and file a report with the police.

Arrest

The police have broad powers to arrest someone, but maybe not as broad as you think. They cannot do so simply on a slight suspicion.

The police can arrest you if they believe you are about to commit an indictable offence, are actually committing an offence, or if there is a warrant outstanding against you.

Police officers can search you during the process of an arrest, in order to determine if you are carrying a weapon and also to see if there is any evidence of the alleged offence.

They can also stop and ask you to provide identification, and request that you accompany them to the police station voluntarily, without charging you.

If there is an official arrest, you must be advised of the reason for the arrest, and must be told about your right to talk to a lawyer. If you are arrested, you should ask to speak to a lawyer immediately. The police must provide you with a telephone, if possible, and not question you further until you have had a chance to speak to your lawyer. If you don't have a lawyer, the police must provide you with a referral.

Anyone who is arrested and taken into custody has the right to appear before a justice of the peace or a judge as soon as possible, usually within 24 hours, and to discuss the possibility of being released on bail. This means that you or a benefactor can put up a sum of money that assures the court you will not leave town before your trial.

Citizen's Arrest

It is possible for you to make a citizen's arrest—if you see someone who is committing a crime or trying to escape after committing a crime, for example—but in most cases the police recommend that citizens do not attempt to prevent someone from fleeing. The risk is simply too high for the would-be hero.

Police generally recommend that if you witness a crime, you should attempt to take note of the suspects' physical descriptions and the description of their vehicle, rather than try to stop them. Naturally, if someone is in danger, you are expected to provide help if you could do so without risking your own safety or the safety of anyone else.

Legal Aid

Legal Aid in Canada operates as an independent, non-profit organization to help defend or represent those who don't have the financial resources to defend themselves. First, applicants for legal aid must prove they cannot afford to pay for a lawyer. They may be asked to provide recent pay stubs, social assistance stubs, income tax returns, and bank records. Applicants for legal aid may also be asked to sell some assets to pay for legal services.

If individuals should come into some income as a result of legal aid representation, they may be asked to contribute something back to society. If you feel you need the services of a lawyer or simply some guidance or advice, contact the Legal Aid Society nearest you.

At the Trial

Although most criminal cases in Canada are tried by judges without a **jury**, a person who is charged with a criminal offence for which he or she could face a prison sentence of five years or more has the right to a trial by jury. A jury consists of a panel of 12 randomly selected members of the community in which the court is located. Jury members must be adults who possess Canadian citizenship, so you might find yourself serving on a jury after you become a citizen.

At the trial, the accused is either found guilty or not guilty. If found guilty, the judge will decide on an appropriate sentence, which could consist of one or more of the following: a fine, probation, community service, or imprisonment. Most civil and criminal court decisions can be appealed to a higher level of court.

Small Claims Court

If you should run into a problem with someone who owes you money, such as a contractor or a former employer, your best option is to try to negotiate a settlement rather than go to court. Similarly, if you owe someone money, but perhaps not as much as he or she thinks you owe, again your best option is to avoid court by trying to settle by yourselves. Most of these disagreements (in fact more than 90 percent of them) are settled out of court between the parties involved. The simple threat of a lawsuit frequently encourages people to settle such disputes quickly. This can save everyone a lot of aggravation and money.

Even if you have to settle for payment over an extended period of time or you receive something less than you feel you deserve, you might be better off settling out of court to avoid the time and expense of a court hearing. If you can arrange some kind of compromise, put it in writing and have both parties sign it.

If all else fails, **Small Claims Court** might be your next option. It provides a relatively quick, informal, and cheap way to solve disputes involving less than $10,000. You should, however, ask yourself a few questions before proceeding to Small Claims Court. Is the hassle worth it? Do I know where to find the person I want to sue? Do I have documents to support my claim? Does he or she have the money to pay if I win?

If you feel you want to pursue the matter, you can pick up a form at the Small Claims Court, which is generally located at the provincial courthouse. The person who brings the lawsuit or civil action to the courts is called the plaintiff, while the person being sued is the defendant. The plaintiff must start the court action within a specified period of time from the offence, usually one year, although the limit varies for different matters.

Types of Courts		
Traffic Court	Municipal	Accepts payment of provincial offence fines, schedules and supports provincial offence trials.
Small Claims Court	Provincial	A branch of the Superior Court of Justice dealing with civil disputes up to $10,000.
Youth Criminal Justice Court	Provincial	For youth aged 12 to 17 who are charged with a criminal offence.
Supreme/Superior Court of the Provinces	Provincial	The superior trial court. Deals with divorce cases and family law matters where there are claims for the division of matrimonial property, or support or custody matters. Hears appeals from Ontario Court of Justice in summary conviction matters.
Supreme Court of Canada	Federal	Final general court of appeal. Covers both civil law and common law. Supreme Court of Canada can hear cases in all areas of the law.
Federal Court	Federal	Deals with legal disputes arising in the federal domain, such as claims against the Government of Canada, civil suits in federally-regulated areas, and challenges to the decisions of the federal tribunals.

You may attend Small Claims Court without a lawyer if you feel adequately prepared to present your case. Most jurisdictions offer a lawyer referral service, which usually allows you to speak to a lawyer about the validity of filing a claim without actually hiring him or her to represent you. As well, some jurisdictions offer a guidebook to help people file a claim in Small Claims Court. Don't hesitate to ask at your provincial courthouse for assistance in this process.

If you are ever served with a Small Claims form, you become the defendant and should reply accordingly. Whatever you do, do not ignore such legal documents. The hearing could proceed without your input, and this could have negative results for you.

> In the spring of 1826, the city of St. John, New Brunswick announced it was looking for men "of good character" to work as policemen. On March 20, it hired six applicants who became members of the first paid police force in North America.

Youth Criminal Justice Court

Young people aged 12 to 17 who commit crimes are prosecuted under the *Youth Criminal Justice Act*, which was designed to extend some leniency to youths so they could pay for their crime without becoming habitual criminals. The act therefore extends some rights and safeguards to which older criminals are not entitled, such as a reduced maximum limit on the time a young offender can serve.

Court proceedings are held in youth courts before a judge, not a judge and jury. And a number of alternative sentencing possibilities are available to judges who deal with the youths.

Young persons over the age of 14 who are accused of more serious offences such as murder can be raised to adult court where they will face the same kind of severe sentencing as an adult.

Traffic Court

Traffic Court deals with offences under the motor vehicle acts of each province, which establish driving speed limits, seat belt laws, and penalties for careless driving.

Supreme Courts of the Province

Each province has a higher level of court that hears civil matters dealing with sums greater than $10,000 and also hears serious criminal matters. Judges at this level hear appeals from lower courts, such as Small Claims Court. Persons appearing at this level of court will usually require a lawyer to represent them.

Supreme Court of Canada

The highest court in the country is the Supreme Court of Canada. It is composed of a chief justice and eight appointed judges in Ottawa, who hold court for three sessions per year, each lasting three months. Among the cases they hear are those involving matters of public importance, matters that raise an important question of law, or matters that concern the constitution.

Federal Court of Canada

The Federal Court of Canada is composed of the appeal and trial divisions. The court reviews the disputed decisions of federal boards, commissions, and tribunals, as well as inter-provincial and federal-provincial disputes, intellectual property proceedings, citizenship appeals, and appeals under certain federal statutes.

Testifying in Court

If you witness a crime or have information that could be of assistance in a court case, you might be called to **testify** in a civil or criminal trial. If you have such information, it is your responsibility to come forward to the police or the courts and present that information. All court testimony is given under oath or by affirmation.

It is also possible that you could be ordered to give evidence in court. A subpoena commands you to give evidence at a particular time and place, whether you volunteer to do so or not. You will face a penalty if you do not show up to testify.

Common Law and Civil Law

Canada's criminal and private law is partly based on **common law**, or the English system of precedent law: decisions made by judges are based on previous court decisions and may be used in any following court decisions to guide judges. As a result, the law is constantly evolving. This system is used throughout Canada, with the exception of Quebec, where a system of

civil law is used when dealing with provincial laws. Civil law is derived from the French judicial system and is based on a code of principles that can be applied to a wide range of legal matters. However different the two law systems are, the *Criminal Code*'s definitions of offences and penalties apply equally to the entire country.

Children's Rights

Canadian children's health, safety, and rights are constantly being monitored by teachers, doctors, and even neighbours. Parents or guardians must provide for their children or the children in their care, nurture them, and protect them until they reach the age of 16. Parents who fail to do so risk having their children removed from the home by social workers.

Parents cannot abuse their children, or any other children, physically, psychologically, or sexually. Abuse may include spanking, humiliating, or striking children in any way. Parents also cannot neglect their children or leave them without supervision. Regardless of other cultures' traditions or customs, Canadian law does not allow for the exploitation of children.

Women's Rights

Under the *Canadian Charter of Rights and Freedoms*, women have the same rights as men. Women who are abused, either mentally or physically, or who are threatened by their husbands, boyfriends, relatives, or acquaintances can seek assistance and, if necessary, legal protection. Immigrant organizations, crisis centres, or the police can help women in such situations find assistance, whether they need emergency short-term shelter, counselling, or legal advice.

There are also rape-relief centres and sexual assault support centres listed at the front of the phone book, and many of these centres are open 24 hours per day. There is help available to anyone who seeks it.

arrest: (used about the police) to take somebody prisoner in order to question him/her about a crime

bylaw: a law that is made by a municipal government

charge: to accuse somebody officially of doing something that is against the law

civil law: law that does not involve criminal matters but deals with the rights of private citizens

common law: a system of laws that have been developed from usage and custom of the courts rather than by parliament

compensation: money that you pay to somebody, especially because you have injured him/her or lost or damaged his/her property

convict: to declare in a court of law that somebody is guilty of a crime

courthouse: a building where courts of law and other offices of a county are located

criminal act: an action that breaks a law

equality: the situation in which everybody has the same rights and advantages; being equal

freedom: the right to do or say what you want

guilty: having broken a law; being responsible for doing something wrong

indictable offence: criminal behaviour that can cause somebody to be officially charged with a serious crime

innocent: not having done wrong; not guilty

jail: to put somebody in prison

judge: a person whose job is to apply the law and decide what punishment should be given to somebody found guilty in a court of law

jury: a group of twelve people in a court of law who listen to the facts about a crime and decide whether the accused person is guilty or not guilty

justice of the peace (abbr. JP): an official who judges less serious cases in a court of law and performs marriage ceremonies, etc.

legal aid: legal services provided by the government or another organization to people that do not have enough money to hire their lawyers

liberty: the freedom to go where you want, do what you want, etc.

offence: (formal) a crime; breaking the law

presumed innocent: considered not guilty of a crime even before there is actual proof to support the defendant's innocence

private law: the part of law that deals with relationship between individual persons and private property

probation: the system of keeping an official check on a person who has broken the law instead of sending him/her to prison or after he/she has left prison

public law: the part of law that affects the public as a whole and deals with the relationship between the government of a country and its people

small claims court: a court that deals with cases involving small amounts of money, where people do not need lawyers to speak for them

summary offence: a petty crime that is tried without following the normal legal process

testify: to make a formal statement that something is true, especially as a witness in a court of law

witness: to see something happen and to be able to tell other people about it later

Note: Entries taken or adapted from the Oxford ESL Dictionary

Creating Your Canadian Experience

1. Find out which city department you would call to find out about local bylaws.
   Tip: enter the name of your city and "Bylaws" into a search engine.

   Department name: _____

   Phone number: _____

2. Does your area use the number 911 for emergency calls? Check at the front of your local phone book to find out.

   Yes _____   Other Number _____

3. Research the nearest police station to your home.
   Tip: type the name of your city and "Police" into a search engine.

   Address: _____

   Contact Information: _____

4. Locate the Legal Aid Society nearest your home.
   Tip: type the name of your city and "Legal Aid Society" into a search
   engine.

   Address: _____

   Hours: _____

   Contact Information: _____

Chapter 14

Income Taxes

In This Chapter

- How much tax will you pay on your income?
- What if you're self-employed?
- What should you do if you can't pay your taxes?
- Do you have to reveal your foreign earnings?

Don't believe everything you hear about the Canadian **tax system**. It may be true that some **high earners** pay a lot of taxes, but there are many, many benefits derived from those taxes. As well, you can take advantage of many tax deductions—once you figure them out.

Let's start with a couple of tables showing the estimated total taxes payable in each province, as created by the Fraser Institute. The first table shows a variety of taxes charged to **income earners** and consumers in Canada and includes **income tax**, sales taxes on goods purchased, the so-called **sin taxes** on alcohol and cigarettes, automobile-related taxes, **property taxes**, import **duties**, taxes on **profits**, and natural-resource levies.

Taxes of the Average Family (of Two or More Individuals) 2005											
	NF	PEI	NS	NB	QC	ON	MB	SK	AB	BC	CAN
Average Cash Income	59,324	61,956	65,350	63,231	68,684	83,265	71,065	66,911	90,338	69,701	76,634
Average total income before tax	94,606	97,709	101,194	97,025	107,689	126,258	109,822	110,255	142,146	111,427	119,076
Income tax	8,848	8,483	10,489	9,469	11,862	13,715	11,120	9,489	14,893	10,248	12,637
Sales tax	5,335	5,779	5,595	5,411	6,232	7,073	5,707	5,336	3,549	5,309	6,269
Amusement taxes[1]	2,428	2,172	2,339	2,066	2,208	2,331	2,596	2,233	3,472	2,414	2,474
Automobile taxes[2]	1,179	1,240	1,059	1,273	934	991	927	1,445	867	875	1,010
Payroll taxes[3]	5,094	5,342	5,790	5,765	8,148	9,162	6,224	5,660	7,967	6,734	8,169
Property taxes	1,060	1,847	1,470	1,861	2,105	2,130	2,185	2,167	2,082	3,116	2,128
Import duties	191	204	224	211	254	320	250	227	344	247	286
Profits tax	1,552	2,193	2,082	1,763	2,759	2,428	2,628	2,530	2,561	2,798	2,448
Natural resources	610	9	56	135	25	29	139	1,632	3,206	1,303	570
Other taxes	1,215	559	309	433	383	658	1,688	888	1,291	1,201	777
Total taxes	27,512	27,828	29,411	28,388	35,002	38,835	33,463	31,607	40,232	34,254	36,769

Note 1: Amusement taxes include liquor, tobacco, amusement, and other excise taxes.

Note 2: Automobile taxes include automobile, fuel, and motor-vehicle license taxes.

Note 3: Payroll taxes include social security, pensioon, medical, and hospital taxes.

Note 4: The Fraser Institute's Canadian Tax Simulator 2005.

Source: Tax Facts *by Niels Veldhuis and Michael A. Walker, The Fraser Institute*

This table also shows average provincial incomes and the taxes paid by a family of two or more. The highest average income earners are in Ontario, Alberta, Manitoba, and BC, while the lowest income earners are located in Newfoundland and PEI.

As shown, both tax rates and average incomes can vary widely across the country, as each province regulates its own level of provincial income tax and **tax credits**. As you can see from the second table, the average income after tax ranges from about $23,000 to $93,000.

Average Income After Tax	
	2005
Economic families, two people or more	64,800
Elderly families	48,200
Non-elderly families	67,600
Married couples only	62,700
Two parent families with children	73,000
Married couples with other relatives	92,900
Lone-parent families	38,800
All other non-elderly families	56,500
Unattached individuals	27,000
Elderly male	27,000
Elderly female	23,200
Non-elderly male	29,900
Non-elderly female	25,200

Source: Statistics Canada

Basic Income Tax

As you can see, no matter where you go in Canada, you can't escape paying taxes. Let's start with the basics: your responsibility regarding the payment of income tax.

Although income tax was introduced in 1917 as a short-term financing plan during World War I, it has stayed with us ever since. And it's not likely to go away. So grin and bear it, as the saying goes.

The **Canada Revenue Agency** (CRA) is the federal department responsible for collecting the income taxes for federal and provincial spending.

The province of Alberta has the country's lowest gasoline tax and the lowest combined provincial and municipal taxes in the country. In addition, Alberta is the only province with no provincial sales tax and the first and only province that has paid off its provincial debt.

April 30 is the annual deadline to file your **income tax records** for the previous year, although **self-employed** persons have until June 15 to file their records. Income tax is filed in the province in which you lived as of December 31 of the previous year, not where you live at the time of filing. Everyone over the age of 15 who earned an income in the last year must file their income tax.

Your income tax records must report all the income you earned during the previous year, from January 1 to December 31, showing the allowable tax deductions. Income means not just salary, but **commissions**, employment **benefits**, business income, pensions, investment income, child tax benefits, and cash gifts earned in Canada or anywhere in the world.

Your income tax payment is determined on a sliding scale, based on your **net income**. Generally speaking, if you made less than $7,000 you won't have to pay income tax.

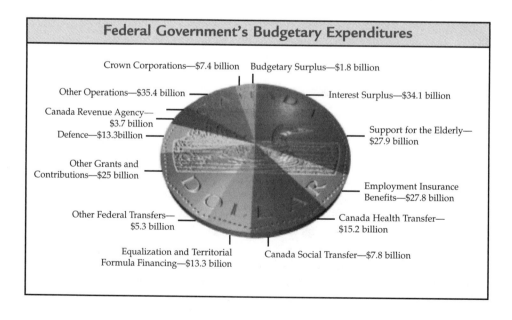

Federal Government's Budgetary Expenditures

Crown Corporations—$7.4 billion   Budgetary Surplus—$1.8 billion

Other Operations—$35.4 billion

Interest Surplus—$34.1 billion

Canada Revenue Agency— $3.7 billion

Defence—$13.3billion

Support for the Elderly— $27.9 billion

Other Grants and Contributions—$25 billion

Employment Insurance Benefits—$27.8 billion

Other Federal Transfers— $5.3 billion

Canada Health Transfer— $15.2 billion

Equalization and Territorial Formula Financing—$13.3 bilion

Canada Social Transfer—$7.8 billion

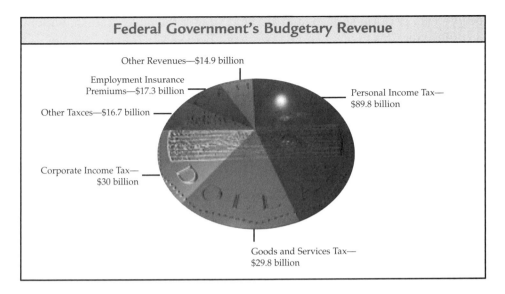

Federal Government's Budgetary Revenue

Other Revenues—$14.9 billion

Employment Insurance
Premiums—$17.3 billion

Other Taxces—$16.7 billion

Personal Income Tax—
$89.8 billion

Corporate Income Tax—
$30 billion

Goods and Services Tax—
$29.8 billion

Source: Department of Finance Canada

Before I get into the nitty-gritty of a few major components of the income tax structure in Canada, I'll advise you to learn as much as you can about the tax system here and take it very, very seriously. If, after completing your income tax return, you discover that you owe money to the CRA, try to submit a cheque for the amount owing with your tax papers by the April 30 deadline. However, no one is about to arrest you if you don't submit the money you owe by that date.

It is always best to at least file your income tax return, even if you can't pay what you owe at that time. But be aware that after April 30, interest begins to build on the amount of taxes that remains unpaid.

If you have a temporary cash shortage and cannot pay the amount owing, it is always a good idea to propose a payment plan to the CRA and try to pay the sum off over a period of months. If you don't, the agency will eventually find a way to get you to pay what you owe. The agency can charge non-filers with **tax evasion**, failure to disclose income, or refusing to file. They can impose fines, make third-party claims, seize property, and lay criminal charges. Fines can vary from $1,000 to $25,000 and those convicted can even go to jail for up to 12 months. In 1998, the Canada Revenue Agency laid more than 2,000 charges related to non-filing of income tax.

Also, in recent years, the agency has made an effort to reduce the **underground economy** in Canada. This drive is focused on the number of people who perform services and are paid "under the table" in cash, with no official receipts given, and no taxes paid. Between 1992 and 1999, the CRA recovered about $2.3 billion in unpaid taxes from people performing such illegal transactions. People caught accepting payment under the table could face criminal charges. Among the industries most affected by this are the construction and renovation, hospitality, and auto sales and repairs industries.

If you are having trouble paying your income taxes, the best plan is to contact a **collection officer** at the Canada Revenue Agency by mail or phone, and try to work out a payment plan. You can also pick up a copy of the CRA's pamphlet entitled "Canada Revenue Agency's Collections Policies" to see what your rights and obligations are under the *Income Tax Act*.

Hanif Muljiani: Ismaili Accountant Grows Business

Hanif Muljiani, a Ugandan immigrant and chartered **accountant**, landed the job as controller for an exhibit marketing company called The Portables in 1991. "As controller, I was involved in production right off the bat," he says. Four years later, with his extensive knowledge of the way the company worked, he was promoted to general manager and opened new locations across the country. "We're from Victoria to Halifax," he says. In 1991, sales were $2 million; under Muljiani's guidance, revenues were up to $10 million in 2000.

At that time, the owner asked Muljiani to buy the business. "The purchase price of the company was $5 million, and I was exactly $5 million short," Muljiani says, with a laugh. "I had no idea how I was going to raise the money."

With the help of his accountant, Muljiani put together a report on the future of the company, found an investor, and put his plans to diversify the company into action. The Portables soon moved up to $12 million annually in revenues.

Named one of the top 40 business people under 40 by a business newspaper in 2002, Muljiani remains modest. "I basically took over a company, raised a bunch of money, and have started the process of changing it."

—*Margaret Jetelina*

Every phone book in Canada lists the contact information for the tax department in the back of the telephone book under Government of Canada, Canada Revenue Agency. You can also access a great deal of information on the agency's website at www.cra-arc.gc.ca, or by calling the Canada Revenue Agency's Tax Information Phone Service (TIPS) at 1-800-267-6999.

Salaried vs. Self-Employed

Salaried employees are those who work for someone else and receive approximately the same payment for their labour every month. They never get to see the full amount of their hard-earned wages, because employers are required by law to **deduct** income tax from employees' salaries and send it to the federal government. This can come as a big surprise to a new employee who is looking forward to a cheque for $2,000 and instead gets one for about $1,400.

In addition to withholding income tax for the federal government, employers must deduct employment insurance premiums and Canada Pension Plan (CPP) contributions from their employees' wages. The employer must submit these funds to the CRA and keep standardized records of these contributions. The good news is that by the time employees file income tax papers in the following spring, they will likely owe the government nothing, owe a small amount, or even have a refund coming back to them. It is worth noting here that employers also contribute to the CPP and the Canada Employment Insurance Commission on behalf of their employees.

Every February, the employer must also present each employee with a **T4** slip, which is a standard statement of wages paid, showing the amount of the employee's wages for the year, as well as contributions made to the CPP and EI (Employment Insurance). Employees who do not receive this slip by April should request it from their employers. If, however, the slip is not provided before the deadline for tax filing, the employee still has an obligation to complete and file an income tax form, estimating the amount of income and deductions. Estimates should be based on the information on the employee's pay stubs, with a photocopy of all stubs submitted with the income tax form. Also, of course, the employee should include the name and address of the employer to enable CRA to press for the T4 slip.

A word of advice: Canada's income tax filing forms are at best tedious, and at worst, more complicated to understand than the launching of the last space shuttle. Many Canadians hire an accountant or other professional tax preparer to complete their tax forms for them.

If you can't afford to hire an accountant, you can use the services of a community volunteer tax preparer, who is trained by the CRA to provide assistance with income tax filing. In addition, free tax clinics are provided throughout the community in the weeks or months leading up to the tax deadline. Call the CRA for a list of the clinics near you.

As an example of the complexity of the tax filing system, tax deductions may include daycare expenses, disability expenses, some school tuition, interest paid on student loans, some medical expenses, moving expenses (if you had to move to take a new job), some car expenses (if you must use your car for work), child support payments, union and professional dues, business investment losses, and perhaps the biggest one for Canadians, payments made to Registered Retirement Savings Plans (RRSPs). It is best to keep all documents relating to your income and expenses in a safe place— and then hand them over to your accountant. Be aware, however, that if you perform a lot of the sorting and filing of the papers before you dump it on his or her desk, you'll save money on the accountant's fee.

Q: If I work at home can I get a tax break on some of my monthly expenses?

A: Yes, one of the advantages of working from home is the fact that you may deduct some of your home expenses. A portion of your mortgage or rent, hydro, and heating, as well as some cleaning supplies may be deducted. Check with your accountant for details.

Self-Employed

If you are working for yourself, you must submit approximately 25 percent of your estimated annual tax bill to the CRA every three months. You will also have to pay your CPP contributions, both as an employer and as an employee—so you really pay twice as much as you would if you were just an employee. As a self-employed person, you don't have to pay EI, but that also means you're not eligible to collect EI if you are ever out of work.

Self-employed persons and business owners must also be aware of the **Goods and Services Tax** in Canada, which is a 5 percent tax that must be added to nearly all goods produced and services performed in Canada, except food, medical services, and public transportation fees. This tax applies across Canada, except that in Nova Scotia, Newfoundland and Labrador, and New Brunswick, it is included in the provincial taxes and called the Harmonized Sales Tax, or HST. The HST adds up to 13 percent.

Every self-employed person who makes more than approximately $30,000 per year must obtain a Goods and Services Tax registration number from the CRA and include this GST number on all invoices. Whenever you perform a service for someone or sell a product to someone, you must add the

Theresa Cabreza-Cruz: Self-Employed Florist

Theresa Cabreza-Cruz owned a flourishing Legaspi Village flower shop in Makati, Philippines, when she, her husband, and her son decided to move to Canada in 2001.

"We came for my son. We wanted to have a better future for him," she says.

The Cruzes had to start from scratch, without the luxuries they had enjoyed in the Philippines, such as a housekeeper. "We had a brand new car there; here we had to buy a second-hand one. We asked ourselves, 'Did we make the right move?'"

But the businesswoman told herself, "If others can do it, I can do it."

Still a shareholder in the family-owned flower shop back in Makati, she used the flower shop's website, WorldofPetals.com, which she had set up while still in the Philippines, to start marketing to potential North American customers who wanted to send flowers to relatives and friends in the Philippines. "There's no other florist that offers delivery to the Philippines," she explains.

Once she receives orders here, she forwards them to her shop, which has a staff of ten people who package and deliver the flowers.

Cruz is also considering opening a storefront flower shop. "It's very competitive; there are lots of flower shops around, so we'll see."

—Margaret Jetelina

5 percent GST to the bill and show this amount as a separate calculation; you must also keep records of this GST and submit the amount you collect to the CRA. This means, however, that you can deduct from that amount any GST you have had to pay in the operation of your company. This can become quite a bookkeeping nightmare unless you, or your accountant, keep very good records.

Obviously, self-employed persons need to keep detailed records of all their income and related expenses, and budget roughly one-third of their income for income tax.

Goods and Services Tax Credit

As mentioned earlier, the 5 percent GST is paid by everyone on most products and services. The tax is rebated, however, to individuals in the year they become permanent residents, as well as many corporations, foreign visitors, and low-income earners who are 19 years or older, through a GST tax credit system.

According to Canada's Department of Finance, the federal government collected $222.2 billion in taxes and other revenue during the 2005-2006 **fiscal year**. Approximately 46 percent of this came from personal income taxes.

In order to receive the credit, new permanent residents must fill in form RC151 from the Canada Revenue Agency. The only way for other individuals to apply for a GST tax credit is to check the appropriate box when filing an income tax form. Even if you have no income to report, you have to file the income tax form to receive any GST credit. The basic credit is currently just over $200, but the amount you receive may differ depending on the number of children you have registered for the Canada Child Tax Benefit or the GST/HST credit and your family's net income.

Note that the GST credit will only go to one spouse in a family, and the credits are paid quarterly. For information on GST, call the Canada Revenue Agency at 1-800-959-1953.

Foreign Income Verification

In an effort to discourage Canadian residents from avoiding paying their due taxes, the federal government implemented foreign income verification rules in April 1999, to the frustration of many new Canadians.

It requires that Canadian residents, corporations, trust companies, and partnerships report, on CRA form T1135, any foreign asset valued at more than $100,000. There are several important exclusions regarding this requirement. They include property held to carry on a business, registered pension plan funds, personal use property, and shares in foreign affiliates.

Any income derived from any foreign asset is subject to taxation in Canada, including interest in any foreign bank account.

International Security Benefits

Canada currently has social security agreements with about 50 countries around the world, mostly in Europe and the Caribbean. These agreements mean that former residents of those countries who immigrate to Canada might be entitled to Canada's OAS retirement benefits, disability benefits, and survivor benefits if they or their spouses have contributed to the social security program in one of those countries. In other words, the period during which you contributed to your originating country's pension plan may be used to help you qualify for Canada's OAS.

For information on whether such an agreement is in place with your country of origin, contact Human Resources and Skills Development Canada.

Key Words

accountant: a person whose job is to keep or examine the financial records of a business, etc.

benefit: an extra payment or service that is given to an employee in addition to his/her salary

Canada Revenue Agency (also CRA; formerly known as Revenue Canada): Canada's federal department responsible for income tax and trade laws

collection officer: a person in a position of authority whose job is to get back the money owed to the government

commission: money that a person gets for selling something

deduct: to take something such as money or points away from a total amount

duty: a tax that you pay, especially on goods that you bring into a country

fiscal year: a period of twelve months that a company or government uses to calculate its accounts, taxes, etc.

Goods and Services Tax (also GST): a tax that is added to the price of goods and services

high earner: somebody who earns more money than the average person

income earner: a person who earns money for a job he/she does

income tax record: a written account of a person's tax return, which is an official document that details the amount of money he/she has earned and calculates the amount of tax he/she has to pay

income tax: the tax that you pay on the money you earn

net income: the money that a person earns from which nothing more needs to be taken away after taxes, etc. have been paid

profit: the money that you make when you sell something for more than it cost you

property tax: the money that a person has to pay to the government for real estate he/she owns so that the government can provide public services

salaried employee: a person who gets paid regularly by an organization for the work he/she has done

self-employed: working for yourself and earning money from your own business

sin tax: a polite expression for a tax added by the government to products or services that are traditionally seen as immoral, such as alcohol, tobacco, and gambling

T4: an official document supplied by your employer that shows how much money you have earned in one year so that the amount of tax you owe to the government can be calculated

tax credit: a reduction in the amount of tax a person or a company has to pay in particular situations

tax evasion: the illegal action of underpaying or not paying the taxes you should pay

tax system: a set of legal rules for assessing and collecting taxes

underground economy: secret or illegal business transactions that are not reported to the government to avoid taxes

Note: Entries taken or adapted from the Oxford ESL Dictionary

Creating Your Canadian Experience

1. Look at the tax chart on page 274 and find the following information for your province.

    Average income: _____

    Income tax: _____

    Sales tax: _____

    What is the next largest tax paid?

    _____

2. Research the tax service office nearest your home.
    Tip: type the name of your city and "Tax Service" into a search engine.

    Address: _____

    Hours: _____

    Contact Information: _____

3. Locate a free tax clinic nearest your home.
    Tip: type the name of your city and "Free Tax Clinic" into a search engine.

    Address: _____

    Hours: _____

    Contact Information: _____

Chapter 15

Customs and Etiquette

In This Chapter

- How should you act when you first meet someone?
- What should you talk about with someone you just met?
- How should you address your boss?

Canadian **customs** may not be familiar to all newcomers when they first arrive. It can leave a person feeling out of place or confused. Take the time to ask questions of different people and observe the things going on around you. Before long you will not only understand the customs and **etiquette** of your new country, but you will be able to help others who have just arrived.

Below are some ways to get familiar with Canadian customs and etiquette and some that we thought were important for you to know. Feel free to write us with your own suggestions or comments on some of the peculiarities that you find in this country.

Communities

Living in a new country can be very lonely if you do not know about the many resources available to you.

The library is an important source of assistance for newcomers. The programs and services available include the following:

- Homework clubs to help children with schoolwork
- Toy libraries and storytelling for children
- Activities related to health and fitness—which are a great way to meet people!
- Newspapers, magazines, books, and DVDs in various languages
- Computer and Internet access

Some of these services may charge a fee, but many are available for free.

Another way to connect with your new community is through a religious or ethnic association. They will allow you to meet people with backgrounds similar to yours. You can find lists of such organizations at settlement agencies and local community centres. Volunteering at one of these organizations can be a great way to strengthen your connections with a group and make new friends.

For many newcomers, finding a local place of worship is a very important step in the settlement process. Aside from being the centres of their religious communities, temples, mosques, synagogues, and churches can provide a lot of valuable information and support to new Canadians. Places of worship are where many newcomers meet new friends with similar interests, and this can be extremely important to someone who is in a strange new country.

Places of worship may provide information about where to find stores that understand the dietary needs of a particular religious group. They may also give newcomers advice and assistance about the immigration process, and many religious groups often defend the rights of immigrants and refugees.

Temples, mosques, synagogues, and churches often provide social services to the community. They may serve meals or collect food or clothing for the homeless. If you are interested in assisting the less fortunate in your area, volunteering to help with these services can be a great way to do this while getting to know the members of your religious community.

You can locate local houses of worship by looking in your phone book or online under "Churches, Mosques, and Synagogues." Many community centres will be able to provide this information as well.

Julia Krasnopevtseva: The first step is hard; the second is harder

"When I first arrived to Canada, an enormous amount of different feelings filled me. Excitement, joy, relief, fear," says European immigrant Julia Krasnopevtseva.

"When you arrive in Canada, you bring your own cultural touchstones that reflect the way you see things, think, and solve problems. Since then, you have inevitably encountered ways of doing, perceiving, or valuing things, which are different than the way you have become accustomed to seeing the world. Things appear less predictable. Rules of behaviour seem unclear. It took time to realize that now my life is in Canada: my school, my work, and my home."

Krasnopevtseva recommends that newcomers use the support services available to them: school instructors, new friends, people who are in the same situation with them. "Don't feel that it's not important enough to discuss, and don't be embarrassed about seeking help. With timely and caring advice, you will soon be ready to enjoy your Canadian experience completely! And when you do, you become proud that you made it and proud to live in Canada."

—*Margaret Jetelina*

I have a word of advice here: I do understand that moving to a new country can be very scary. A lot of immigrants tend to move into an ethnic community that matches their own background. While this may be comfortable, I personally believe your true growth in a new country will come from moving out of your comfort zone. When you have friends of all nationalities, you will learn a lot more. If all of your friends are from your own country, many of your discussions will focus on the past and life "back home."

You need to look at the future and at Canada—your new home!

Everyday Manners

Politeness and good **manners** are highly valued by most Canadians. In fact, many people believe that Canadians say "thank you" and "excuse me" more than the rest of the world combined. Americans in particular enjoy poking fun at our polite manners.

Both men and women generally shake hands when being introduced to someone or when greeting someone they already know. This is common in the business world, although is not always practised in more casual situations among friends. Make sure you don't try to impress someone with an overly firm grip. Friends will frequently give each other a hug or a quick kiss on the cheek.

It is not a common practice to visit someone without an invitation, except perhaps your neighbours or very close friends and family.

Families

Common-law couples, or couples who live together without being married, are widespread in Canada. After one year of living together, such couples acquire legal status as common-law partners. Canadian law recognizes marriage between both heterosexual and same-sex couples.

Many couples find that both partners have to work outside the home to earn a decent living, and therefore place their children in daycare or with a nanny.

Some Canadian couples divorce and end up sharing or splitting time with their children. It is common for the kids to spend weekends with one parent and weekdays with the other. Either partner can initiate divorce proceedings. Single-parent families are fairly common, and most of them are headed by women.

Many adult children leave home after completing school to live on their own before getting married.

The age at which Canadians marry has been increasing over the years. In 1981, the average age of brides was 24 and in 2002, it was 31.5. The average age of grooms was 26.8 in 1981, and 34 in 2002.

Social Behaviour

Lineups for the bank, grocery store, or public transit are controlled by custom and good manners. Always look to see where the line ends; that's where you should line up. If you do not look to see where the line ends, you might be embarrassed to hear someone point the back of the line out to you.

Punctuality for business appointments and school is mandatory, and for social appointments you should not be more than five or ten minutes late. If a real emergency causes you to be late, you should call and apologize.

There is nothing wrong with breastfeeding in public. You should always feel comfortable feeding your baby wherever and whenever you need to. You may find, however, that some people are not entirely happy about this practice and will try to discourage it.

When you need to diaper your baby, you should do so modestly and discreetly, if possible. In many places—such as large office buildings and shopping malls—there are quiet and private areas for parents to do this. If no such area is available, try to find a quiet site off the beaten path and do what you have to do.

The wearing of heavy perfumes and colognes is becoming less acceptable in Canada, as more and more people seem to be suffering from intolerance to such odours.

Most public places have washrooms or toilets, but some restrict their use to paying customers. The washrooms at gas stations are generally also available for use.

Many cities have bylaws that require dog owners to clean up after their dogs in public places. And the following practices, aside from being very offensive are also illegal: littering; urinating or defecating anywhere except in a public or private toilet; and now, in most public spaces, smoking.

Lighting up a cigarette is now forbidden in any federal building, elevator, airplane, bus, or theatre. In many places, it is also forbidden in restaurants. You should never light up a cigarette when you are visiting someone's home, even if you know that person is a smoker. Frequently, people don't even smoke in their own homes. While the serving of alcohol is common at public and private functions, drunken behaviour is considered in very poor taste, and drunk driving is illegal.

Q: I have an office party to go to. Any suggestions?

A: Confirm your attendance, dress appropriately, bring money, watch your alcohol consumption, be punctual, and be sociable with everyone.

Making Small Talk

One person who had a huge impact on me was an immigrant friend, John, who I met within the first few days of landing. He had been in Canada for a while and had become very familiar with Canadian **society** as a whole. It was interesting to watch John in action. He would start a conversation with almost everyone he met. In the streets, at malls, supermarkets, and even gas stations John would talk to them about anything under the sun. It was fascinating watching him.

Here is an example of John's chat with a man at the bakery:

John: Time was when a loaf of bread was a loaf of bread! Now they have sixteen shelves!

Shopper: Yeah, but you should try the twelve-grain variety—I used white bread until recently when I learned how many preservatives they contain and what they do to our digestion.

John: Really?

Shopper: Yeah, I left a loaf in a cupboard and forgot about it for two months. When I did find it, it hadn't rotted! Imagine how many chemicals are in that stuff! Take it from me—get the twelve-grain variety.

John: Gee, thanks! I will.

This was classic John. He would talk about the weather when it was good and when it was not, or about recent hockey games—I suspect he sometimes had no clue what he was talking about, but the opportunity to chat was irresistible!

I learned from John how easy it is to make small talk. John treated it like a sport, and like many sports it takes practice but after some time it becomes easy. Small talk is essential to success and I often suggest that immigrants should practise it.

Keeping in touch with **current events** will help you start conversations with "What do you think of…." or "Have you heard…?" Stay away from negative topics, or sensitive topics like religion.

Business Etiquette

In the workplace, or at company events, it's important to maintain a professional image at all times. Pay careful attention to personal hygiene and dress neatly and appropriately. If you are unsure about what clothing is appropriate at your workplace, you can check the company's policy or ask your employer.

Always be on time for business meetings. If you are seated when other people enter a meeting room, stand up and shake their hands. Make eye contact and smile while you do this; it will make others feel comfortable.

Men and women should be treated equally, both in the workplace and elsewhere. Never assume anything about a person's position in a company based on gender. When meeting someone for the first time, use "Mr." or "Ms" and a last name until you are invited to use the person's first name. This is especially important during a job interview. When introducing people to each other, always introduce the highest-ranking person first. For example, you would introduce the company's president first, then an associate.

Try to return phone calls and emails as quickly as possible. Keep your voice mail messages and emails brief and clear. When writing an email, always use proper spelling and grammar. If you have written a very important email, you may want to wait for a while before sending it. By working on something else in the meantime, you'll be able to come back and look at your message more clearly, and you'll be more likely to catch any major errors.

If you attend a business lunch or work party, behave as well as you would if you were at your workplace. Be prepared to make small talk, which is important at these events. Try to avoid controversial issues such as politics and religion; instead focus on topics such as positive world news, food, or hobbies. Limit yourself to no more than one alcoholic drink.

Q: I am invited to dinner at my employer's home where alcohol will be served and I do not drink alcohol. How do I handle this?

A: Simple. Just say "I do not drink alcohol. May I have a soft drink or juice?" You will find many people who do not consume alcohol for a variety of reasons, including health or religion. Declining will not make you stand out in any way.

You'll probably want to keep some business cards with you to hand out to your contacts; make sure the cards have up-to-date information on them. Only give out your card when people ask for it or give you theirs. If you receive someone else's business card, place it in a notebook, planner, or business card holder—never your wallet or pocket.

Key Words

common-law: a person who has been living with a person of the opposite sex for a long time but who is not married to him/her

current event: something that happens in the present time that is in the media

custom: a way of behaving which a particular group or society has had for a long time

etiquette: the rules of polite and correct behaviour

manners: the way that sb behaves toward other people

punctuality (also on time): doing something or happening at the right time; not late

society: the people in a country or an area, thought of as a group, who have shared customs and laws

Note: Entries taken or adapted from the Oxford ESL Dictionary

Creating Your Canadian Experience

1. Make a list of topics you could make small talk with. Come up with a starting sentence for the conversation and a point you would like to make.

Topic	Starting Sentence	Point You Want to Make

2. Use the following list of questions to ask your friends and other people you know about Canadian customs. Add two questions of your own.

   a. Do you greet your friends in a different way than the people you work with?
   b. How well do you need to know someone before you drop in for a visit?
   c. How quickly do you expect a response to an email?
   d. Is punctuality important to you?

   e. _____

   f. _____

Chapter 16

Becoming a Citizen

In This Chapter

- When can you apply for citizenship?
- How do you apply for it?
- How do you get a passport?
- When can you start voting?

Canada is a land of immigrants, with about 250,000 newcomers welcomed from other countries each year. While Ontario, Quebec, and British Columbia are the destinations for the vast majority of immigrants, every region of Canada is attracting people and cultures from around the world, and most immigrants are eventually **sworn in** as Canadian citizens.

With citizenship comes many **privileges**, as well as many **responsibilities**. This chapter will outline some of the most important of each, although you will still want to contact Citizenship and Immigration Canada for complete instructions and a list of the documents you will need to attain citizenship.

The very first Canadian citizenship ceremony was held on January 3, 1947, and the very first recipient to be declared a Canadian citizen was then–Prime Minister William Lyon Mackenzie King. Prior to this time, Canadians were members of the Commonwealth and viewed as British subjects.

Who is Eligible for Citizenship?

Before applying for Canadian citizenship, you should determine if you will have to give up citizenship in your former country or if you can hold **dual citizenship**. Canada has no restrictions on dual citizenship, although many countries forbid it. If your birth country does not recognize dual citizenship, you could be detained in that country if you return to visit and, in some countries, you could possibly be forced to complete a period of compulsory military service.

Certain circumstances will prevent you from becoming a Canadian citizen.

You may not obtain citizenship if you

- are considered a risk to the security of Canada;
- are under a deportation order;
- are in prison, on parole from prison, or on probation;
- have been found guilty of a serious crime within the past three years; or
- are under investigation for war crimes.

John Halani: Passionate Philanthropist

In his native Uganda, hotel operator and community worker John Halani helped acquire loans to build a secondary school in Masaka, Uganda, which was named after the Aga Khan. Now, in Canada, Halani continues to dedicate his time and endless energies to helping his community recognize multiculturalism, while hosting newcomers in his hotel, the Tropicana.

"There is a tradition of volunteering among the Ismaili community. So my social work started when I was young. People who come here need help and guidance."

His importance to the community in Uganda can only be matched by his importance to his new community in Canada. While Halani is chair of both the Ethno Business Council and an advisory council on multiculturalism for the Government of British Columbia, he still has time to participate in several organizations such as the Greater Vancouver Citizenship Council, Gordon Neighbourhood House, Alexandra Housing Society, and Salamat Housing Society.

It's his hard work and inability to slow down which puts Halani at the top of any list of immigrants who have left their mark on the state of diversity in Canada, and he has passionate intentions for the future. "I'm hoping one of my sons will soon be ready to take over the hotel business so I can continue to do more social work."

—*Sarshar Hosseinnia*

On the more positive side, you will need to meet all of the following criteria before you can be sworn in as a citizen.

You must

- be able to speak and understand either of Canada's two official languages, English or French;
- be 18 years of age or older to apply on your own behalf;
- be a permanent resident;
- have knowledge of Canada, including its history, politics, and geography;
- have lived in Canada for a total of three of the four years preceding your application (if you are older than 18);

- understand your rights and responsibilities as a Canadian citizen; and
- be prepared to take an **oath** (or affirmation) of citizenship.

A citizenship judge will determine whether you meet these requirements.

Privileges of Citizenship

As a citizen you will be entitled to

- vote and run for political office in federal and provincial elections;
- travel outside of Canada on a Canadian passport;
- enjoy full economic rights;
- receive some pension benefits; and
- enjoy equal treatment and protection under the law without discrimination.

Your Responsibilities

You will be expected to learn and obey Canadian laws. You should also be familiar with, and respect, the *Canadian Charter of Rights and Freedoms*, a summary of which is included in this chapter.

Good citizenship also means getting involved in your community and your country. This means participating in elections, volunteering for charitable or community organizations, and keeping informed about current affairs.

What Do I Do?

You can obtain an application for citizenship by contacting the nearest Citizenship and Immigration Canada office, listed in the blue pages of your telephone book. It may take the office at least two weeks to deliver the application to you. Only one application is required per family, and it will include detailed instructions on how to complete the form and how to pay the fee.

Currently, the fee for processing the application is $200 per adult and $100 per child under the age of 18. The application will also explain what photographs and documents you need.

Once you have completed the form, you must pay the required fee at a financial institution, as explained in the application's instructions. You can

Daniel Igali: Wrestler Devoted to Canada

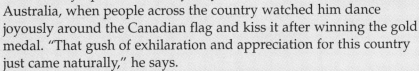

Canadian Olympic wrestler Daniel Igali, who was born in Nigeria, loves Canada and even ran as a candidate in the BC provincial election in 2005.

Igali became a household name during the 2000 Olympic Games in Sydney, Australia, when people across the country watched him dance joyously around the Canadian flag and kiss it after winning the gold medal. "That gush of exhilaration and appreciation for this country just came naturally," he says.

As a child in Nigeria, Igali escaped the harsh realities of daily life through wrestling, which is a longstanding tradition among his people, the Ijaws. "It's a traditional kind of wrestling. It goes hundreds of years back," he explains. When he travelled to Victoria, BC, to represent Nigeria in the 1994 Commonwealth Games at the age of 20, he decided to stay and seek refugee status.

Today he is proud of being accepted into Canada as one of its own. A few years ago, he was amazed when the police knocked on his door to ask him some questions about a neighbour. "They asked 'Can we come in?' I couldn't believe it. The cops were begging me to come into my house," he says, with a chuckle of disbelief. "Back home, my door would have been broken down. People here will never understand that."

—*Margaret Jetelina*

then send the application, with your receipt, required documents, and photographs, to your local case processing centre.

The processing of your citizenship application could take as long as ten months. After it has been processed, you will be notified by mail when and where to write your test, and you could possibly also be scheduled for an interview with a citizenship judge. All adults between the ages of 18 and 54 must pass a citizenship test to demonstrate their knowledge of Canada and their proficiency in English or French.

Citizenship and Immigration Canada	Citoyenneté et Immigration Canada		For official use only	PAGE 1 OF 5

Application for Canadian Citizenship -
Adults (18 years of age and older)
Under Subsection 5(1)

UCI no.

Certificate no.

Before you start, read the instructions

Please PRINT in ink or TYPE   Protected when completed

1 I want service in   English ☐   **OR** French ☐   Please check (✓)one

2 I have special needs   No ☐   Yes ☐   ▶ If yes, explain: _____

3 I have applied for Canadian citizenship before   No ☐   Yes ☐   ▶ When? _____ Year

For official use only

4 A Name (**exactly as is shown on my immigration document**)
Surname/Last name _____
Given name(s) _____

B Name to appear on citizenship certificate (supporting documentation required)
Surname/Last name _____
Given name(s) _____

C Other names used (example maiden name or name at birth) These names will not appear on your citizenship certificate
Surname/Last name _____
Given name(s) _____

Use another piece of paper if you need more space.

5 A Birth details as shown on your immigration document
Date   Day ___ Month ___ Year ___   Place   City, town, etc. ___   Country ___

B Personal information
Sex   Male ☐   **OR** Female ☐   ▶ Height ___ OR ___ cm / ft in   ▶ Colour of eyes ___

Marital status   Single ☐   Married ☐   Common-law ☐   Widowed ☐   Divorced ☐   Separated ☐

6 A Home address _____ Postal code _____

B Mailing address (if different from home address) _____ Postal code _____

C Telephone number(s)   Home (___) _____   Work (___) _____ Ext. ___   Cell (___) _____

D I have lived at this address ___ year(s) and ___ month(s)

CIT 0002 (07-2005) E

(AUSSI DISPONIBLE EN FRANÇAIS - CIT 0002 F)
AVAILABLE ON CIC WEB SITE AT: http://www.cic.gc.ca

Canada

7 **(a)** Date you became a permanent resident?

Day	Month	Year

(b) When did you first come to live in Canada if different from (a)?

Day	Month	Year

(c) Are you a citizen of any other countries?

No ☐ Yes ☐ ▶ **If yes,** please list the country (countries).

(d) Do you have permanent resident status in any other country?

No ☐ Yes ☐ ▶ **If yes,** please list the country (countries) and provide the dates you acquired this status.

(e) Note: If you use the **online Residence Calculator**, you are not required to complete this section. You must check the box below, print and attach a copy of the completed online calculation page(s) with your application.

☐ Residence Calculator results submitted with my application.

ABSENCES FROM CANADA:
Have you left Canada in the last 4 years?

No ☐ Yes ☐ ▶ **If yes,** please list all of your trips outside of Canada, even if accompanied by a family member who is a permanent resident or citizen of Canada in the last 4 years. You must list all the trips you have taken outside Canada in the last four (4) years including trips for the purpose of business, pleasure or vacation, visits to family members, trips to the United States, etc.

FROM Y M D	TO Y M D	DESTINATION	REASON FOR ABSENCE	TOTAL # DAYS
			TOTAL	

Use another piece of paper if you need more space.

(f) **ADDRESSES IN THE LAST 4 YEARS:**
List all of your addresses in Canada and foreign addresses in the last 4 years. If you were residing, employed or attending school outside Canada in the last four years, you must **also** indicate all your foreign addresses.

FROM Y M	TO Y M	ADDRESS	CITY, PROVINCE, COUNTRY

Use another piece of paper if you need more space.

CIT 0002 (07-2005) E

7 (g) **Note:** If you use the **online Residence Calculator**, you are not required to complete this section. You must check the box below, print and attach a copy of the completed online calculation page(s) with your application.

☐ Residence Calculator results submitted with my application.

HOW TO CALCULATE RESIDENCE

The *Citizenship Act* requires a person to reside in Canada 1095 days (3 years) in the 4 years immediately before the date of the application. You may count ½ time (up to a maximum of 730 half days which equals 365 days) for the time you resided in Canada before you became a permanent resident. The time you resided in Canada after you became a permanent resident counts as full time. **Remember, you count only the last 4 years.** For example, if you apply for citizenship on November 1, 2004 you calculate your time in Canada from November 1, 2000. Any time in Canada before November 1, 2000 is not counted. **To assist you in calculating your residence in Canada complete this form and include it with your application.**

Criminal activity may affect your residence. If you think this may apply to you, please contact the call centre.

SECTION 1   CALCULATION OF TIME AFTER PERMANENT RESIDENT STATUS
Everyone must complete this section.

A Enter the date you became a permanent resident on Line A.
(See box 45 on your IMM 1000).
Note: If you have been a permanent resident for more than 4 years, enter 1460 on Line C.

A [   ]

B Enter the date you will sign your application on Line B.

B [   ]

C Total the number of days between the date you became a permanent resident (A) and the date you will sign your application (B). Enter this number on Line C.
IMPORTANT: If this number is more than 1460 (4 years) then enter 1460 on Line C. If this number is less than 730 days, you are not eligible yet.

C [   ]

D If you were outside Canada between the date in A and the date in B, enter the total number of days absent on Line D.
Note: If you have been a permanent resident for more than 4 years, enter on line D the total number of days you have been absent from Canada in the four year period immediately before the date in B.

D [   ]

E Subtract Line D from Line C (C - D = E). Enter this number on Line E.
If this number is at least 1095 days, you do not have to complete Section 2. You are eligible to apply for citizenship. If the total is less than 1095, go to Section 2.

E [   ]

SECTION 2   CALCULATION OF TIME BEFORE PERMANENT RESIDENT STATUS
Complete all of Section 2 if you were in Canada <u>before</u> becoming a permanent resident.
Remember: <u>You count only the 4 years preceding the date you will sign your application</u>. If you were not in Canada prior to becoming a permanent resident, write "0" on Line K and complete Line L.

F On Line F enter <u>either</u> the date you arrived in Canada
<u>or</u> the date 4 years prior to the date on Line B if you arrived in Canada more than 4 years ago.
Example: The date you arrived in Canada was October 20, 1999. The date on Line B is November 1, 2004 and 4 years prior to this date is November 1, 2000. November 1, 2000 is the date you enter on Line F.

F [   ]

G Enter the date you became a permanent resident on Line **G**.
(Same date as Line A)

G [   ]

H Total the number of days between the date in F and the date in G. Enter this number on Line H.
If this number is more than 730 (2 years), enter 730 on Line H.

H [   ]

I If you were outside Canada between the date in F and the date in G, enter the total number of days absent on Line I.

I [   ]

J Subtract Line I from Line H (H - I = J). Enter this number on Line J.

J [   ]

K Divide the number in J by 2 (J ÷ 2 = K). Enter this number on Line K.
If this number is more than 365, the calculation has not been done correctly.

K [   ]

L Add the number in E to the number of days in K (E + K = L).
If this number is at least 1095 days, you are eligible to apply.

L [   ]

The *Citizenship Act* requires a person to have accumulated 3 years (1095 days) in the past 4 years on the day before the application. If you have less than 1095 days in Canada <u>because of absences outside of Canada</u> you may still apply for citizenship. It will be up to a judge to determine if those absences affect your application. There is no refund of the processing fee if your application is not approved because you do not meet the residence requirement.

CIT 0002 (07-2005) E

---

8 PROHIBITIONS UNDER THE *CITIZENSHIP ACT*

1. Are you now or have you ever been in the last 4 years:
   - an inmate of a penitentiary, jail, reformatory, or prison?
   - on probation?
   - on parole?

2. In the past 3 years, have you been convicted of an indictable offence (crime) or an offence under the *Citizenship Act*?

3. Are you now charged with a crime, or a crime under the *Citizenship Act*?

4. Are you now, or have you ever been, under a removal order (have you been asked by Immigration officials to leave Canada)?

5. Are you now under investigation for or charged with a war crime or a crime against humanity or have you ever been convicted of a war crime or a crime against humanity?

6. In the past 5 years, have you had Canadian citizenship which has been taken away (revoked)?

I have read and understand the prohibitions under the *Citizenship Act*. I declare that these prohibitions:

☐ Do not apply to me.

☐ Do apply to me.   ▶ Provide details:

_____

_____

_____

_____

9 CONSENT TO DISCLOSE PERSONAL INFORMATION

CONGRATULATORY LETTER:

Request for authorization
Federal Members of Parliament (M.P.s) send a letter of congratulations to new citizens in their ridings. Do you authorize Citizenship and Immigration Canada to forward your name, address and preferred official language to your Member of Parliament? No other information will be forwarded.

☐ YES   ☐ NO

This information will be disclosed once your Canadian citizenship is granted.

10 CONSENT TO DISCLOSE PERSONAL INFORMATION

(a) NATIONAL REGISTER OF ELECTORS:

Request for authorization
Canadian citizens who are 18 years of age or older have the right to vote in federal elections and referendums.

Elections Canada needs your authorization to add your name to the National Register of Electors to ensure that you are included on the list of electors for federal elections and referendums.

Do you authorize Citizenship and Immigration Canada to forward your name, address, gender and date of birth to Elections Canada so that this information can be added to the National Register of Electors?

☐ YES   ☐ NO

No information will be forwarded to Elections Canada until you acquire Canadian citizenship. By law this information will be used for electoral purposes only.

For more information, please refer to Section 10 of "How to Complete this Form".

CIT 0002 (07-2005) E

(b) QUÉBEC'S PERMANENT LIST OF ELECTORS:

Request for authorization
To make sure that you are on the list of electors for provincial, municipal or school elections, the Chief Electoral Officer of Québec needs to add your name to Québec's Permanent list of electors.

Do you authorize Citizenship and Immigration Canada to forward your name, address, gender and date of birth to the Chief Electoral Officer of Québec so that this information can be added to the permanent list?

☐ YES   ☐ NO

No information will be forwarded until you acquire Canadian citizenship. By law this information will be used for electoral purposes only.

For more information, please refer to Section 10 of "How to Complete This Form".

11 SIGNATURE OF APPLICANT

I agree to advise Citizenship and Immigration Canada if any information on this form changes before I take the Oath of Citizenship. I understand the contents of this form. I declare that the information provided is true, correct, and complete, and that the photographs enclosed are a true likeness of me. I understand that if I make a false declaration, or fail to disclose all information material to my application, I could lose my Canadian citizenship and be charged under the *Citizenship Act*.
I have indicated in Section 8 whether the prohibitions apply to me.

Signature of APPLICANT _____ Place _____ Date

Day	Month	Year

IMPORTANT NOTE:
Remember to make sure that you are eligible to apply for citizenship on the day before you <u>SIGN</u> this application.

12 INDIVIDUAL, FIRM OR ORGANIZATION WHO ASSISTED IN THE <u>COMPLETION</u> OF THIS APPLICATION
(The applicant does not complete this section)

Name of individual who assisted in completing this application form: _____

Name of firm, organization _____

Address _____

_____

Signature of Individual _____ Date

Day	Month	Year

REMEMBER:
If you are sending more than one application, send all of them together in one envelope. The applications will be processed together.

Source: Citizenship and Immigration Canada

Q: If I fail the citizenship test can I try again?

A: Absolutely! If you do not pass the written test, you will receive a notice telling you to appear for a short interview with a citizenship judge. At that interview, the judge will ask you the test questions orally so you can show that you meet the language and knowledge requirements. A small percentage of applicants fail this test, but it is easy to reapply.

A brochure called "How to Become a Canadian Citizen" is available at any citizenship court or by contacting Citizenship and Immigration Canada, Communications Branch, Ottawa, Ontario, K1A 1L1, Fax: (613) 954-2221.

The Citizenship Ceremony

The final step in obtaining citizenship is the oath-taking ceremony, usually presided over by a citizenship judge. All adults and children over the age of 14 must swear the oath of citizenship to receive a certificate of Canadian citizenship. Community groups are often involved in hosting these ceremonies, which take place across Canada and can involve hundreds of new Canadians taking their oaths together.

On December 10, 1985, Canada awarded its first ever honorary citizenship to Raoul Wallenberg, a Swedish diplomat who worked courageously to save the lives of thousands of Jews during World War I. Canada has also given honorary citizenship to former South African president Nelson Mandela, and Nobel Peace Prize winner and Dalai Lama of Tibet, Tenzin Gyatso.

Obtaining a Passport

Once you become a citizen, you can obtain an application for a passport through Passport Canada, which is an agency of Foreign Affairs and International Trade Canada. Passport office phone numbers are listed in the blue pages of your local telephone book. Passports must be renewed every five years. Most countries require a valid passport for entering and leaving, although if you have no intention of travelling outside Canada, you may not require a passport. It is still a good idea, however, to obtain one to use as identification, and to have in case of unexpected travel.

Registering to Vote

Once you become eligible to vote, you must register with Elections Canada in order to cast ballots in provincial, federal, and municipal elections.

Sandra Wilking: Citizenship Judge

It's difficult to define citizenship judge Sandra Wilking in just a few words. "Sometimes my family members are embarrassed to answer the question 'What does she do?'" says Wilking.

What she does and who she is are questions Wilking has often asked herself since arriving in Canada. Wilking can easily list off some of her most prominent achievements, such as becoming the second female Chinese-Canadian in all of Canada to be voted to public office, opening her own cultural and racial diversity consultancy firm, volunteering in the community, and being appointed a citizenship judge. But she says it took her time to figure out where she fit in.

"The process of becoming Canadian is a long one—I've experienced it myself and I've seen it on a day-to-day basis as a citizenship judge," explains Wilking. She calls the process a "personal journey."

Her own journey began as an international student from Hong Kong. She arrived in Canada in 1968 to attend university. In 1973, she became a landed immigrant and four years later, a citizen.

But, even after taking her citizenship oath and marrying a Canadian, Wilking's sense of being "Canadian" was still uncertain. "It's a mental mindset—one day I switched and knew I was no longer a foreigner," she says. "I was complaining about something to my husband about 'those Canadians,' when he said, 'Excuse me, but you're Canadian, too.' It sounds like a small thing, but it's a big challenge for those not born here to include themselves as Canadians."

—*Margaret Jetelina*

Registration for federal elections is automatic when you file an income tax return; you may simply grant approval for the Canada Revenue Agency to provide your name and address to Elections Canada, to include your name in the National Register of Electors.

Canadian Charter of Rights and Freedoms

As a citizen of Canada, you will be governed by, and subject to, the *Canadian Charter of Rights and Freedoms*. The *Canadian Charter of Rights and Freedoms* was established in 1982 and states that Canada's people have freedom of expression, the right to a democratic government, the right to equality, and the right to use either of Canada's two official languages (French or English). These and other rights and freedoms reflect the values that Canadians feel are important in a free and democratic society.

The Charter guarantees the following, within reasonable limits:

- Freedom of conscience and religion
- Freedom of thought, belief, opinion, and expression, including freedom of the press and other media
- Freedom of peaceful assembly
- Freedom of association
- The right to vote or run for office in federal and provincial elections
- The right to enter, remain in, and leave Canada
- The right to life, liberty, and security of the person
- The right to equal protection and equal benefit under the law

Many other rights are guaranteed by the Charter. You can get a copy of the *Canadian Charter of Rights and Freedoms* from Canadian Heritage, Communications Branch, Ottawa, 25 Eddy Street, 10th Floor, Hull, Quebec, K1A 0M5. Tel: (819) 997-0055.

Key Words

dual citizenship: the state of being a citizen of two countries at the same time

oath: a formal promise

privilege: a special right or advantage that only one person or group has

responsibility: a job or duty that you must do

sworn in: made to declare that he/she will accept the responsibility of a new position

Note: Entries taken or adapted from the Oxford ESL Dictionary

Creating Your Canadian Experience

1. Research the Citizen and Immigration office nearest to your home. You can find this information on the department's website at www.cic.gc.ca.

    Address: _____

    _____

2. Locate your local passport office. Office addresses will be listed on Passport Canada's website at www.ppt.gc.ca

    Address: _____

    Hours: _____

3. Research the provincial elections office so that you can register to vote. Tip: type the name of your province and "Elections Office" into a search engine.

    Address: _____

    Hours: _____

    Contact: _____

4. Research the municipal elections office so that you can register to vote. Tip: type the name of your city and "Elections Office" into a search engine.

    Address: _____

    Hours: _____

    Contact: _____

Appendix—Useful Websites

Federal Government

Service	Website Address
Government of Canada	**www.canada.gc.ca**
Canada Child Tax Benefit	www.cra-arc.gc.ca/benefits/cctb/menu-e.html
Canada Pension Plan	www.sdc.gc.ca/en/isp/cpp/cpptoc.shtml
Canada Revenue Agency	www.cra-arc.gc.ca
Canada Savings Bonds	www.cis-pec.gc.ca
Canada Student Loans	www.hrsdc.gc.ca/en/gateways/nav/top_nav/program/cslp.shtml
Canadian Firearms Centre	www.cfc-cafc.gc.ca
Canadian Food Inspection Agency	www.inspection.gc.ca
Canadian Heritage	www.pch.gc.ca
Canadian Human Rights Commission	www.chrc-ccdp.ca
Canadian Rural Information Service	www.rural.gc.ca/cris
CITES Office, Canadian Wildlife Service	www.cites.ec.gc.ca
Citizenship and Immigration	www.cic.gc.ca
Going to Canada	www.goingtocanada.gc.ca
GST/HST Information	www.cra-arc.gc.ca/tax/business/topics/gst/menu-e.html
Health Canada	www.hc-sc.gc.ca
Human Resources and Social Development Canada	www.hrsdc.gc.ca
Immigration and Refugee Board of Canada	www.cisr-irb.gc.ca
Integration-Net	integration-net.ca
Legal Aid	www.justice.gc.ca/en/ps/pb/arr/legal_aid.html
Old Age Security	www.sdc.gc.ca/en/isp/oas/oastoc.shtml
Passport Canada	www.ppt.gc.ca
Service Canada	www.servicecanada.gc.ca
Youth.gc.ca	www.youth.gc.ca

Provincial and Territorial Governments

Province	Website Address
Alberta	www.gov.ab.ca
British Columbia	www.gov.bc.ca
Manitoba	www.gov.mb.ca
New Brunswick	www.gov.nb.ca
Newfoundland and Labrador	www.gov.nl.ca
Northwest Territories	www.gov.nt.ca
Nova Scotia	www.gov.ns.ca
Nunavut	www.gov.nu.ca
Ontario	www.gov.on.ca
Prince Edward Island	www.gov.pe.ca
Quebec	www.gouv.qc.ca
Saskatchewan	www.gov.sk.ca
Yukon Territory	www.gov.yk.ca

Employment

Service	Website Address
Monster	www.monster.ca
Public Service Commission	www.jobs-emplois.gc.ca
Working.com	www.working.com
Workopolis	www.workopolis.com

Education

Service	Website Address
Association of Canadian Community Colleges	www.accc.ca
Association of Universities and Colleges of Canada	www.aucc.ca
Canada Language Council	www.c-l-c.ca
Canadian Bureau for International Education	www.cbie.ca
Canadian Universities.net	www.canadian-universities.net
National Association of Career Colleges	www.nacc.ca
National Educational Association of Disabled Students	www.neads.ca

Foreign Credential Assessment

Centre	Website Address
Canadian Information Centre for International Credentials	www.cicic.ca
International Credential Assessment Service of Canada	www.icascanada.ca
International Qualifications Assessment Service (AB)	www.advancededucation.gov.ab.ca/iqas/iqas.asp
BC Internationally Trained Professionals Network	www.bcitp.net
International Credential Evaluation Service (BC)	www.bcit.ca/ices
Comparative Education Service (ON)	www.adm.utoronto.ca/ces
Service des évaluations comparatives d'études (QC)	www.immigration-quebec.gouv.qc.ca/en/education/comparative-evaluation/index.html

Workplace Rights and Safety

Organization	Website Address
Canadian Human Rights Commission	www.chrc-ccdp.ca
Alberta	www.wcb.ab.ca
British Columbia	www.worksafebc.com
Manitoba	www.wcb.mb.ca
New Brunswick	www.whscc.nb.ca
Newfoundland and Labrador	www.whscc.nf.ca
Northwest Territories and Nunavut	www.wcb.nt.ca
Nova Scotia	www.wcb.ns.ca
Ontario	www.wsib.on.ca
Prince Edward Island	www.wcb.pe.ca
Quebec	www.csst.qc.ca
Saskatchewan	www.wcbsask.com
Yukon Territory	www.wcb.yk.ca
Intercede (ON)	www.intercedetoronto.org

Language Assessment

Province	Centre	Website Address
Alberta	Norquest College	www.norquest.ab.ca
British Columbia	Chilliwack Community Services	www.chilliwack.com/leisure/ comm-programs/ccs.html
	College of New Caledonia	www.cnc.bc.ca
	Continuing Education – Quesnel School District	www.sd28.bc.ca
	Gladwin Language Centre	www.gladwinlanguagecentre. com
	Intercultural Association of Greater Victoria	www.icavictoria.org
	Ki-Low-Na Friendship Society	www.kfs.bc.ca
	North Island College	www.nic.bc.ca
	Okanagan University College	www.ouc.bc.ca
Manitoba	Manitoba Department of Labour and Immigration	www.gov.mb.ca/labour/ immigrate
New Brunswick	UNB English Language Programme	www.unb.ca/extend/elp
Newfoundland	Association for New Canadians	www.anc-nf.cc
Nova Scotia	Metropolitan Immigrant Settlement Association	www.misa.ns.ca
Northwest Territories	Aurora College	www.auroracollege.com
Ontario	Guelph and District Multicultural Centre	www.gdmc.org
	Kitchener-Waterloo YMCA Language Assessment Centre	www.kwymca.org/Contribute/ immigrant/program_ language.asp
	Settlement and Integration Services Organization	www.siso-ham.org
	Community Development Council Durham	www.cdcd.org
	The Career Foundation	www.careerfoundation.com
	YMCA of Simcoe/Muskoka	www.ymcaofsimcoemuskoka. ca
	YMCA-YWCA National Capital Region	www.ymcaywca.ca
	YMCA of Toronto	www.ymcatoronto.org

Province	Centre	Website Address
Prince Edward Island	PEI Association for Newcomers to Canada	www.isn.net/newcomers
Quebec	Tyark College	www.tyark.com
Saskatchewan	Cypress Hills Regional College	www.cypresshillscollege.sk.ca
	Moose Jaw Multicultural Council	www.mjmulticultural.com
	Parkland Regional College	www.parklandcollege.sk.ca
	Regina Open Door Society	www.rods.sk.ca
	Saskatchewan Institute of Applied Science and Technology	www.siast.sk.ca
	Saskatoon Open Door Society	www.sods.sk.ca
	University of Regina	www.uregina.ca/langinst

Newcomer Assistance

Province	Centre	Website Address
Alberta	ASSIST Community Services Centre	assistcsc.org/traditional/main.htm
	Calgary Bridge Foundation for Youth	www.calgarybridge foundation.com
	Calgary Catholic Immigration Society	www.ccis-calgary.ab.ca
	Calgary Immigrant Aid Society	www.calgaryimmigrantaid.ca
	Calgary Immigrant Women's Association	www.ciwa-online.com
	Catholic Social Services	www.catholicsocialservices.ab.ca
	Central Alberta Refugee Effort and Catholic Social Services	www.intentr.com/immigrantctr
	Centre for Newcomers	www.centrefornewcomers.ca/index.shtml
	Changing Together: A Centre for Immigrant Women	www.changingtogether.com
	Edmonton Immigrant Services Association	eisa-edmonton.org
	Edmonton Mennonite Centre for Newcomers	www.emcn.ab.ca

Province	Centre	Website Address
	Lethbridge Family Services—Immigrant Services	www.lethbridge-family-services.com
	Millwoods Welcome Centre for Immigrants	www.mwci-edmonton.net
	YMCA of Wood Buffalo	www.ymca.woodbuffalo.org
British Columbia	Abbotsford Community Services	www.abbotsfordcommunityservices.com
	Burnaby Family Life Institute	www.burnabyfamilylife.org
	Burnaby Multicultural Society	www.bby-multicultural.com
	Campbell River and Area Multicultural and Immigration Services Association	www.misa.crcn.net
	Central Vancouver Island Multicultural Society	www.cvims.org
	Chilliwack Community Services	www.comserv.bc.ca
	Collingwood Neighbourhood House	www.cnh.bc.ca
	Comox Valley Multicultural and Immigrant Support Society	www.island.net/~cvmiss
	DIVERSEcity Community Resources Society	www.sdiss.org
	Family Services of Greater Vancouver	www.fsgv.ca
	Family Services of the North Shore	www.familyservices.bc.ca
	Frog Hollow Neighbourhood House	www.froghollow.bc.ca
	Hispanic Community Centre Society of BC	www.vcn.bc.ca/hispanic
	Immigrant and Multicultural Services Society	www.imss.ca
	Immigrant Services Society of BC	www.issbc.org
	Inter-Cultural Association of Greater Victoria	www.icavictoria.org
	Intercultural Society of the	www.interculturalkelowna.

Province	Centre	Website Address
	Little Mountain Neighbourhood House	www.lmnhs.bc.ca
	Mennonite Central Committee of BC	www.mcc.org/bc
	MOSAIC	www.mosaicbc.com
	North Shore Multicultural Society	www.nsms.ca
	Options: Services to Communities Society	www.options.bc.ca
	Pacific Immigrant Resources Society	www.pirs.bc.ca
	Progressive Intercultural Community Services Society	www.pics.bc.ca
	Ray-Cam Cooperative Community Centre	www.raycam.com
	Richmond Multicultural Concerns Society	www.rmcs.bc.ca
	South Vancouver Neighbourhood House	www.southvan.org
	SUCCESS	www.successbc.ca
	The Lower Mainland Purpose Society for Youth and Families	www.purposesociety.org/index.html
	Vernon and District Immigrant Services Society	www.vdiss.com
	Victoria Immigrant and Refugee Centre Society	www.vircs.bc.ca
Manitoba	International Centre of Winnipeg	www.international-centre.ca
	Jewish Child and Family Service	www.jcfswinnipeg.org
	Manitoba Immigration and Multiculturalism	www.immigratemanitoba.com
	Manitoba Interfaith Immigration Council	www.miic.ca
	Success Skills Centre	www.successskills.mb.ca
	Ukrainian Canadian Congress	www.ucc.ca
New Brunswick	Multicultural Association of Fredericton	www.mcaf.nb.ca
	Multicultural Association of the Greater Moncton Area	www.multicultural-association-moncton.com

Province	Centre	Website Address
	YMCA Fredericton	www.ymcafredericton.nb.ca
	YMCA Saint John	www.saintjohny.com
Newfoundland and Labrador	Association for New Canadians	www.anc-nf.cc
Nova Scotia	Metropolitan Immigrant Settlement Association	www.misa.ns.ca
	YMCA of Greater Halifax/ Dartmouth	www.ymcahrm.ns.ca
Ontario	Afghan Association of Ontario	www.afghanao.ca
	Arab Community Centre of Toronto	arabcommunitycentre.com
	Bloor Information and Life Skills Centre	www.bloorinfo.org
	Brampton Neighbourhood Resource Centre	www.bnrc.org/index2.html
	Canadian Ukrainian Immigrant Aid Society	www.cuias.org
	Catholic Community Services of York Region	www.ccsyr.org
	Catholic Cross-Cultural Services	www.cathcrosscultural.org
	Centre for Information and Community Services of Ontario	www.cicscanada.com
	Centre for Spanish-Speaking Peoples	www.spanishservices.org
	COSTI Immigrant Services	www.costi.org
	CultureLink	www.culturelink.net
	Dejinta Beesha Somali Multi Service Centre	www.dejinta.org
	Dixie Bloor Neighbourhood Centre	www.dixiebloor.ca
	Ethiopian Association in Toronto	www.ethiocommun.org
	Folk Arts Council of St. Catharines	www.folk-arts.ca
	Guelph and District Multicultural Centre	www.gdmc.org
	Halton Multicultural Council	www.halton-multicultural.org
	India Rainbow Community Services of Peel	www.indiarainbow.org

Province	Centre	Website Address
	IInter-Cultural Neighbourhood Social Services	www.icnss.ca
	Jamaican Canadian Association	www.jcassoc.org
	Jewish Family Services of Ottawa	www.jfsottawa.com
	Kababayan Community Centre	www.kababayan.org
	Kitchener-Waterloo YMCA	www.kwymca.org
	Lebanese and Arab Social Services Agency of Ottawa	www.lassa.ca
	Malton Neighbourhood Services	www.mnsinfo.org
	Mennonite Central Committee	www.mcc.org
	Mennonite New Life Centre of Toronto	www.mnlct.org
	Midaynta Community Services	www.midaynta.com
	Multicultural Council of Windsor and Essex County	www.themcc.com
	New Canadians Centre – Peterborough	www.nccpeterborough.ca
	Northwood Neighbourhood Services	www.northw.ca
	Ottawa Community Immigrant Services Organization	www.ociso.org
	Quinte United Immigrant Services	www.quis-immigration.org
	Rexdale Women's Centre	www.rexdalewomen.org
	Riverdale Immigrant Women's Centre	www.riwc.ca
	Scadding Court Community Centre	www.scaddingcourt.org
	Settlement and Integration Services Organization of Hamilton	www.siso-ham.org
	South Asian Family Support Services	www.safss.com
	South Asian Women's Centre	www.southasianwomens centre.ca
	Sudbury Multicultural/Folk Arts Association	www.sudburymulticultural. org
	Thunder Bay Multicultural Association	www.thunderbay.org

Province	Centre	Website Address
	The Cross-Cultural Community Services Association	www.tccsa.on.ca
	UJA Federation of Greater Toronto	www.jewishtoronto.net
	WoodGreen Community Services	www.woodgreen.org
	Working Women Community Centre	www.workingwomencc.org
	YMCA of Cambridge	www.ymcacambridge.com
	YMCA of Niagara	www.ymcaofniagara.org
	YMCA of Windsor and Essex County	www.windsor.essex.ymca.ca
	Youth Assisting Youth	www.yay.org
Prince Edward Island	PEI Association for Newcomers to Canada	www.peianc.com
Quebec	Carrefours d'integration du Quebec	www.immigration-quebec. gouv.qc.ca/fr/index.asp
Saskatchewan	Moose Jaw Multicultural Council	www.mjmulticultural.com
	Regina Open Door Society	www.rods.sk.ca
	Saskatoon Open Door Society	www.sods.sk.ca

Aid Organizations

Province	Organization	Website Address
British Columbia	Vancouver Association for Survivors of Torture	www.vast-vancouver.ca
Ontario	Canadian Centre for Victims of Torture	www.ccvt.org

Provincial Auto Insurance

Company	Website Address
Insurance Corporation of British Columbia (ICBC)	www.icbc.com
Manitoba Public Insurance (MPI)	www.mpi.mb.ca
Saskatchewan Government Insurance (SGI)	www.sgi.sk.ca

Credit Bureaus

Bureau	Website Address
Equifax Canada	www.equifax.ca
Northern Credit Bureaus	www.creditbureau.ca
TransUnion Canada	www.transunion.ca

Tenancy Laws

Province	Contact	Website Address
Alberta	Service Alberta – Landlords and Tenants	www.servicealberta.gov.ab.ca
British Columbia	BC's Residential Tenancy Office	www.rto.gov.bc.ca
Manitoba	Manitoba's Residential Tenancies Branch	www.gov.mb.ca/finance/cca/rtb
New Brunswick	New Brunswick Department of Justice and Consumer Affairs	www.gnb.ca/0062/index-e.asp
Newfoundland and Labrador	Residential Tenancies Newfoundland and Labrador	www.gs.gov.nl.ca/cca/tp/residential-tenancies
Northwest Territories	Northwest Territories' Rental Office	www.justice.gov.nt.ca/RentalOffice/rentalofficer.htm
Nova Scotia	Service Nova Scotia's Residential Tenancies	www.gov.ns.ca/snsmr/consumer/resten
Ontario	Ontario's Landlord Tenant Board	www.ltb.gov.on.ca
Prince Edward Island	Prince Edward Island's Office of the Director of Residential Rental Property	www.irac.pe.ca/rental
Quebec	Quebec's Landlord and Tenant Information, Régie du Logement	www.rdl.gouv.qc.ca
Saskatchewan	Saskatchewan's Office of Residential Tenancies	www.justice.gov.sk.ca/officeofresidentialtenancies
Yukon Territory	Yukon's Landlord and Tenant Resonsibilities	www.community.gov.yk.ca/consumer/landtact.html

Other Websites of Interest

Organization	Website Address
National Ethnic Press and Media Council of Canada	www.nepmcc.ca
Operation Red Nose	www.operationnezrouge.com
The Canadian Immigrant Magazine	www.canadianimmigrant.ca
Welcome Wagon	www.welcomewagon.ca

Index

Boldface page numbers indicate definitions of key words

Gross Domestic Product (GDP), 3, 13, **14**
Guaranteed income supplements, 91, 129

H

Halifax, 37–39
Harmonized sales tax (HST), 154, 281
Health Canada, 149
Health care. *See* Doctors; Hospitals; Medicare;
    Public health
Heirlooms, 48, 52, **60**
Help centres, 84, 85
Holidays, statutory, 5, 210, 211
Home repair scams, 183
Homesickness, 46–47, **60**
Hospitals, 69, **79,** 104, 107–108
Host programs, 63
Household costs. *See* Expenses
Household goods
    disposing of, 157, 158
    importing, 52, 54–55, 64, 65
    insuring, 178–179
    packing and moving, 48–50
    See also Appliances
Housing
    apartments, 120, 122–128
    condominiums, 121, 134–135, 139, 141
    costs of, 58, 119–120 (*see also names of cities*)
    types of, 120–121, 123, 128–129
    See also Renting; Utilities
Housing purchase
    about, 129–130
    arranging financing, 130–131
    checklist, 136–138
    choosing a realtor, 133–134
    considerations, 134–135
    legal information, 139–140
    making the offer, 138–139
    role of a realtor, 131–132
    and RRSPs, 177
Human development index ranking, 3
Human Resources and Skills Development
Canada (HRSDC), 66, 89, 91
Human rights. *See* Legislation; Rights

I

Identification, xi, **254**
    credit cards, 46, 170
    driver's licence, 178, 240
    social insurance card, 65
    See also Passport; Permanent Resident Card
Identity papers. *See* Documents
Identity theft, 182
Immigrant agencies, 66
    help for professionals, 192
    help for women, 269
    and meeting people, 287
    names of, 88, 96, 97
    programs, 63, 95

    resources, 63, 78, 202, 259
Immigrant loan programs, 94–96
Immigration, xiv, 2, 46, 47–48, 289, 296
Immunization, 51, 52, 53, 71, **79**
Importing
    firearms, 51
    household goods, 48–50
    pets, 50–51
    vehicles, 242–243
Income, average, 200, 228, 274
Income assistance, 91, 96–97, **99,** 109, 129
Income tax, 209, 247, 274–279, **284,** 307
Industry. *See* Economy; *names of cities*
Infant mortality, 107, **114**
Insurance, **60, 185**
    employment, 87–89, 209, 211, 212
    life, 109, 178–179, **186**
    moving, 49
    property, 178–179, **186**
    vehicle, 51, 244–247, 248, 252
    See also Medical insurance; Medicare
Interest rates, 130, **140,** 171, 172, **186,** 243
Internet
    access, 48, 168, 196, 202, 287
    banking, 166, 168
    fraud, 181–182
    and job search, 198, 202
    service providers, 78–79, 147
    telephone directories, 76
    wireless devices, 77
Inventions, 48, 70, 105, 109, 158

J

Jewellery, 48, 52, 72, 168
Jobs. *See* Employment
Judicial system. *See* Legal system

L

Landing. *See* Arrival
Landing papers, 64, 66, **79,** 93
Languages, 7, 34
Language training, 85–87
Laws. *See* Legal system; Legislation;
    Regulations
Lawyers, 227, 263, 264, 265, 268
Legal aid, 264, 267, **270**
Legal system
    about, 11, 259–261, 265–269
    and citizens, 259, 263, 268
    municipal bylaws, 259, **269**
    settling out of court, 265
    testifying in court, 268
Legislation, **14**
    criminal, 260, 267, 269
    and government, 10, 12
    human rights, 208, 298, 307
    medicare, 104
    multiculturalism, 3

Pedestrian safety, 249
Pensions, government, 89–91, **99**
Permanent Resident Card, 65
Personal effects. *See* Household goods
Pets, 50–51, 291
Pharmacare programs, 110–111
Pharmacies, 71, **115,** 159
Phone cards, 145
Physicians. *See* Doctors
Places of worship, 85, 287–288
Police, 250, 261–262, 263, 267, 269
Population, xi, 7, 13, **41.** *See also names of cities*
Population growth, 23, 26, **40**
Postal system, 159–160
Post-traumatic stress disorder (PTSD), 47
Pregnancy, 105, 108
Prescription drugs, **79, 115**
    how to receive, 70–71, 104
    and medicare, 68, 105
    provincial benefit plans, 110–111
Prime Ministers, 10, **15,** 106, 252, 296
Prince Edward Island, 111, 119, 155, 221, 228, 246, 274
Professional associations, 55, 191, 192
Professional credentials, 55–56, 190–192
Professional sports teams. *See names of cities*
Professions, regulated, 191–192, **214**
Provinces, 6, 11–12, 94, 110–111. *See also names of provinces*
Provincial sales tax (PST), 154, 155, 242, **255,** 274, 276
Public administration. *See* Government
Public health, 71, 150. *See also* Immunization
Public libraries, 48, 78, 201–202, 287
Public transit, **40, 41,** 71–72, 243. *See also names of cities*

Q
Qualifications, 230, **236.** *See also* Credentials
Quebec
    about, 7, 34
    average income, 228, 274
    benefits, 89
    biggest cities, 34–37
    damage deposits, 126
    education, 220, 221, 226
    house prices, 34, 36, 119
    prescription drug plan, 110
    regulations, 151, 152, 268–269
    taxes, 155, 274
Quebec City, 36–37
Quebec Pension Plan (QPP), 89

R
Realtors, 122, 131–132, 133–134
Record of Employment, 87, **99,** 211
Record of Landing, 66, 93
Recycling, 158–159
Reference letters, 51, 52, 190, 195, 245

Refugees, 11, 69, 94–96, 151, 229, 299
Regina, 27–28
Registered Retirement Savings Plans (RRSPs), 176–177, 280
Regulations
    alcohol, 151–152, 250–251
    driving, 240, 248–249, 252
    employment, 209–211
    food safety, 149–150
    importing, 50–51
    for professions, 55–56, 191
    public health, 71
    See also Legal system; Legislation
Religion, 3, 85, 287–288, 293
Renting
    costs, 58, 120 (*see also names of cities*)
    damage deposit, 126, **140**
    finding accommodation, 122–24
    legal information, 125–128
    types of housing, 120–121, 123, 128–129
    utilities, 145–146, 280
Resume, 190, 194–198, 200, 202
Retirement, 89–91, **99,** 176–177, 283
Retraining, 205, 212, **214**
Rights, 125–128, 208, 263, 267, 269. *See also Canadian Charter of Rights and Freedoms*

S
St. John's, 39–40, 160
Sales tax, provincial, 154, 155, 242, **255,** 274, 276
Saskatchewan
    average income, 228, 274
    capital city, 27–28
    education, 221
    house prices, 27, 119
    medical coverage, 105–106, 110
    taxes, 155, 274
    vehicle insurance, 246, 247
Scams, 180–185
Schools
    enrollment, 73–74, 223–224
    first impressions, 49
    and immunization, 51, 52, 53, 71
    parent involvement, 221–223
    parent-teacher interviews, 224–226
    private, 73–74, 220
    public, 13, 73–74, 220–221
    See also Education; Self-education; Training
Self-education, 14, 47, 193, 204, 259
Self-employment, 280–282
Seniors
    discounts for, 156
    government pensions, 89–91
    medical benefits, 68, 71, 105, 110, 111
    public transit, 28, 72
    subsidized housing, 128–129
Service organizations, 84, 85, 87, 93, 113–114, 230, 297
Settling in, 46–48, 277–278

Shopping
        centres, 26, 31, 37, 153–154
        comparison, 46, 144, 149, 153
        direct debit, 167
        refunds, 156, **161**
        telephone or Internet, 170, 182
        tips, 147–149, 153–157
Skills upgrading, 205, **214,** 234
Smoking, 207, 291
Social assistance, 71, 91, 96–97, **99,** 105, 283
Social insurance card, 63, 65, 66, 178
Social Insurance Number (SIN), 66, **79,** 178
Social safety net, 85, 96
Social services, 84, 97, **99,** 288
Society for Worldwide Interbank Financial
        Telecommunication (SWIFT), 46
Sports and recreation. *See names of cities*
Standards, employment, 209–211
Standards of practice, 191, **214**
Statistics
        average income, 200, 228, 274
        credit card use, 169, 170, 175
        education, 220, 226, 234, 235
        housing costs, 119, 120
        immigration, 2, 296
        marriage, 290
        on moving, 121, 127
        See also Population; Taxes; Unemployment
            rate
Statutory holidays, 5, 210, 211
Stress, 47, 204
Students, 12, 156, 287. *See also* Education:
        post-secondary; Schools
Survival job, 95
Survivor benefits, 89, 90, 91, 283

T
Taxes, 274, 275. *See also* Goods and services tax
        (GST); Harmonized sales tax (HST);
        Income tax; Provincial sales tax (PST)
Teachers, 205, 222, 224–226
Telemarketing, 78, 171, 182
Telephone
        emergency numbers, 70, 261
        etiquette, 77, 293
        long-distance calls, 75, 76, **79,** 145
        service, 74–78, **79,** 145, 147
        voice mail, 75, **79,** 293
Telephone book
        blue pages, 66, 77, **79,** 84
        emergency numbers, 70, 77
        Internet directories, 76
        white pages, 77, **80,** 84
        yellow pages, 63, 77, **80,** 84
Television, cable, 146, 147, 174
Tenants. *See* Renting
Territories, 6, 12, 13, **15,** 94, 155. *See also*
        Northwest Territories; Nunavut; Yukon
        Territory

Tips
        banking, 178
        for job interviews, 206–208
        for settling in, 46–48
        shopping, 147–149, 153–157
Toronto, 7, 30–32, 76, 120, 127, 234
Tourist attractions. *See names of cities*
Trade associations, 55, 191, 192
Trade journals, 201, 202, **214**
Trades, 191, 192, **214**
Training, 193, 202, **214,** 226, 234–235
Trans-Canada Highway, 241
Transportation. *See* Public transit
Transportation loan, 94–95
Traveller's cheques, 46, 166, **186**
Tuition fees, 74, 220, 227, 229–234, **237**

U
Underground economy, 277–278, **285**
Unemployment rate, **41.** *See also names of cities*
Unions, 209, 212, 222, 230
United States, xi, 7, 233, 242
Universities, 22, 227–230, 231, 233
Utilities, 74–78, 144–147, 167–168, 174, 235

V
Vacations, employee, 210
Vacation scams, 184
Vaccination. *See* Immunization
Valuables. *See* Documents; Heirlooms;
        Jewellery
Vancouver, 7, 19–21, 72, 120, 135, 234
Vehicles. *See* Driving
Victoria, 20, 21–23
Vision care, 108, 111
Volunteer organizations, 63, 66, 93, 97, 193
Volunteer work, 193, **214,** 287, 288, 297
Voter registration, 306–307

W
Water, safety of, 145, 150
Weather. *See* Climate
Welcome Wagon, 98
West Edmonton Mall, 26, 154
Will, **115**
Winnipeg, 29–30
Women, 12, 85, 169, 235, 265, 269

Y
YMCA, 87
Youth Criminal Justice Act, 267
Youth Link (publication), 234
Yukon Territory, 12, 111, 119, 228, 246

Credits

Photo Credits

1 iStock International Inc; 2 Citizenship and Immigration Canada; 3 Human Development Report, United Nations Development Programme/iStock International Inc; 13 Canada, Department of Justice, Canada's System of Justice (Ottawa: Supply and Services, 1998), 20.; 18 iStock International Inc; 19–39 Statistics Canada (At a Glance boxes); 20–40 Temperature and precipitation statistics courtesy of Environment Canada (http://www.weatheroffice.gc.ca); 54 Canada Border Services Agency; 57 "Skilled Workers and Professionals—Who Can Apply," http://www.cic.gc.ca/english/immigrate/skilled/funds.asp, Citizenship and Immigration Canada 2007. Reproduced with the permission of the minister of Public Works and Government Services Canada, 2008; 62 iStock International Inc; 83 iStock International Inc; 88 The Maytree Foundation; 90 Service Canada Website (http://www1.servicecanada.gc.ca/en/isp/pub/factsheets/rates.shtml). Reproduced with the permission of the Minister of Public Works and Government Services, 2008.; 94 Canada Revenue Agency; 102 iStock International Inc; 118 iStock International Inc; 119 Canadian Real Estate Association/*Step Forward Canada*, Oxford University Press Canada; 120/1 iStock International Inc (all housing photos); 124 iStock International Inc; 128 Settlement.Org; 133 Canadian Real Estate Association; 143 iStock International Inc; 159 Canada Post; 165 iStock International Inc; 189 iStock International Inc; 201 iStock International Inc; 219 iStock International Inc; 221 Council of Ministers of Education, Canada; 228 "Earnings Groups, Full-Year, Full-Time Workers by Level of Education (Canada, Provinces and Territories)," from the Statistics Canada product "Earnings of Canadians: Highlight Tables, 2001 Census," Catalogue 97F0024XIE2001013 Released March 11, 2003, URL: http://www12.statcan.ca/english/census01/products/highlight/Earnings/Index.cfm?Lang=E; 231 *Maclean's* magazine; 232 Human Resources and Social Development Canada. Reproduced with the permission of Her Majesty the Queen in Right of Canada 2007; 239 iStock International Inc; 241 Ontario Ministry of Transportation, http://www.mto.gov.on.ca; 258 iStock International Inc; 273 iStock International Inc; 274 "Average income after tax by economic family types, 2005," from the Statistics Canada website http://www40.statcan.ca/101/cst01/famil21a.htm; 275 From *Tax Facts* by Niels Veldhuis and Michael A. Walker, The Fraser Institute, www .fraserinstitute.org; 276–7 Department of Finance Canada. Reproduced with the permission of the Minister of Public Works and Government Services, 2007; 286 iStock International Inc; 295 iStock International Inc; 300–4 "Application for Canadian Citizenship—Adults," http://www.cic.gc.ca/english/pdf/kits/citizen/CIT0002E.pdf, Citizenship and Immigration Canada 2005. Reproduced with the permission of the minister of Public Works and Government Services Canada, 2008

All other photos courtesy of the authors.

Personal profiles appearing in this book first appeared in the *Canadian Immigrant* magazine. They are reprinted and abridged with permission from the magazine and authors.

Literary Credits

49 Lachman Balani; 88 Sarshar Hosseinnia; 111 Sarshar Hosseinnia; 169 Ben Roth; 181–184 Better Business Bureau of Mainland BC, originally printed in the *Canadian Immigrant* magazine, 2006; 297 Sarshar Hosseinnia

All other immigrant experiences written by Margaret Jetelina.